Gisele Marie Thibault

The Dissenting Feminist Academy

A History of the Barriers
to Feminist Scholarship

HQ
1426
.T53
1987
West

Arizona State Univ. West Campus Library

PETER LANG
New York · Bern · Frankfurt am Main · Paris

Library of Congress Cataloging-in-Publication Data

Thibault, Gisele Marie
    The dissenting feminist academy.

    (American university studies. Series XI, Anthropology/
sociology; vol. 9)
    Bibliography: p.
    1. Feminism—United States—History—20th century.
2. Women—Education (Higher)—History—20th century.
3. Sex discrimination against women—United States—
History—20th century.   4. Dissenters—United States—
History—20th century.   5. Women's studies—United
States—20th century.   I. Title.   II. Series.
HQ1426.T53   1987   305.4'2'0973   86-33774
ISBN 0-8204-0396-2
ISSN 0740-0497

CIP-Kurztitelaufnahme der Deutschen Bibliothek

Thibault, Gisele Marie:
The dissenting feminist academy: a history of
the barriers to feminist scholarship / Gisele Marie
Thibault. – New York; Bern; Frankfurt am Main;
Paris: Lang, 1987.
    (American University Studies: Ser. 11,
    Anthropology and Sociology; Vol. 9)
    ISBN 0-8204-0396-2

NE: American University Studies / 11

© Peter Lang Publishing, Inc., New York 1987

All rights reserved.
Reprint or reproduction, even partially, in all forms such as
microfilm, xerography, microfiche, microcard, offset strictly
prohibited.

Printed by Weihert-Druck GmbH, Darmstadt, West Germany

To my parents

Dissent

...v. (L, : dis-, apart + sentire, to feel) ...1: To think or feel differently; disagree; differ...n.2. The refusal to conform to the authority or doctrine... noncomformity.

The Heritage Illustrated Dictionary

CONTENTS

Acknowledgements

This book culminates my research, teaching and thinking over the last five years about women and education. But its strengths, where they exist, must be accredited to many whose valued input have made the work a published reality. I am deeply indebted to more people than I can name here for various kinds of help in going above and beyond the call of duty in supporting and encouraging this project.

Specifically I have been lucky to have had the advice, dialogue and support of Toni Laidlaw, Susan Sherwin, Alison Prentice, Martha MacDonald, Ann Manicom, and James Manos, during the embryonic and middle stages of this research. Each in their own way contributed enormously to the production of *The Dissenting Feminist Academy* and their unique dissent has found a vital place within these pages. They illustrate by example, what such an academy can do, and impressed upon me the importance of describing it accurately, honestly, and fully. I would like to thank the University of Calgary's Faculty of General Studies for supporting and sustaining the final stages. It has provided me with a "room of my own", a helpful library, and a stimulating haven in which to write. Of the many people who made that experience a positive one, I would like to thank the Dean, Marsha Hanen, for giving me kind encouragement in my ideas and for offering intellectual food for thought in the writing. The efforts of Richard Johnson's time, rigor, and technological pioneering, made this book a first-generation, lazer-printing production. His contribution to this work has been vital. I would like to mention Diane Potter at the onset; Debbie Proskrow, who has unconditionally given me more help than she will even know and: Barbara Howe, my typist, for her patience, level-headedness and capabilities. Without your calm Barb, I might have dropped my pen forever at Chapter three's end. Most importantly, thank you for agreeing to type the book with deadlines, lazer codes and all! I would like to thank Winnie Tomm for her kindness, and her friendship: your moral support was indespensible. I would like to mention the academic advisors in the Faculty of General Studies, especially Judy Horan, Laura Martineau, Beverly Schevchenko, Patti Konschuh, Beth Goldstone, Anna Marie Becker, Diane Boychuk (technical assistant) Marion Benaschak, Marguarite Brooker, and Margaret Walker. Thank you for making my year writing this book a pleasant one. To Eli Silverman, Women's Studies Co-ordinator: Thanks for the use of your office, your friendship and your confidence. I feel we will always be true sisterhood in action. To Heather Walker: Let us please do this again, only this time I will edit for you. To my editor-in-chief, Jay Wilson: Thanks for the confidence in the manuscript and your accessibility and guidance in its preparation. Finally, but not lastly, Edna Houdle and Lorne MacIntyre have shared in their respective ways, their affection and time: Edna for her photography and her friendship; Lorne for his brotherly concern. I love you both.

To all these people I am grateful, but I have discovered that in writing a book, one has daily cause to be thankful to people who reappear from the past to teach once again the lessons that have been the unconscious guideposts of a lifetime. Among these I would like to thank first and foremost, John M. Willinsky, who gave me the confidence to undertake this project in the first place and without whose daily patience, sponsorship, professionalism, acumes and wit, this volume would not be completed. To John: you are a rare and a precious friend. To Jim Calder whose combination of scholarly brilliance and eliptical humor has brightened my outlook on more than one occasion. To Pierette Martell (deceased) who knew this could be done. To Jim MacIntyre for promising to re-read this book with me in twenty years.

Closer to home, I would like to thank my parents. In the preparation of this volume, as in all my enterprises, I have had their unfailing encouragement, and their astute advice and love. These are only part of the many reasons I have dedicated the book to them. I'd also like to mention Mary Ellen Reynolds, my grandmother, my aunt, Ann Reynolds, who did not see this book to its completion, and the rest of my wonderful family for encouraging me to dissent when I was too young to vote.

Finally, this book would never have been written if it were not for those women whose feminist spirits, relentless intelligences, and courageous words made possible feminist dissent in educational institutions today. Their struggles and their dissent lives here.

Gisele M. Thibault   August 1986

Calgary, Alberta

1

INTRODUCTION

Barriers have been erected and while outside
them there is an enormous amount of activity which is yielding challenging stimulating, and useful data, inside the old order is
preserved —at the moment

Dale Spender.

This book is about universities—and how they have thought about
women—and it is about feminists' rejection of university discrimination. It is about feminist dissent and the paradox of academic
survival. Its concern is with the work of the university—both in
what it has intended and in what it accomplishes in terms of gender
and equally, with the sense which feminists have made of that
work.

Why should such a book be written? The question of feminist
dissent in academe is not just a superficial or intellectually interesting one. Historically, the access to and acquisition of higher education has perhaps been the most pervasive and ongoing issue of the
nineteenth and twentieth century feminist movement. From the
perspective of women, higher education has been a mixed blessing:
it has been a vital and necessary component in social change and in
bringing about shifts in economic and political policy. At the same
time, women have found it difficult to appropriate their potential
strength in educational sites which are deeply enmeshed in a culture which prescribes women's "proper sphere" as outside the public
domain. The dilemma is a highly complex one. In many respects,
feminist ideas have had to rely on the very academic structures that
feminism's philosophy inherently rejects. But this contradiction,

too, shifts as the social context changes. The extraordinary dialogue between feminism and academe over time constitutes a process which scholars now term "epochal" and educators coin "revolutionary." And indeed, as the proliferation of feminist scholarship grows in Canada and in the United States, and as the full impact of that scholarship begins to be felt in the media, the government, the law, the medical profession and the schools, the need becomes greater to understand its genesis in order to better understand its present agenda.

As Dale Spender (1983) asked in her *Women of Ideas*: "why didn't we know about the dissent?" After all, educators, politicians, critical theorists and students have explicated to us what is wrong with universities, but scant attention has been given, particularly in the academic literature, to women's unique relationship to the university. And virtually no subject has been more misrepresented by omission in that literature than the way in which the university sustains and supports prevailing attitudes toward women in our culture.

One reason for this is that critical scholars, along with politicians and the media at times, have primarily questioned and emphasized the social class and racial bigotries which motivate universities. For example, much has been written about the function of educational systems in teaching white, Anglo-Saxon virtues and in extolling the importance of learning specific forms of knowledge, values, economic imperatives—all of which perpetuate a kind of intelligentsia elite (Apple, 1979; Bowles and Gintis, 1976; Karabel and Halsey, 1977). The university's role in maintaining the interests of the upper class has occupied a central position during the past decade in most of the critical analyses in education. And all of the analyses were true enough in what they said concerning the university.

When dealing with the wider social and political context of academe directly, the tendency has again been to stress the university's "elitist" character without fully identifying who is affected by such "elitism" and why. For instance, in 1967 Theodore Roszak published *The Dissenting Academy*. North American journalistic circles as well as academic circles widely acclaimed the book because it presented a coherent critique of the "accepted" scholarship and because it offered an alternative role for American scholarship. The nature of the dissent was to expose the connection between military, corporate and governmental interests and to show clearly the ways in which the university expresses those interests. The dissent was considered "radical in the truest sense." However, there is no mention in the book of the role of the university as a social institution which is organized and constructed around patriarchal values. Nor is there acknowledgement of the fact that since the nineteenth century, feminists have, in varying ways, exposed that role by showing how discrimination inherent in the economic, social, political and educational systems expresses itself in academe.

One aim of this book is to chronicle a different dissent: a dissenting academy that has most recently re-emerged with the advent, in the late 1960's, of the women's movement and the feminist perspective which accompanied it. Contemporary feminists have taken Roszak's dissent one step further. They argue that the university does indeed reflect society's "wrongs" (as Roszak names them) and that one of these "wrongs" can be coined "patriarchy"—or the predominance of a systematic male perspective.

In a wider sense, a feminist perspective itself must be understood in relation to the university, especially as that perspective has both flourished in and been thwarted by academe. The core of this relationship presents a paradox: in the effort to expose and combat sexism, feminists have ultimately tried to appropriate their potential strength in an environment deeply enmeshed in the culture it challenges. The Dissenting Feminist Academy was born out of this contradiction: the same institution which has, within limits, permitted feminists to dissent, has generally reinforced expectations that women should conform to traditional roles.

This study is fundamentally concerned with understanding this contradiction as it is analyzed in feminist literature and revealed at various historical periods. More explicitly, the study attempts to describe the tension between the philosophy and structure of feminism and that of the university. For as O'Brien notes,

> When we speak of feminism and education, we are immediately confronted by a contradiction. On the one hand, education is seen as a necessary and important part of action directed towards social transformation. On the other hand, educational systems and school curriculum are structured hierarchi-

cally ... educational institutions are bastions
of male supremacy ruling class power. (1984,
p. 3)

The specifically feminist recognition that traditional scholarship has omitted women—left them out or peripheralized them—broadly characterizes the feminist dissent described in this book. In light of its contradictory relationship to the university, however, it is inadequate and inaccurate to suggest that the feminist dissent has been the passive recipient of the academy's barriers. What has become much clearer over the past few years, as one sees the contemporary scene against the backdrop of a rich and dynamic history, is that feminists have acted against the barriers and in turn, wrought significant changes in the context and content—the structure and content of academia. Moreover, the very fact that feminists have dissented implies that the university is not simply an institution where domination of one group and their ideas over another is completely successful. Rather, the university has been a site where continuous struggle has occurred between and within dominant groups and feminist scholars.

It is also limiting to single out any one group of feminists' interpretation of the problems in this interaction at any one time. Such an approach obscures our understanding of how feminists experience the barriers at different times and in different settings. The result of using this traditional social science method is that both feminism and universities are rendered fixed and unchanging, and both are torn from their socio-historical contexts. Another consequence of taking this perspective is that it leaves no room for understanding or implementing social change. Equally, the reality of how feminists as subjects and their complex histories interact is ignored. The study which follows, then, poses the question: What have feminists at different times identified as constraining their work, and how have they struggled against those constraints?

In order to answer this question, this book explores three time periods in which North American feminists visibly proliferate in the academy: (a) the late nineteenth and early twentieth century; (b) the late 1960's and early 1970's and; (c) the current decade. During each period feminists have attempted to define and explain the problems they face in academe. During each period those explanations have shifted because the social/political/ historical contexts were different and because the needs and concerns of feminists were distinct. Finally, during each period three major facets of the university were challenged: the institutional practices and policies of academe; the problems inherent in academic disciplines; and the tensions posed by the private/public dichotomy.[1]

The selection of these three time periods has been guided specifically by Rosenberg's (1982) work, but also by other historical accounts of women in academe.[2] Furthermore, it might be helpful to note here that the study's focus on different time periods does not imply the concern to explore the whole historical period per se. Rather, the main intent is to examine the experiences of feminists in the university within the context of each time period. The use of the word "Stage" is not so much representative of an historical setting in its entirety as it is denotive of a change in feminist thinking. Because of this, the period between 1920 and 1960 is not dealt with here. As Rosenberg (1982) points out:

> Throughout the 1930s, 1940s, and 1950s a number of scholars carried on the spirit of early, dissident social scientists . . . Despite these continuities . . . however, feminist-minded researchers from the fifties enjoyed less influence than earlier feminist scholars had. A full explanation of this declining influence must await further research . . . . (p. 238)

The three historical junctures are not entirely discrete although distinctive features highlight each. The First Stage witnessed the entry of women into higher education.[3] In late nineteenth century America, and indeed in Canada, many women (and some men) spoke out against the dominant ideology which held women to be inferior to men. The First Stage dissent was comprised of some of these women who were intent on challenging that ideology, and who did so at a time when the society was undergoing enormous change. Most notably, educational institutions and their practices had begun to be profoundly transformed (Prentice, 1974; 1977).

One of the developments which has central relevance to this study was the admission of women to universities that had previously excluded them. Prior to the First Stage, single-sex colleges for women had been in existence for roughly four decades. But these institutions were frequently designed to enhance women's skills as future mothers and wives. In this sense, such establishments worked actively to support the status quo and its notion that women belonged "naturally" in the private sphere. The opportunity for dissent was more available in the co-educational institution, not because of its rejection of the status quo, but because of its novel nature, its ambivalent philosophy and its ambiguous plebiscite. Three factors in particular worked to the advantage of feminists. One was the growing demand by reformers, politicians and educators, for institutions of learning more pragmatic and accessible than existing models. The research university was one structure which answered this need. Its original title reflected its *avant garde* agenda which sought to provide an environment in which reform could be translated into research and theory in order to study the environmental causes of a society in transition (Haskell, 1977; Oleson and Voss, 1979).

Another factor and related to the first, was the decision of some research universities to admit women. While debates about co-education were legion, a growing tendency to see women as badly needed economic resources, especially for establishments not as yet fully viable, gave impetus to admitting women (Rosenberg, 1982).

Equally important was the interest stirred in women, themselves, who saw their role in reform movements compatible with the referendum of the fledgling social sciences that were beginning to emerge within research academies. Within this context, some feminists attacked the larger dominant ideology of women's inferiority which they found supported by social science research.

What was the distinct nature of their dissent? The answer is difficult to pinpoint precisely, yet certain general trends can be observed. On the whole, nineteenth century feminists recognized institutional discrimination and experienced conflict between their private and public roles, but most of their energies were channelled into refuting social science research which supported the notion of women's inferiority. Within the university, they demanded both an extension of the services provided to include a wider selection of courses and programs available to women, as well as equal treatment as researchers, students and, in a few isolated instances, faculty.

The Second Stage dissent emerged from the social setting of the late 1960's. The political momentum characteristic of the period provided women (some of whom had rejected the sexism of the Left) with the chance to carry the "personal is political" motif over to a strategy for equal opportunity in universities. Because women were again struggling to become admitted as faculty as they had been in the late nineteenth century, the main focus of the critiques during this period were the problems posed by the institutional practices of universities. Not unlike their nineteenth century counterparts, the feminists in this period were aware of other kinds of barriers, particularly the private/public dichotomy whose rejection had largely defined the politics of the larger women's movement from which the academic arm had its roots. However, the absence or invisibility of women as faculty precipitated an immediate concern to challenge the institutional practices which perpetuated that invisibility.

The nonlinear evolution of the Third Stage witnessed a shift in feminist criticisms of the academy. The shift is not abrupt and in numerous ways appears nebulous. Yet we can see profound alterations in both the dissent's focus and in its manifestations.

The period, generally, is characterized by the movement of feminism into social science, arts and humanities research, and the full development of Women's Studies. This development involves examination of the underlying philosophies and assumptions of patriarchy itself — the ideology which creates and maintains the notion that women are inferior, the institutions which structure male dominance and female subordination, and the social sciences which are, in many respects, the study of men, by men, for men. Specifically, the concern here is with the problem of academic knowledge and with the academic disciplines which determine, select, construct and produce that knowledge. In this latest stage, feminists have, to some extent, gained access to faculty ranks, have fought and sometimes won battles with university administration, but the problem of what knowledge they teach has become the central concern. The distinct feminist response here, however, is the revelation that knowledge, practice and the separate sphere ideology are interdependent.

The following research, then, attempts to go beyond those studies which have isolated, and then studied, the ideas of one group of feminists in a particular time period to analyze how the *Dissenting Feminist Academy* has, over time, perceived and described patriarchal influence in universities. It is, secondly, an attempt to understand the dissent's contradictory relationship to academe, as well as an attempt to unravel some of the tangled roots of the contradiction, for within those roots lie the purposes and ideological functions of universities as well as the significance of feminist scholarship.

The dissent of feminist educational ideas is hardly new, but over the last ten years, this movement has filtered down into the classroom, suffusing along the way educational journals, conferences, curriculum guidelines and experimental programs. However, recent retrenchment in the economic climate has been matched by a swing back among educational interests.

If the dissent has seemed to be slowing down in momentum, then it would appear to be the right moment to look back at its impact. As I discovered over the course of the study, universities, in unsequenced cadences, have risen and fallen with particular political/economic tides and taken feminism with it. But in its moments of flux, the university has cared or worried about feminism for reasons that have more to do with its potential instability, than its political "correctness." The gap between this interest and official university policy regarding gender is the issue underscoring my interests in this book, and one, I believe, with which many feminists are concerned. It also begs the main questions implicitly addressed: Why have some of the major needs articulated by women been ignored by the educational institutions of our society and why has education in universities taken the particular forms it has with regard to gender? Hence, an examination of the structure, form and content of academe is central to both these questions.

The history of the dissent begins in Chapter Two covering the period from approximately 1880 to 1920 in North America, particularly the United States. The First Stage is examined in the context of the emergence of the research university and the subsequent evolution of the social sciences. It stresses the role of feminist scholars in the move away from biologically-based theories to environmental explanations of human behaviour. In the chapter, I examine both the changes that are taking place in the late nineteenth century university and its virtues which underwrite its claim as superior to the earlier learning academies. Such virtues helped to establish the university's well-earned place in the social order of things. But beyond attracting feminists, the qualities of the new co-educational institutions have, since the nineteenth century, become entangled in the debate over social inequality which troubles, time and time again, the conscience of the democratic state.

Chapter Three examines the period from the late 1960's to early 1970's. In it, I consider the agenda of Second Stage feminists whose writings and ideas primarily exposed the sexist nature of the university's institutional practices. These ideas are considered within the context of the larger dissent taking place in most universities in North America. Specifically, the dissent stressed the need to recruit women as faculty, to ensure their tenure, to encourage promotion. These issues affected the development of such matters as affirmative action and equal pay for equal work. As in the earlier period, feminists were aware of the other barriers but focused more on one to the relative exclusion of the others. Their focus was concentrated more on the university's institutional polity than on academic disciplines.

After examining and discussing what and how the university teaches, I turn in Chapter Four to the main issue occupying feminists, or, what is learned in academe. Chapter Four looks at the most recent shift in the dissent. The Third State critique of academe concentrates on the processes of knowledge formation, construction and dissemination within and across academic disciplines. In large part, the social context of the Second Stage gave rise to the current one by laying the groundwork for the Third Stage to go beyond earlier analyses and argue that the three categories of barriers form an interrelated web. After modifying, bending and pulling at theories to make them work after women were abruptly added to them, feminists began to question whether or not there is not something more problematic. Throughout analysis after analysis, feminists illustrate that patriarchy has extended more deeply than the surface level of knowledge: it has a firm hold on the very underlying philosophy of virtually all theory, if not the practice. And in both the theory and the practice of theory, we find we once again confront an ideology that women and men belong to two, separate and necessarily unequal spheres. By the late 1970's, the undercurrent of discontent among feminists reached an intellectual stalemate. Where do we turn from here? The response called for is the construction of feminist epistemology.

In the final chapter, I discuss the history of the dissent first in general terms and then consider its recent manifestations and its possibilities for the future. Taken as a whole, the history is enriched by the fact that it takes place in educational institutions where constraints, obstacles and overt forms of oppression are frequently very directly flaunted, but in which academic freedom, (or freedom to be and to exist are as meaningful as they can be in any context) reform, and recourse to political solutions have never completely ceased to be real for feminists. Though reformation does not necessitate transformation, I suggest that to expose the misconceptions of academic knowledge may well offer students a different future in academe. In unearthing some of the political, social and economic issues entailed in a patriarchal body of knowledge, the curriculum may come to offer knowledge as a more employable social resource, and one in which the oppression of gender — for both men and women — will cease to be an academic reality.

Finally, it is intended that this work, which is explicitly grounded in the Third Stage and by the time it goes to press, the Fourth, already too new to define, document the record of women's confrontation with higher education as part of the larger aim to halt the academic process of women's historical denial. However, until the university sees feminism's goal as one of its own, it will be a site where feminist dissent is necessary.

2

THE FIRST STAGE:
THE MID TO LATE NINETEENTH CENTURY

Blackberry Winter, the time when the hoar frost
lies on the blackberry blossoms; without this frost
the berries will not set. It is the forerunner of a
rich harvest

Margaret Mead.

The nature, issue and question of women's "right" to education has
been the bane of conservatives, the focus of liberals, the topic of
numerous historical tracts and, the subject of debate, controversy
and analysis amongst feminists. Because of its controversial nature,
women's institutional learning has been one of those reminders of
an historical problem that has not, and will not go away.

The prolific accounts of this subject however, have taken particular forms that Dyhouse (1984) describes as "the optimistic ver-
sion of women's educational history which imagines a clear path
from Victorian "revolutions" to late twentieth-century "equality"." I
believe Dyhouse is quite correct in pointing out that such a notion
problematically paints women in a linear historical process and
eludes the contradictory effects of higher education on women:
"For whilst it seemed in the beginning (as now) to secure valuable
space for women to think and experiment, it operated at the same
time to constrain and control them" (Acker and Piper, 1984, p. x).
Contrary to what traditional accounts have indicated, the "hidden
curriculum" of women's early higher education is especially significant with respect to this contradiction and "featured male dominance of the governing structure of the academies, differential
treatment and expectations for males and females and overt differences in curricular material and curricular choice. In this regard,

higher education was a double-edged sword insofar as it mirrored sexual divisions in the society outside."

In another sense, mainstream history has, in its insistence on this one-dimensional view of women's education, denied how women themselves "looked in" as they coped with the "ambivalence of educational provision." As feminists have pointed out, all too often women are presented (or mispresented) as having simply accepted the terms in which their education were given. Again, this is a overly simplistic view and it ignores the question of how women have constructed an academic and personal identity within structural constraints. And again it overlooks the paradox of women's educational experience, where marginality enforces limitations but ironically provokes opposition and resistance.

This chapter deals with "a moment" in the late nineteenth-century when some women tried to work through this paradox within the setting of the Research University. Together the barriers they faced, and the ways in which they responded to them comprise "The First Stage Dissent" of feminist scholarship. It will examine some of the debates, issues and developments within higher education which played an important part in both facilitating the dissent's rise and contributing to its decline. When I use the terms "rise" and "decline" I am not suggesting that the struggle for equity in education began and ended on a determinate date. Rather I am intending to map a piece of the ongoing process of dissent during a period that is historically specific in terms of its unique social setting. In terms of that setting, I will focus on the period of the 1870's to the 1890's, in which feminists attempted to articulate a social ideology, espoused by reformers and antedating democratic liberalism. The model they attempted to carve, was as paradoxical as the educational provision they fought so ardently to obtain. Inspired by scientific principles of symmetry, feminists described the tenets on which an egalitarian society could rest, including: intellectual equality for women, cooperation and sharing, moral conformism and the improved physicality of the sexes. Through their espousal of these ideals, they clung to the prevailing liberal philosophy of the period's reformists. Their arguments for a cooperative social community belied their fundamental rejection of some of liberalism's central claims, even as they held *to* the liberal legacy and even *as* they sustained the superiority of women's moral virtues.

Equally I am concerned to examine the women who became

caught in this transition, particularly those who championed "equal educational opportunities" for both sexes in the public realm. Here too, it is imperative that one places this evolution within the wider strategy of the middle-class reconstruction of all institutions. When seen within this larger incline; the notion that women spent all of their energies fighting for space in the so-called public domain, seems overly simplistic. For one thing, such a notion obscures what it was precisely that women were engaged in: for another, it does not allow for the *fluidity* of the public sphere. The public sphere was indeed an objective set of structures, but it was also an individual invention, subject to varying definitions. Leach (1980) provides an interesting insight into the "public" activities of feminists during this period. He suggests that "it was in the realm of *civil* society, the area of political struggle that we ordinarily think of as private, that feminists sought, and in some degree captured, power" (p. 9). He continues that in this sphere, feminists established their alliance with reformist intellectuals and formulated their critique of liberalism's "possessive individualism". In a unique and complex manner, feminists used their "private" definitions in the attempt to remodel the "public" domain. They did this in order that the male world of the professions and institutions become egalitarian.

Set against this intricate backdrop, I wish to focus in on the dissent's emergence in higher education. I will quickly retrace the parameters of the controversy surrounding education for women, including the debate amongst women themselves about the merits and/or disadvantages of coeducation and single-sex institutions. The differences between the two types of provision are largely a matter of individual opinion and, controversy about the impact of the two is as lively as it was in the nineteenth century. It is not my intention in this chapter to discuss the differences between single-six and coeducational institutions, nor am I inclined to try and settle the debate. Rather, I do want to point out that the dissent manifested, in differing ways, in both separate and mixed-sex colleges and universities. Both "choices" were sometimes inspired to intellectual equality with men and both kinds of provision strengthened, more than they weakened, academe's male genre. Within the context of both, some women were utilizing the power of their "private" definitions to forge a distinctive feminist tradition. I will examine, specifically the dissent's appearance in the coeducational research universities, whose gradual deference to reform lobbying, led to the installation of social science, as a fixed, permanent fixture in the academic world. My emphasis on this occasion, stems from the symbiotic affiliation of organized, nineteenth-century feminism, with the reform-undergirding of social moralism, later legitimized as social science.[1] In fact, women's early role in founding the American Social Science Association (1869) for instance, had cemented their alliance with social science, sometime before its establishment in the academic agenda. These coincidences, combined with the enthusiasm of feminists' toward coeducation, make the coeducational context of the experimental academics, (such as the famous University of Chicago and Stanford) ideal places in which to understand the dissent's relationship to academe. Both the barriers they encountered, and the responses they offered, shaped and gave shape to the nature of women's dissidence in the nineteenth century. In the midst of this contradiction, and despite the fact that women often took on a kind of domestic feminism to assert their "rights", their implicit attempt to propound a theory of social reality based on humanistic, cooperative principles reveals a familiar contemporary concern to create a "feminist epistemology".

The Beginnings

In order to clearly understand its significance, it is necessary to situate the First Stage in the social milieu of the late nineteenth century.

The entrenchment of commercial industrialism, the replacement of cottage and domestic economy with a centralized manufacture mode of production, the loss of authority by the Church and the ever-growing spread of urban development all combined to create intense upheavals in the lives of men and women. Not only were people's homes and work redefined, but notions of self-definition, identity and personal roles became confused and ambiguous. The resulting social dislocation left many impoverished, and many others concerned about the growing instability and deterioration of the "human condition" (Berkin and Norton, 1979).

Much of the confusion surrounding these social changes, sprang from the apparent inconsistencies that existed in the prevailing liberal preponderance with "possessive individualism". From a reformist point of view, the impact of this individualism had created social conditions to the detriment of men and women. Bringing the liberal tradition into question, movements for reform (of which women comprised a substantial proportion) proposed a critique that reflected their general, overall confusion with the ideals of liberal democracy on the one hand, and the realities of social chaos on the other. Adhering to much of that same tradition, progressive reformers tried to construct a revised model of social democracy which came to be "physically expressed" in the various social reform activities they engaged in. "After the Civil War, innumerable, apparently contradictory reform groups, overtly feminist or with feminist sympathies, labored to construct a new world view that offered an alternative to classical liberalism" (Leach 1980, p. 12). Within a strictly social framework, these groups directed their political attention to "school, asylums, libraries, hospitals, and prisons, to the professions and to the home, and - perhaps most of all to political interpretation - to human biology, to the bodies of men and women, to sexuality" (p. 12). Significantly, these attentions were prompted by the perceived hope reformers had in the emerging theories of science, of organization, and of the potential they envisioned in institutional and professional structures. In the interests of harnessing these forces, feminist reformers, (like the abolitionists before them and the Progressives which followed them) turned to the principles of science to contour their quest for social coalescence. For women, not only would this lead to a better understanding of how to ameliorate the decay of public order, but it would facilitate the growth of their own, personal roles which had become scrutinized. For the reform sector generally, the scientific rationalization of society would allow a humanitarian ethic to re-organize the sociality, and would mean an organization in which people's lives and roles could be ordered and regulated. The apparent implications for *women's "role"*, including of course the women who zealously supported this vision, had not as yet become visible; for in the meantime, feminists with ties to this commitment, were turning a selected eye to the question of higher education, both because of its exposure to scientific knowledge and because they believed social symmetry must involve intellectual equality with men.

Using the rhetoric of equality, reformers carried their concern and fear of social "chaos" over to issues of abolition, prohibition, legal reform and education. Education, and particularly higher education during this period, became a center of attention for reformers. The main role of education, especially from the 1860's on, was to respond to the numerous economic and social changes in North American society. Adjustment to change was essential, argued reformers, educators, and political authorities, in diminishing social disorder, creating public order and, moving progressively toward the future. Indeed, the "progress" of society was the touchstone of the transformations of the educational system in the United States and in Canada.

Earlier, universities had served to maintain an established social order and were strictly elitist by nature (Oleson and Voss, 1979). However, institutions of higher learning eventually would follow and accelerate the social changes advocated by social reformers. By the end of the nineteenth century, politicians and educators expounded the polemic that education was more an instrument for shaping a new type of society than the means of maintaining the old established order. Consequently, initiatives were more frequently taken in the name of progress or "usefulness" than in the name of education (Prentice, 1977).

The altruistic concern for amelioration by way of education was double-sided. On one hand was the expression of a genuine need to provide necessary changes in education. On the other was the desire and indeed the need for institutions which could effectively manage and control the social order. The extent to which this ambivalence characterized the issue of women's education speaks implicitly to the general contradictory tenor of nineteenth century ideologies concerning women's "proper sphere".

Although by the 1870's many women were involved in paid employment outside the home, the access to higher education was still predominantly restricted to middle-class men. The was due in large measure to the prevailing ideological notion that "women were biologically inferior to men — they were weak, frail, incapable of strenuous mental and physical exertion" (Gordon, 1971, p. 36). It was argued that too much study, like employment outside the domestic sphere, would fatigue women (because they had smaller brains) and ruin their reproductive organs. The paradox of such a notion is evident in the way working women were seen: "Women who worked as domestics, factory workers and farm hands were often accused of immoral behaviour, thought to be the result of their working conditions and environment causing a disordered biology" (Kealey, 1974, p. 8).

The Entry of Women into Higher Education

New developments in women's educational provision went hand in hand with larger reforms in secondary education (Rosenberg, 1982). These developments took various forms.

In Britain, (though not our particular focus) certain North American trends manifested in the change-over from small domestic academies for women, to the development of Ladies' Colleges and Collegiate schools. The founders of the Ladies' Colleges believed that "women's education ... (was) important because women were not expected to earn their own living - as dependent wives they were expected to use their leisure time to cultivate "refinement", to indulge in aesthetic or social activities which would lend prestige or distinction to the family as a whole" (Dyhouse, 1984, p. 54).

Such views were cross-culturally ubiquitous, though the forms they took varied across social contexts. The notion that education would sharpen women's domestic skills was highly characteristic of the overall rationale for women's educational provision and as Dyhouse (1984) says, such views "were expressed time and time again by middle-class advocates".[2] These advocates included the reformers who were making enormous dints in the fabric of educational ideology. In many respects, the *forms* of provisions offered were novel, but the *aims* of those provisions were not altogether different from earlier ones: in both the predecessing schools and the new colleges, a central objective was to "turn out cultivated ladies of leisure" (Dyhouse, p. 54).

It is here particularly, in the reform advocacy of women's scholastic development, that we find the emphasis on regulating women's roles as wife and mother and, the reformers' determination to institutionalize that regulation. As Dyhouse points out, because of the patriarchal nature of late Victorian society, even the reconstruction of social institutions tended to be "conservative" if not in the structure, in the underlying assumptions and motives. But they cannot be seen as wholly conspiratorial or unilateral in their practice. Such institutions did not exist to simply reinforce the sexual division of labour. Rather, in some cases they "supplied women with valuable space for learning and self-expression and played a crucial role in the history of the feminist movement.." (Dyhouse, p. 55).

Generally speaking however, both the type and the form of education which women received propounded "femininity for domesticity". Miriam David's (1978) excellent study shows how the State, through new kinds of contingencies, employed the "family-education couple" to maintain sexual divisions in the late nineteenth century. The State sought the help of the family in reproducing the school's work. Even opponents of women's higher education, "justified" their challenge by arguing that the mental strain of intellectual endeavor would cause undue damage to women's maternal and conjugal functions.

Opponents of women's education found convenient backing for their position in scientific "discoveries" ostensibly proving that "prolonged education would lead to mental and physiological derangement in women students, especially those who attended college" (Burstyn 1984, p. 65). While lay persons frequently found these arguments irrelevant or inaccurate, educators nevertheless "amended the curriculum and the social environment in schools and colleges to allay fears and forestall prophesied ill-effects" (p. 65). Even those who would support women's education participation, argued that the "need to educate women was as great, if not greater, than the need to educate men, because women had to learn a anew how to use their brains to the full in order to reverse a process of evolution that had already begun." Clearly these "proofs" of women's evolutionary inferiority, spurred on by the dissemination of Darwin's *Origin of Species* (1859), gave impetus as well, to the establishment (in some academies)of separate, specially-devised curricula. According to Burstyn, the authority attached to the medical profession and the convincing evidence it provided of the dangerous physical effects of educational strain to women's reproductive functions, made women and men reformers especially vulnerable to these kind of claims. Combined, the desire to promote women's domestic skills as mothers and wives, the use of the "family-education couple" and the scientific, evolutionary-premised delineations of women's physical retribution, worked to shape both the structure and the content of women's provision.

The British experience was by no means exempliar in its execution of higher learning. The reasoning behind philanthropists', educators' and statesmen's (sic) concession to higher education for women in the United States and Canada, was concomitantly double-edged and ideological. The importance of physical health, the maintenance of moral values and domestic agility and, the promulgation of women's special position in the nuclear family unit framed the tone of controversy between challengers and defendants of women's intellectual training. The kinds of actual training which were made available to women however, were not always as explicit in their thinking about women's roles. Two types in particular, offered women advanced education beyond the secondary school level.

The first kind of provision was made accessible in single-sex institutions or within larger male-dominated universities through separate, "female" colleges. In the former, women were offered Latin and Greek; they studied arts subjects, particularly history and were exposed to religious studies and domestic science. In the latter, similar programmes emphasized the development of women's moral, as well as intellectual and physical character (Dyhouse, 1984; Rosenberg, 1982). Later, some of the "ladies departments" merged with the formal structure of large universities. Colleges for women only, such as Pennsylvania Female College, Elmira College in New York and Wesleyan Female College, and later Mount Holyoke, Smith Vassar and Wellesley, had curricula "equal in rigor and quality to that of the best male schools" (Leach, 1980, p. 76). Their iniative came, on a parochial level, from doctors, clergy or prominent businessmen (Dyhouse, 1984).

Though the debate about separate institutions has revealed both the advantages and more commonly, the disadvantages of single-sex provision, here I would again point to the features it shared with the coeducational experience (itself a variation of similar forms of gender maintenance and never a radical alternative). One of those distinguishing features which it held in common with coeducation was its rationale for specially-suited curricula, segregated classes, activities and accommodations. Special examinations were frequently instituted and these along with separate requisites, were considered necessary in light of women's biological infirmities. In the same spirit, medical opinion in *favour of* women's colleges held that there women would not be tempted to overstrain themselves. Mental collapse, could be avoided by physical excercise.

The "separate college idea" however, and the actual experience of single-sex education was by no means one-sided. Despite the rhetoric, women were often provided with female role models who rejected the sanctions and limitations of cultural standards of "femininity". Freed from the constraints of "male culture", a woman often found within the separate college community, a distinctively female culture. Burnstyn (1984) proposes though, that such environments were subject to decline, not only for financial reasons, but also because in a patriarchal society, institutions of male domination, such as universities, are accorded higher status because they are male-dominated. Hence the separate strategy could not (although it certainly attempted to in some instances) challenge the overall perpetuation of sex roles. It may, in fact, have interrupted it by providing a "haven in a heartless world", but in using gender as a basis for allocating women, separate institutions were often forced to promote the same ideology which held women to be inferior.

Feminists who fought through reform movements for women's educational equity were themselves often divided about the type of higher education they felt would best promote equality. Of those who avowed the advantages of a learning environment unhampered by the presence of male distraction; the separate, single-sex institute provided a marvelous opportunity for women to sharpen their academic, intellectual skills, without the fear of male bullying, male-oriented competition or intrusion, and with the support of other women. To this end, states Spender (1983), feminists such as Mary Astell, cryptically acclaimed the possibilities for intellectual development inherent in single-sex establishments. In her invitation to women, Astell said: "You are therefore, Ladies, invited into a place, where you shall suffer no other confinement but to be kept out of the road of sin: you shall not be deprived of your grandeur, but only exchange the vain pomps and pageantry of the world, empty titles and forms of state, for the true and solid greatness of being able to despise *them*" (cited in Spender 1983, p. 59). That male values dominated most of the society, was a point taken up by many feminists. The "woman-only" college in this view, would allow women to acquire a new value system, based on "woman-centered" characteristics and in the process, women educators could impart to women the fact of the deficiencies in patriarchal forms of organization and, the futility of demanding a greater share of male power in institutions controlled by men. In response to her challengers, Astell defended her proposal to establish a college for women with these convictions: "The Ladies, I am sure, have no reason to dislike this Proposal; but I know not how the men will resent it, to have their enclosure broken down, and women invited to taste of the Tree of Knowledge, they have so long unjustly monopolised. But they must excuse me, if I be as partial to my own sex as they are to theirs, and think women as capable of learning as men, and that it becomes them well" (cited in Spender, p. 59).

Irrespective of the provisional-type, and as the "progressive" notion of education became more widespread, women were considered "able" to participate in higher education, though class-bias was evident in the fact that it was primarily middle class women who were considered "able" (Acton, 1974). Many advocates of higher education for women argued that because women were "better" and "purer" than men, education *itself* would improve when "good", "ladylike" women were allowed to participate. Thus Victorian sexist stereotypes were used as a basis for middle class arguments about women's education.

It is important to understand that while educational opportunities for women were on the rise in the mid-nineteenth century, in many sectors, opposition thrived. In the 1850s and early 1860s, women in the United States for example, were permitted to enter some Midwest coeducation universities such as Iowa and Wisconsin, though these institutions were the exception, not the rule. In Canada during the same time, women were beginning to form the ranks at McGill, Dalhousie and Mount Allison Universities. Predominantly though, women's formal education consisted of common or elementary school provision, or academies designed from the "Victorian ideal of segregated respectability" (Light and Prentice, 1980, p. 204).

The question of coeducation began to attract the growing attention of reformers as the doctrine of separate spheres for women and men became increasingly expounded and as the distinction between public and private spheres itself became increasingly differentiated. As Light and Prentice (1980) point out, while "The home came ... to be regarded as the preserve of women ... many women ... were nevertheless escaping, if only temporarily, from the private sphere of home and family" (p. 181). In the coeducation institution, feminists thought they would be able to work in the world of men on an equal basis. For some, education in single-sex institutes posed little threat to the sanctity of separate spheres and therefore could not be counted on to achieve equality. In fact, the education received was considered inferior because it *was* given in an all-woman environment. Coeducation, on the other hand, was considered more attractive to some feminists.

Despite the opposition to it, coeducation became increasingly supported by feminists and by male reformers. As Leach (1980) suggests, most feminists took the coeducational position, but received a great deal of support from educators in their demands that women receive precisely the same education as men students, that they study the same curriculum, have the same teachers, and "contend together for the same rank and honors" (p. 76). Paradoxically though, the arguments they put forward to justify these demands were grounded in "hygenic-scientific" terms. Citing the medical evidence, coeducationists argued that women's health would improve in a coeducational system. Single-sex schools, they proported, segregated women in "dreamy, claustrophobic domesticity" and kept "the flame of the sexual imagination alive far beyond healthy psychological limits, stimulating morbid sensitiveness, hurtful reveries and a false consciousness of sex" (Leach p. 76-77). Egalitarian coeducation, in comparison, "erased the intellectual and moral differences between the sexes in a simulated natural-family context that made potent social forces subject to rational influences. In a coeducational setting ... self-centered sexuality and sexual polarization disappear" (p. 77).

The feminist beliefs that cooperative, fully integrated human beings could develop freely in such a climate; that open exchange between the sexes promoted less conflicted sexual relations; that coeducation improved possibilities for better marriages and; that women's equality with men would only come through the integration of the sexes in institutional forums; were part of their larger commitment to the scientific doctrines of symmetry and to their espousal of the reformists' concern with developing the professions. In fact, some time before they were given the coeducational option, feminists were already involved in education, household reform, health and social reform, newspaper and magazine work for women and so on (Kealey, 1974). Organizations such as the Association for the Advancement of Women in 1873, the American Woman's Industrial Congress, the Chicago Woman's Club and the American Social Science Association, promoted the inclusion of women professionals in all institutions. Insisting that women were temperamentally suited for professional work, feminists who were especially keen to social science reformism pointed out that "women's older caretaking and educational functions had been plucked from the home by the state, that social institutions as well as the state had acquired a domestic complexion, and that women, therefore, should follow their functions out of the home" (Leach, p. 189).

Such was the nature of feminists' reform-influenced ideas about institutional reconstruction and about women's role in that reconstruction. These ideas in turn, influenced to a great extent, their position on coeducation. Many shared their position.

While the debate about women's higher education raged on the case for coeducation was building momentum. An article written in it The Educational Review (1887), entitled "Educational Advantages for Girls in the Maritime Provinces", suggested that Canadian *educators* saw the benefits of providing women with access to educational institutions. The article, cited in Prentice and Houston (1975), extolled the impressive and progressive record of Maritime universities:

> Dalhousie College, in Halifax has for five years admitted ladies on exactly the same footing as male students, and of the (five) ladies who have been graduated there every one came off with honors, three winning the degree of B.A., one that of B.Sc., and one that of B.L. But beside there have been about one hundred ladies who have taken special courses not leading to degrees (p. 259).

It also appears evident that such records came some time later than the openings accorded by American institutions of higher education, though this made the Canadian concession to women no less double-edged, or free of ideology. In an 1867 document (again found in Prentice and Houston (1975)) the coeducational tendency of increasing numbers of American universities was greeted with mixed feelings, and while the author of this document conceded that there were certain advantages to this policy, he argued that, "We may content ourselves, however, for the present, with the Arts course. Happily, our young Dominion is not yet ripe for throwing open the Bench, and the Bar, ... to the gentler sex, however well our fair Portias might become the Doctor's gown, or even the Episcopal silks and lawn" (p. 256). It was apparent that from the perspective of educators, coeducation posed problems to preserving both working class and middle class women's role in the private sphere, where, it was purported, they belonged. However pervasive this notion may have been, it is clear that women's educational opportunities were expanding just the same. As I have mentioned, among those who saw the benefits of coeducation, for example, were groups of women who had ties to larger reform movements, but who were also advocates of women's rights.[3] They saw education as one key, and because they believed sex-segregated education would always be unequal, they supported coeducation.

These same women shared in the reform notion of progress and unlike their working class counterparts, they were optimistic about the potential of higher education in freeing women from the ideological bonds of domesticity (Rosenberg, 1982). These women saw the importance of gaining access to the public sphere and relentlessly pursued the campaign for women's *equal* education. They were by no means a negligible group. In her introduction to Elizabeth Smith's diaries, for example, Strong-Boag (1980) points out that Smith was one of several women in the third quarter of the nineteenth century in Canada who set out to get a medical education and succeeded in that effort. We see from Smith's individual battle that she was not alone in her struggles for admission to a male-dominated medical school: "There were large numbers of nineteenth-century women who were determined to break male monopolies in education, the professions, and business, and demanded the right to live uncloistered lives" (Strong-Boag, 1980, p. ix). Similarly in the United States, many women who struggled in the spirit of feminism were determined to examine, criticize, and "occasionally applaud their own and society's slow progress towards perfection" (p. ix).[4]

Amidst the various larger developments we have seen, many of those women, who were bent on proving their equal abilities in the public world of education as in the private, found a novel welcome in the new American coeducation policy of many universities. These feminists argued that women were equal to men, required similar, not different opportunities and could lead similar lives. These ideas were compatible with their reform commitments and with their shared belief in the progress of society and hence the "improvement" of women. Their fundamental *challenge* to the attitude that women were *biologically* predisposed to weaker intelligence was, moreover, compatible with a wider belief of reformers, and educators, that the biological nature of humans could indeed be controlled and ameliorated by education.

These events, coupled with the gradual spread of coeducation provisions in several of the new research universities in the United States, made it possible for women to challenge the notion that women were biologically, and therefore intellectually inferior to men. The social context provided by reform, by a society in transition and by the liberal notion in equality, facilitated a particular manifestation of the First Stage of feminist dissent within academe (Rosenberg, 1975; 1979; 1982).

It is apparent that despite the continuous arguments against it, coeducation was put into practice by some universities, most notably the research academies. It is also evident that a change in thinking had occurred in women to the extent that once admitted, they managed to dissent. But how had women's experiences in the university facilitated their dissent? What specifically was it about the new research academy that allowed women in, but led them to dissent? And most importantly; what *was* the specific nature of that dissent?

The Research University

Beyond the obvious significance of its frequent support of coeducation, the research university of the late nineteenth century was novel in numerous ways. Unlike its predecessors, it was defined (at least in the beginning) as an institution dedicated to the pursuit of scholarly research and scientific development (Haskell, 1977). It was to be committed to attracting reformers who would undertake research on the "special problems plaguing American society at the end of the century" (Rosenberg, 1982, p. 28).

The commitment to attract reformers and indeed the fact that reform had largely created the new university was central to the new university's designated role in late nineteenth century society. Above all, the research university was seen as a vital mechanism in cohering some of the fragmented elements of the social order. As such, neither its *ideological* role nor its function was altogether clear-cut (Touraine, 1974). More important, because the problem of constructing a new social order outweighed the larger concern for preserving pre-existing social relationships and ideologies, the research academy initially was in a state of flux. This state meant that it was not as yet equipped nor deeply involved with *social selection* and *state legitimization* at the outset of its development. Though short-lived, the academy's inchoate organization lasted long enough for groups who had previously been excluded from parochial and privately-financed institutions, to become part of what was considered a "maverick" community.

The new agenda of the research academy reflected the ideology of "progress", which explains in part its attraction to and for liberal reformers. Though this ideology was not completely autonomous from the hold of the dominant ruling class, it nevertheless corresponded to the expectations of students from quite varied backgrounds. It was during these beginning stages of growth that one group in particular was granted access to the academic community. These were feminists who were often struggling for women's right to education and who were often involved in issues or movements for reform and/or philanthropy. They were also the same women who saw the equal educational right of women as one facet of a larger struggle to refute the "biology is destiny" dictum. The new agenda of the research university and the coeducational policy which accompanied it (in many cases) presented a golden opportunity for the dissent to formulate its feminist-reform ideas within an academic context.

But if the research university consisted of enough supporters of coeducation, there were still those who resited the idea. To those academics schooled in earlier doctrines and established norms, the traditional order was the only order. How then, did these male faculty members and educators respond to the numbers of women who were entering? For the less heterodox, the proliferation of women in the academic system could *de facto* only prove deleterious to the reverence which academe commanded. The phenomenon of such comparatively large numbers of women led them to fear what one university president called "The Feminization of Academe" (Eliot, 1937).

On one level the concern over female enrollment reflected the university's parochial desire for status, but on another level it echoed the ubiguitous fear of "feminization" that plagued that society in the nineteenth century. As economic and social upheavals of industrialization brought social dislocation, North American society clung more ardently to its basic assumptions about sexual identity. Within universities, and despite its liberal rhetoric, similar assumptions loomed large. After women had gained access to the university, they discovered the establishment of separate spheres within its governance that reflected conventional notions of sexual difference and upheld the growing demarcation of private/public forms of organization.[5]

At the same time, the maverick nature of the university, allowed room for iconoclasm to survive, and evoked a tenor of freedom which made it possible for feminists to scorn and reject these assumptions: "For these deviant scholars, academia became a prism through which sexual differences could never again be seen in quite the same way as they had been seen before" (Rosenberg, 1979, p. 373).

Given the juxtaposed novel aims of the coeducational university and the equally orthodox character of the factions within it, how did feminists fare in it during these early stages and what were the effects of later developments on women?

Initially the feminists who entered were interested in explaining women's "nature" but did not feel compelled to understand their own activities in terms of that "nature" (Rosenberg, 1982). And because the academic institutions had not as yet erected rigid sex-role divisions, feminists did not perceive the need to articulate a female sphere within that institution. For a short while, they received relatively "equal" training, carried out similar work, and functioned apart from the ever-growing private public divisions of the larger society.[6]

Such was the paradoxical nature of the university's early development; its more advanced organizational expansion was no less contradictory in terms of its impact of feminists. Among the structural novelties of these academic systems, three tendencies stand out, particularly as they affected women: (1) they combined advanced training and research, and encompassed not only undergraduate and graduate instruction in the same institution, but also professional training (Haskell, 1977; Oleson and Voss, 1979; Rosenberg, 1982); (2) they came to be characterized by the desire — indeed the economic necessity — to serve as many interests as possible, and the commitment to provide an "egalitarian" education[7] (Curti, 1967; Haskell, 1977), and; (3) they introduced the "elective" system which expanded the curriculum and created specialization in the development of scholarship. This last creation precipitated the early emergence and later crystallization of the social sciences as academic disciplines (Curti, 1967; Haskell, 1977; Ross, 1979).

The second aim was especially advantageous for women who had been previously denied access to universities. Admitting women was also advantageous to academies which had not as yet become financially viable. Badly needed tuitions gave deeper conviction to providing "egalitarian" education and gave impetus to opening the university's doors to women (Touraine, 1974).

The first aim however, was less double-edged and more one-sided. The innovation of graduate studies was one step toward tighter internal organization of the university, and as it became more regulated and managed, graduate studies took on a selecting and sorting function. At this point feminists had accumulated in large numbers in the undergraduate population. For example, "When the University of Chicago opened in 1892, women comprised ... 40 percent of the undergraduate student body. By 1902 the enrollment of women had out-stripped that of men ..." (Rosenberg, 1982, pp. 43-44).

The graduate enrollment was a different story, if only because "most universities refused women admission to graduate studies, or admitted them only as auditors ..." (Rosenberg, p. 52). Some of the new research academies were willing to break precedent. The University of Chicago was one such exception and to the charge that women had no interest in graduate work, Marion Talbot (then the dean of women and assistant professor of sociology at the University of Chicago) argued that "... 12 percent of the male undergraduates and 14 percent of the women went on to graduate study. Of those with fellowships, 41 percent of the men and 36 percent of the women completed doctorates" (Rosenberg, 1982, p. 47).

Gradually, the earlier reform-oriented purpose began to take a back seat to the proliferation of science claims. The shift was gradual, but was evidenced by the consolidation of the academy whose now "... distinct purpose was to develop productive scholars and scientists" (Rosenberg, 1982, p. xii). Its renewed purpose manifested itself in a renewed agenda. No longer would scholars be expected to simply teach an outdated curriculum of little practical relevance, but would now combine a program of teaching *and* research, more relevant to the problems of urban, industrialized nineteenth and twentieth century society. This agenda had direct implication for the professor's role: "... they assumed a new identity as specialists aware of the inherent obligation of the scholar to advance as well as disseminate learning. Increasingly their promotion and status depended on their contribution to research as judged by their disciplinary peers" (Oleson and Voss, 1979, p. xii).

One final point concerning the dual emphasis on research/teaching is significant in this context. Shils (1979) argues that the university's dual function of teaching and research helped to establish its dominance as a learning institution which legitimates "true" knowledge. Contrasted with the older academy which merely taught an outdated and monolithic curriculum, the new research university was an institution "... that produced its own *nachwuchs*[8] and staff" (p. 28). In other words, there was kind of "circle effect" system put in place, whereby professors became both producers and disseminators of knowledge to students who became the proceeding producers and disseminators. In this way, the research universities assured themselves centrality in the system of learning. The rise of the "real pillars" of research academe such as John Hopkins University in 1876, Clark University in 1887, and the University of Chicago in 1892, marked the inauguration of a deep commitment to make research an integral and major part of the university's program (Rosenberg, 1982; Shils, 1979). The expectation of upholding this commitment and retaining the importance of teaching did not succeed however. Shils stresses:

> Then as now, there were some who did a great deal of research, many who did a little, and others who did none ... there emerged a division of labor between the younger teachers who were assigned the more elementary courses and their older colleagues who taught the advanced courses that were more directly related to research (p. 29).

At the same time, even though junior faculty had heavier teaching responsibilities, they were especially expected to engage in research. The more established senior scholars had less teaching to do and their teaching was more congenial to their own research.

The third and final objective of the academy was like the others, one which later functioned as a help and a hindrance to feminists scholars. The spread of the elective system provided wider choices of study, but also catalyzed the erection of strict boundaries between particular areas and ultimately paved the way for the institutionalization of the social sciences.

The growth of knowledge was marked by a number of sometimes contradictory and sometimes complementary dualisms, depending on who benefited the most or least: teaching and research, amateurism and professionalism, the push for centralized intellectual leadership and the pull of decentralized authority (Haskell, 1977). Part of this tendency to dualism was the fragmentation of knowledge into specialized units, coupled with the standardization of the institutional forms established to advance and transmit knowledge (Oleson and Voss, 1979). While fragmentation was not in itself dualism, it was a piece of the logic which underpinned the university's institutional framework (Shils, 1979).

This growth of knowledge in ever-narrowing fields, (as a result of specialization) produced a proliferation of professional members who shared an interest in raising the cultural standards of the nation; by the early twentieth century, leadership of "learned societies" was firmly in the hands of professional scientists and scholars who were concerned with formalizing, standardizing, and advancing research in their fields (Ross, 1979).

Ross (1979) has charted the emergence of the social sciences as separate, academic, professionalized, and increasingly "scientific" disciplines by distinguishing three distinct groups of intellectuals who were concerned with the development of these fields: the advocates of social, political, economic, and educational reform in the 1870's; the academic pioneers who in the same decade introduced the social sciences into the college curriculum as independent subjects; and the German-trained generation in the 1880's who ultimately took the lead in defining the new professions. Drawing on extensive data, Wirth (1967) also presents a comprehensive examination of the social sciences communities — particularly sociology and psychology. He points out, as does Haskell (1977), that the social sciences had a unique connection to early twentieth century North American society. They arose amidst internal academic debate and controversy, but were united in their concern with external social forces:

> The rapid rate of industrial expansion of the country, the rise of the nation to the position of world power, the growth of ... industrial and busi-

ness combinations ... the asserted challenges of
that power by organized labor and populist —
agrarian movements, the disappearing frontier,
the mass influx of immigrants, the plight of the
Negro, the chaotic growth of cities, the ever-
widening slums, and the existence of widespread
poverty, were part of the scene in which the
nascent social sciences were seeking to make
headway (Wirth, 1967, p. 39).

The problems which these social forces generated, "... furnished
... scientists with the incentives and materials for their scientific
enterprises and they induced the American public ... to take the
social sciences more seriously" (p. 39). The social sciences in turn,
furnished feminist scholars with an *institutional framework* in
which to intellectually pursue their already implanted concerns for
these social problems.

The character of the developing social sciences at the turn of
the century was significantly shaped by the "... dominant philosophy of the period, with its empirical and pragmatic temper, its con-
sequent emphasis upon the actual problems of the developing
American society, its revulsion from doctrinaire metaphysics and
armchair speculation, and its accent upon observation and experimentation, for which William James and John Dewey might serve
as symbolic representatives" (Wirth, p. 44). At the same time while
the theories of Marx and of Darwin also found their way into the
popular literature at this time:

The charge of atheism, materialism and vulgar
mechanism was often invoked against the
fledgling social scientists because of their
methodological emphasis on objectivity, the
scrutiny of *a priori* assumptions, the questioning
of authority, the search for reliable sources, the
attempts at experimentation, and the great
weight given to direct observation and mensura-
tion (p. 44).

Because many social scientists were conspicuous as advocates
of social reform, or as voiced critics of public policy, they were

frequently denounced as revolutionaries, often with the consequence of having their academic positions appropriated. This was
however much more the case *before* the formal division of the various social sciences because the resulting development of professionalization gave legitimacy to radical social science.

Psychologists in the late nineteenth century and sociologists
somewhat later continued individually to maintain their reform
and altruistic concerns, but the nature of specialization led them
more and more to avoid raising or even dealing directly with the
most crucial questions that were troubling the society that supported them; when they did they avoided the most complete or revealing answers to the questions they did raise. But that did not
merely make their curricula banal or innocuous. Specialization also
affected *what* was to be studied as well as *how* it was to be studied.
In the process, it established the "proper" way of dealing with questions deemed important, which questions are more important than
others, what kind of record, datum, document, or witness constitutes evidence and lends authority; and all of this is antecendent to
and more specific than the more general context. The overwhelming concern for scholarship, and the concern for generating rather
than merely transmitting knowledge, represented a move away
from using a prescribed curriculum to the development of an elective system in which faculty members taught a limited number of
courses, all of them in their "specialty". The shift had ramifications
for both the way knowledge was organized and the way teachers
were organized. Faculty members came to attach themselves to certain fields which became increasingly narrow over the years (Graham, 1978).

By 1920 major changes signalled shifts in academic institutions
and the rising professionalism attendant to that development
(Furner, 1975). For one thing, the organizational structure that
would govern the production of knowledge in America was in
place. For another, universities came to resemble one another in
their methods of training, departmental organization, and administrative systems (Oleson and Voss, 1979). Graduate schools established common requirements for advanced degrees, and professional associations adopted common objectives and modes of operation. This was supposedly a move to "... reconcile egalitarian values
with the elitist nature of specialization by adopting standardized
institutional devices: formal requirements of the Ph.D. degree ..."

(Oleson and Voss, 1979, p. xix).

This uniformity of structural arrangements established the basic patterns of academe which exist today. Oleson and Voss (1979) described these patterns:

> American institutions of learning, like industrial corporations, also have been seen as part of a trend towards nationally oriented, impersonal, hierarchical organizations. ... these bodies manifested the distinctive features of specialization: the acceptance of objective criteria for judging individual ability, a division of labor among experts ... (p. xix).

How then did these developments affect feminists? The early period of these "growing pains" saw feminists who were appearing most prominently. And it was centrally within the context of the social sciences that feminists made their appearance and their First Stage dissent. As I have said earlier, women had an alliance with social science that extended deep into their philosophic reform roots. Within the university, the affliation feminists had with social science took on a different form. "... Practitioners of the newly emerging Social Sciences found the health and marriageability of educated women a fertile area of inquiry" (Gillett, 1982, p. 16). Among these was G. Stanley Hall, a distinguished psychologist "whose works were also widely read and frequently used in colleges and teacher training institutions" (p. 16).

For instance, the "new psychology" practiced at the University of Chicago in the 1890's, championed a divorce from biology and heralded empirical studies which could answer the question of whether the mental traits of females and males were as different as most researchers though them to be. Feminist scholars became involved in this science with other male scholars determined to prove the refutability of claims that women were inherently and innately inferior in mental reasoning. "Influenced by John Dewey, Hume, Wilhelm Wundt and Hegel, the new psychology and its feminist practitioners, particularly at the Chicago school in the early 1900's saw personal relevance in psychology and with the advice and support of their professors they used it to reexamine conventional views of sex difference" (Rosenberg, 1982, p. 66).

In the early years of their participation, feminists worked on roughly the same terms as their male peers. Rosenberg (1982) believes this experience shaped their views, while they in turn shaped the views of their associates. Finding themselves in a situation not as yet rigidly categorized by sex, they often made racial intellectual breaks with prevailing notions of women's nature. More frequently however, their own attitudes towards women's roles swayed with the experiences they had *as* scholars. Recalling her graduate experiences at Barnard college in 1920, Margaret Mead (1972) for example, remembers:

> We belonged to a new generation of women who felt ... free ... from the demand to marry ... free to postpone marriage ... free from the need to bargain and hedge ... We laughed at the idea that a woman could be an old maid at the age of twenty-five, and we rejoiced at the medical care that made it possible for a woman to have a child at forty ... we did not bargain with men ... at the same time we firmly established a style of relationships to other women. "Never break a date with a woman for a man" ... We learned loyalty to women, pleasure in conversation with women, and enjoyment of the way in which we complemented one another (p. 116-17).

While women were in the minority, particularly in the graduate schools and more so in the faculty ranks; standard accounts of American social science (such as: Haskell, 1977; Oleson and Voss, 1979; Ross, 1979; etc.) have tended to miss altogether the women who pursued social science during the late nineteenth - early twentieth century. Kohlstedt (1978) points out that the number of women scientists increased dramatically from 1833 to 1874 and from 1884 to 1900. "From 1833 to 1874, there were 36 women and from 1884 to 1900 there were about 400 women publishing articles" (p. 82). Quite aside then, from the research they produced, their sheer numerical composition was significant.

The evolution of the social sciences as academic disciplines then, coincided with the development of the research academy, and because of its reform-directed agenda, social science attracted many women. The connections among the establishment of social science and the topics of its inquiry, the rise of research universities, and the fifty percent enrollment of women in social science during the 1890s and early 1900s, reflect more than mere coincidental parallels. These three phenomena occurred at a time when social changes in North America society especially in the United States, threatened (and succeeded to a large extent) to disrupt what little stability and unity existed. The number of women proliferated in the social sciences because initially, the agenda of the social sciences was parallel to feminists' concerns and, in fact, had been largely contoured by the reform philosophy of organizations which women themselves had helped to create. Both had been shaped by the social structure in which feminists scholars and the social sciences emerged. But that social structure in turn, and its liberal ideals of order, progress and organization, impacted on the social sciences and the universities. As social order paved the way for social roles, women's "sphere" became formulated. It was felt that the perils and satisfactions of professionalization in the world of academe were better suited for males.

Overall, the period was characterized by debates in educational circles about whether women should or could be educated like men. Despite these debates, many feminists found a "room of their own" in academe, but while a room had been provided, forces were at work which threatened its survival. From the perspective of feminists, the *major* problems for their scholarship, (once they were admitted to the university) rested in the research conclusions of social science which supported the nineteenth century biological notion of women's inferiority. But as we shall see, other barriers were also at work.

The Barriers to Feminist Scholarship

The desire for and the struggle to receive academic training was a long haul. Mainly it was rooted in feminists' conviction to understand the scientific doctrines of social science. This conviction in turn, stemmed from the days when their activism in pre-academic social science and their accompanying commitment to moral reform, led them, as other reformers, to turn to scientific knowledge for explanations of sexual symmetry and for help in institutioning public/social order. Despite their prominence inside academe however, feminists soon felt the disjuncture between the liberal ideals of equality they held, and, the reality of marginalized experience. Their notion that coeducation would integrate the differences between the sexes was abruptly confronted by the male hegemony of both academia and traditional liberalism. What were the specific barriers to their work and to their lives that militated against further advance? Most graduates cannot be traced in any great detail. A few, however, have had their lives well-documented. Despite shortcomings in the evidence, it is possible to identify certain clear general trends. For example, the mechanisms developed to maintain standards for professionalization and specialization often contained built-in sex discrimination, as did work organization, and in some cases admission requirements. These processes were largely contingencies of the university's institutional practices. But there were also disciplinary barriers and the private/public split. Underlying these structural processes was the question "What is Women?" Underpinning the barriers was the ideological "answer" : Woman was "the "weaker sex", the bearer of children, in need of protection, fragile on her pedestal, emotional rather than intellectual ... helpmate, domestic servant or companion ... evil temptress, Eve, the whore, the sex object, or she was the very guardian of morality" (Gillett, 1982, p. 1). Educationally, "Woman" was "Lady" - wife, mother, homemaker - and accordingly believed her education should be largely cultural ..." (p. 2). Not all women agreed with such ideas, though the barriers they faced played no favorites.

Institutional Barriers

In the late nineteenth century, universities were by no means overwhelmed at the prospects of female recruits. The controversy notwithstanding, by the 1890s women had gained entry in universities. But acceptance by the universities did not necessitate equal treatment or later equal conditions for women. When feminist scholars won entry, the internal processes of the university were continual reminders of their subordinate status.

The growing insistence on formal and standardized qualifications for acceptance by recognized universities was one especially effective means of excluding women. Oleson and Voss (1979) note the importance of professionalism in assuring middle class status through exclusionary rules, but professionalism was as important to the university's concern with sexual divisions as it was to their concern about propounding class divisions. Once professionalism became firmly established women were offered less rigorous training and less "scientific" training at every level. Too often the elevated status of the social sciences as scientific or specialized meant "a renewed emphasis on masculinity" (Rosenberg, 1975, p. 136). The effort on the part of many academies to alter their curricula to attract male students suggests that professionalism was, at least in part, an effort to give definition to the male sphere and therefore to sustain traditional divisions of sex roles (Rosenberg, 1979).

Those male social scientists, who because of their radicalism (conservative as it was), suffered ostracism from the larger community, were generally accepted and respected by less radical colleagues. Feminist scholars, on the other hand, were often ostracized by the larger community and their male colleagues inside the university. For these women iconoclasm was as germaine to their gender as it was to their reform proclivities.

Rosenberg (1982) discusses how in the latter stages of this development women scholars became caught in the transition from reform to professionalism. It was reform activities that had often informed women's feminism before they entered the research academy; it was their reform commitments that were inevitably abandoned between 1910 and 1930; and it was the same reform allegiances which led them to sociology and psychology — more than any other discipline — in the interim. The irony of this transition is evident in the fact that reform philosophies may have waned under the crunch of scientific theories, but the liberal, reform determination to create order, concretized women's "proper sphere' and its expression in the academy forced many women out of the same environment, they in several ways, had helped to shape.

The woman faculty member was a relatively rare phenomenon. Nevertheless, in some universities women did manage to break through the male monopoly. For those women, another problem involved the academy's new dual agenda of teaching and research. The double work load was arduous for male faculty. But for women the double work load became a double bind. The academy's organization of women's work lives extended from the larger sexual divisions in the society. It tended to hail prevailing attitudes about women's abilities and characteristics which denied them career advancement. After all, it was expected that women received education, *not* for pecuniary profit or career gains, but for the sake of improved demestic skills. This, combined with women's lack of confidence, (an outcome of the double-bind to which they were relentlessly exposed) contributed to the production of a doubly exploited group of workers (Chisholm and Woodward, 1980; Rendel, 1980). Advancement was considered then, as it is now, dependent on publication, research, performance of administrative duties and teaching, in that order (Rendel, 1980). Overwhelmingly, women were relegated to positions which carried enormous teaching responsibilities, and which consequently left little or no time for publication. A familiar story today. Yet publication (or research) was imperative for promotion and often for continued employment. Such was the contradictory nature of one edge of the double bind. The other edge was connected to the sex-role stereotypes and conventions which required that women choose between abandoning either their commitments to rigid academic work or the satisfactions of friendship, support and sexuality (Rendel, 1980). Very often, women were forced to abandon their culture as they entered an academic world dominated by men. It was also significant that the integration into a male world — sexually, professionally, and politically-meant that women were isolated from their culture and lost their old feminine supports (outside academe) with no supports inside the university to replace them. This conflict was psychologically problematic, was legitimized by specific institutional policies, produced within the university's cultural and academic milieu.

Women, when they were hired, were hired as junior faculty often having just received acceptance to the graduate programs. Moreover, the division of labour between female and male faculty was especially clear-cut, as male faculty greatly outnumbered women and because when women *were* hired as professors they were — almost without exception — given lower positions relative to men. Lower positions meant increased teaching loads. The *material* result was that after the Ph.D., women found themselves with little or no time to conduct research. In turn, they were not considered for senior posts. A further element in this vicious circle related to mechanisms for promotion and advancement within faculty ranks. The research university's agenda (of research and teaching) endured that women could never possibly meet the requirements for senior posts.

Significantly, the "in-house" dominance of the university

rested in the hands of men. Women could disseminate knowledge but were prohibited by a set of institutional practices from *producing* knowledge. As Shils (1979) argues this mechanism ensured the perpetuation of a particular kind of knowledge. But it did much more. It ensured that the discovery and diffusion of a particular kind of knowledge remained outside women's grasp.

The exact feminist response to these prohibitions is difficult to pinpoint precisely. It is clear, though, that in the case of Marion Talbot and from the diaries of Elizabeth Smith, for example, feminists often sought to eradicate such problems in a way which left the underlying ideology of universities intact (DuBois, 1975). Talbot, for instance, attempted to forge within the university a niche that could be considered women's "special" contribution to academia. Similarly, women in Elizabeth Smith's era adoped a form of "domestic feminism" which directed interest toward the ways in which women employed the ideals of "ladydom" to augment both personal and public authority. In short, while these women sought to challenge the notion that women did not "belong" in the private sphere, by arguing for a special moral nature for women, they tended to perpetuate rather than eradicate this notion of separate spheres. The feminists here, however, were a product of their unique social context and, quite often, they envisioned integration as they only viable strategy for their acceptance to male bastions (Freedman, 1979). Such a pattern was established early on in women's educational history. Emma Willard, now considered "the" pioneer of female education in the United States, boldly proposed a "Plan for Improving Female Education" in 1819. Her proposal was radical, but her views about women were essentially traditional: women's true place was in the home. Some twenty years later, another reformer, Catherine Beecher, believed that "women should have a professional as well as domestic education" (Gillett, 1982, p. 9).

The commitments these women had developed for reform and philanthropic involvements before entering academe, tended to inform their overall concern for educational reform once inside academe. This tendency, is initially similar to feminists' approaches in the late 1960's. Unlike the latter, however, nineteenth century feminists carried their integration/reform strategy to the difficulties they encountered *within* academic disciplines. They very seldom considered developing a separatist stance. And in failing to recognize the differences between male, and female experience, feminists seemed to be unable to arrive at adequate accounts of *why* separate spheres existed in the first place (Rosenberg, 1982). Following from their preconceived assumptions of equality, feminists were unable to explicate how the institutional practices of excluding women were connected to an intricate system of maintaining separate spheres, and a system which perpetuated patriarchal dominance in the academy.

Disciplinary Barriers

Initially, the contributions of feminists to the development of the disciplines suggested a promising start to a social science which included women. For example, the spread of "environmentalism" in psychology during the nineteenth century contributed to women's early arguments opposing "biological determinist" paradigms. Mary Putnam Jacobi, who in 1876 had written her dissertation on the question, "Do women require mental and bodily rest during menstruation, and if so, to what extent?" (Wood, 1977, p. 95), had been only too aware of what she was up against:

> An inquiry into the limits of activity and attainments that may be imposed by sex is very frequently carried on in the same spirit as that which hastens to ascribe to permanent differences in race all the peculiarities of a class, and this is because the sex that is supposed to be limited in its nature is nearly always different from that of the person conducting the inquiry (p. 95).

The results of her research led her to conclude that

> yes, short rest periods during the working day would be helpful for menstruating women as they would be for women and men during the rest of the month, all of whom would benefit even more by an eight-hour day in place of the twelve or more hours they laboured (p. 95).

In a few academies, women made particularly tremendous

strides in those disciplines that considered questions of sex differences. They also impacted on male social scientists' attitudes about women's nature. Access to coeducational academies and the research that came from it was a profound step, not only because it unbalanced the masculine monoploy on the social sciences but because the methods of the disciplines were used to shed new light on the "women question" by women themselves in a male bastion.

Feminist dissenters like Jessie Taft in sociology, Helen Thompson Woolley and Leta Hollingsworth in psychology, and Elsie Clews Parsons and Ruth Benedict in anthropology (as cited in Rosenberg's study) were especially influential in weakening the hold that evolutionist theories had on scholars and their social sciences. The commitment feminists' had to help create a more equitable relationship between the sexes spurred them to challenge the biological underpinnings of prevailing definitions of women's nature by empirical research on socialization practices, personality development, and individual differences (Dye, 1977; Wood, 1977).

In psychology, for example, women left their imprint in part because they insisted that their male counterparts "practice what they preach" when dealing with the issue of sex differences. In other words, feminists insisted that the *way* in which their male counterparts practiced psychology be consistent with the way they conceptualized psychology. But they did more:

> In focusing on sex, they contributed in an important way to the trend toward environmentalism in American psychology. For most psychologists, the female sex represented the limiting case in how seriously they could question biological determinism. To doubt the physiological basis of feminine psychological differences was considerably to loosen the keystone of the arch of biological determinism (Rosenberg, 1982, p. 108).

Furthermore, researchers such as Thompson Woolley, Hollingsworth, and earlier Calkins, displayed the character of bias in psychological research, particularly in sex differences' research. They ardently denounced the hypothesis that women's intellectual capacities were less than men's.

Feminists also had a profound effect on the direction of intellectual inquiry about sex differences, in terms of studying social and cultural processes. Helen Thompson Woolley for instance, in her celebrated work, *Psychological Norms in Men and Women*, (1903) presented evidence which suggested that intelligence and physiological make-up was shaped by the environment, thus explaining through socialization practices why, if at all, women differed from men.

Elsie Clews Parsons, a sociologist, argued that because women were *perceived* as society's first anomalies, around them existed a series of rules and conventions regulating their behaviour. From Parson's perspective, these rules played a dominant role in maintaining the classification system that was the root of social order. Parson's later training as an anthropologist and her experience as a woman and a mother, led her to pursue what she saw as an "anthropology for women"; the forerunner of "social science for women" in the 1980's.

Parsons is interestingly unique in her attack on evolutionary theory, and her exposition of the biased form and content of male methodology. She observed that ethnography, the primary research tool of anthropology, had been traditionally barred from women, and "... because most male social scientists were themselves convinced of female inferiority, they rarely noticed the many ways in which the lives of women remained bound by patriarchal forms" (Rosenberg, 1975, p. 157). Finally, Jessie Taft refuted theories of women's biological character to provide a social explanation for personality differences. Two individuals could live in the same environment and have different experiences, she argued, and the implications for women's roles are enormous.

Together with other social scientists interested in the question of women's nature, feminist scholars such as Thompson, Parsons, and Taft shifted the theoretical focus of sex differences to a new level. Together, they recast psychology in *social*, rather than *biological* terms: their work propounded the hypothesis that sexual spheres are grounded in *customs* rather than biology. This realization led them to recognize that the barriers they faced in academia were not necessarily due to their failures to cope (although such notions persisted) but that rather they were grounded in the structure of the university and hence in the structure of the existing society. It followed that the resolution of women's obstacles required changes in both.

These same women were some of the many feminists who stated in general terms the kinds of changes in social science that were required to reformulate sexual relations outside academe. The changes they focussed on were mainly to do with research conclusions drawn by their respective disciplines. We can only speculate that they did not scrutinize the disciplines themselves in terms of the various methods, theories and concepts used. It is clear though, that despite the positive initial contributions feminists made, the barriers of the social sciences as separate disciplines had an impact particularly in the later stages of their development.

Feminists found themselves caught between their feminist belief that sex differences were born out of social discrimination, and their commitment to their newly found scientific method, which relied on the validity of their experimental findings. Because they were social scientists, they were forced to rely on the paradigms of their tests. At the same time and as feminists, they persisted in their ideas that their research could not uncover the roots of sexual division nor explain all its causes. They deferred more and more to other scientists for an understanding of the formation of the feminine and masculine personality, particularly as they found their once scholarly acceptance fading within the development of specialized, professional scholarship and the growing gender demarcation that escorted it.

Two contradictions emerged from these tensions. First feminists challenged the "orderliness" of the very traditions people held tightly to, as the explanations which would reveal the "order" of the world, and their places in it. Second, they challenged the disciplinary barriers at the same time as their research was helping to shape and define the academic agenda. One example, of this paradox is found in the fundamental theoretical frameworks which were developed by male social scientists and were embraced and utilized by feminists, to argue against the subordination of women that traditional theory and practice perpetuated. We can in retrospect see how this was problematic.

As Cooper and Cooper (1973) argue in *The Roots of American Feminist Thought*:

> Few feminist theorists contributed significantly
> to the development of their borrowed ideologies
> beyond giving them a feminist dimension; and

> nonunderstandably, created a system of thought especially for feminist purposes ... Thus existing schemes gained a feminist perspective without altering their fundamental thrust ... The feminist theorists, then, ... worked with philosophical materials that were not of their own making ... (pp. 8-9).

However, the use of "borrowed ideologies" was largely, I believe, a function of the social and cultural conditions which made it necessary for feminists (in positions such as those of Jessie Taft, or Helen Thompson Woolley) to adopt such theories in order to succeed. In more general terms and as a central underlying contradiction, utilizing the tools available was a requisite for professional integration into a male world. In order to make any impact on the academy, it was necessary to become part of it. The cutting edge of this catch-22 was highly contradictory:

> When women tried to assimilate into male-dominated institutions, without securing feminist social, economic, or political bases, they lost the momentum and the networks which had made the suffrage movement possible. Women gave up many of the strengths of the female sphere without gaining equally from the man's world they entered (Freedman, 1979, p. 524).

Freedman's point suggests that several consequences of the ways early academic feminists worked contributed to their "rise" and inevitably to their "decline". First, the divisions between the newly formed social sciences served to separate feminists who were forced to work in isolation from other feminists in different fields. Second, the specialization attached to professionalized areas of knowledge worked as an exclusionary device for those women who had been unable to attain professional legitimization by the university. And, finally, it forced those women who were able to attain professional status to abandon their prior commitments to feminism and reform. The latter two consequences were exacerbated by the fact that feminists saw integration within the university and indeed coeducation itself, (as faculty, students and researchers) as the only viable strategy for their acceptance and the only viable option for their equality with men. Of course, these conclusions can be drawn only from the experiences of those women who attended the *research university* and does not describe the experiences of women in single-sex colleges. For those who worked in the research university, such a belief was shattered by the lack of support they received and was made worse by the fact they were cut off from those feminists who worked inside the university in different disciplines and from the larger feminist community outside.

The disciplinary barriers share certain commonalities with the institutional barriers. Both take their distinct character from the rise of the research academy (which set in place institutional practices) and the development of the social sciences (which established appropriate methods, theories, etc. deemed necessary to individual each social science). Both, however, were part and parcel of wider sex role ideologies, larger notions regarding women's "role" and finally, universalistic conceptions of the function of women's education. Feminists approached both sets of barriers with an integrationist stance rather than a separatist one and failed to analyze how the barriers in disciplines were connected to the institutional barriers by a common underlying system of separate sphere maintenance and patriarchal dominance.

Private/Public Spheres

We have seen that the public/private spheres were becoming clearly demarcated in the late nineteenth century. Indeed, nineteenth century feminists took as a given that there *was* a fundamental split between their public life (within the context of their work in the university) and their private life (within the context of their personal lives outside the university). Further, the *reality* of nineteenth century-early twentieth century feminists' lives visibly displayed a *tension* between these two realms. Yet the feminists did *not* discuss this split as a barrier to their work, largely accepting the divisions as "natural".

However, an analysis of the barriers these feminists *do* explicate, and the evidences of the tensions they lived, do suggest that the private/public dichotomy centrally underlined the parameters of their experience in the nineteenth century and early twentieth century university. For example, several overlapping and complex contradictions appear to characterize the nature of the barriers: the need to enter the university in order to obtain knowledge and the institutional constraints imposed by it; the need to integrate social science techniques and the problems imposed by those techniques and the divisions they entailed; the need to gain legitimacy as a professional, in order to stay in the university, and the impossibility of reconciling the "professional" and the "activist". These contradictions were part and parcel of the private/public split which reinforced women's marginalization in society and in academe.

Part of the split worked to separate feminists' personal lives from their lives in the university, but it also served to establish normative boundaries and to set priorities (as in the case of identifying with the "professional"). In this case, identification with philanthrophy was in keeping with women's "private" life while academic life meant for women, identifying with the "public" world of men. While to some extent, it can be argued that women carved out a unique "female" sphere within the male world of reform, politics and education, on both levels it operated as an instrument of ideology to the extent that it ensured patriarchal domination of *both* the public and private realms. They way in which feminists were *treated* in the university reinforced the notion of the private/public split. Normative boundaries within the so-called public imparted the characterization of women in the so-called private realm (e.g., women were often relegated to so-called "feminine" courses such as domestic science etc.). While these various manifestations of the split occurred at different intervals in feminists' lives, it is essential to see how the private/public spheres were not separate or isolated from each other. Their interdependence is evident not only in the sense that they had *both* a material and an ideological base, but because the dividing line was blurred in feminists' actual experience in the academy. Again this is proven by the kinds of course curriculum, student treatment, divisions of labour, expectations, that were at work. The establishment of the research university reveals that as the entry of increasing numbers of women threatened to break down the boundary between the public considered "male" and the domestic sphere considered "female", the response of the university was to assert that: "... once the university succeeded in establishing its professional schools and in identifying the professional utilities of departments ..., it would be able to secure its reputation as a distinctively male institution training men for identifiably male work" (Rosenberg, 1982, p. 49).

Prophetically, this assertion became an eventual reality. As the university gained prestige, it began attracting more men and by 1920 the sheer magnitude of male enrollment was already confining women to a marginal position, or to areas of study considered "female" (e.g., social work, teaching, nursing).

It was not just the fact that the academy was male-dominated. Feminists found that they had to deny their very values as women. Success as a scientist was often "won" at the expense of much that women considered distinctively female. "The values of science and professionalism undercut the very culture and political climate that had given women strength to expand their lives and to look critically at conventional assumptions about their basic personalities" (Rosenberg, 1979, p. 338). Those same values undercut the very culture that had prompted women to fight for access to education in the first place.

Ultimately, the underlying private/public ideology can be seen quite sharply in retrospect as a central organizing feature of feminists' experience in academe and the root of the contradictory nature of that experience: "The ideological change fostered by work in the social sciences freed women from the restrictions imposed by old prejudices about female inferiority, but at the same time undermined the sense of support women had enjoyed as members of a distinctive and self-consciously separate community" (Rosenberg, 1979, p. 338). The breakdown in feminists' ties to the larger community of women outside academe was brought about in part by their newly-pledged allegiance to professionalization, and to more complex theorectical differences between the two groups[9]. Still, the fact of the division between the two testified to yet another manifestation of the private/public split.

In another vein, and as Rosenberg convincingly argues, evidences of the split come from the voices of women whose problems of identity echo the persistent and pervasive problem of women born into a world of separate spheres and sex-role stereotypes and a confusion of what, after all, masculine/feminine does and should mean.

For example, Virginia Robinson (cited in Rosenberg, 1982) argued "I do not know how I shall escape this influence. I simply sit and gasp as one by one the old standbys — the arguments women stake our life on — are cast aside as so much dead wood" (Rosenberg, 1982, p. 116). Similarly Jessie Taft lamented the anguish which was a result of the fact that women's lives were divided between two worlds:

> All this hopeless conflict among impulses which the woman feels she has a legititmate right, even a moral obligation, to express, all of the rebellion against stupid, meaningless sacrifice of powers that ought to be used by society, constitutes the force, conscious or unconscious, which motivates the woman movement and will continue to vitalize it until some adjustment is made (Rosenberg, p. 142).

The definition of the "academic" as male left feminists marginalized for instance, through the university's entrance procedures and hiring practices. In this sense the *economic* function and *material* visibility of the separate ideology becomes evident. Women's relative invisibility as both graduate students and faculty was the immediate result. The professionalization of social science was part of a larger trend toward specialization. It was another mechanism which worked the private/public ideology in terms of erecting gender divided boundaries between fields considered "male" and fields considered "female". Because women were often short of the requirements for professionalization thanks to other processes of exclusion, professional legitimation often eluded them. Because it was necessary to possess this legitimation in order to gain access to senior posts (and hence have time to publish), the result was that women were effectively barred from producing knowledge in the academy. Finally, it is clear that the manipulation and perpetuation of the private/public dualism helped (from the beginning of the research university's existence) to establish the male domination of the academy. In doing so, it established the university as one social institution which was effectively working separate sphere maintenance.

In summary, it can be said that in the late nineteenth century, the research university represented a genuinely novel development in organized scholarship. It was fundamentally different from its predecessors both in its aims and in its organization. The coeducational research academy aimed, on a scale hitherto unknown, to educate the middle classes as well as elites, and to educate men *and* women. Within the coterie of financial, political and ideological reasoning for its existence, its aims were pragmatic and oriented to social problems and thus differed from earlier sectarian, parochial or private academies, which limited education to acquisition of moral, abstract doctrines disassociated from the problems of society. The novel objectives were directly related to the problems wrought by the increasing turmoil of nineteenth century North America society. The social context of the Industrial Revolution and the impact of its aftermath led research institutions to respond to pressures from social reformers and the state, to formulate theories about the effects of the environment on human behaviour. It was within the social and academic context of this reformulation and re-evaluation that feminist scholarship emerged.

The feminist scholars examined in this chapter were women who had rejected the notion that their situation was preordained and biologically inferior. This consciousness was spurred when changes in the production process brought the sex/gender system into contradiction, but nevertheless led to increasingly rigid distinctions between the private world of the home and the public world of waged labor.

As they became gradually exempt from the responsibilities of domestic industry, women's state of sociological and psychological transition pushed those in the middle-classes to seek sharper self-definition. The social setting provided the context for feminists to pursue reform and philanthropic activities. At the same time, the expansion of higher education and the development of social science created an *intellectual forum* where women could re-evaluate the transitions they were undergoing. In this sense the newly emerged academy and a newly emerged feminist consciousness formed a symbiotic relation: the academy needed the economic resources of enrolling women, and women needed the academy to intellectually explore their developing feminism.

What connected the social sciences and feminists together with the research university was their shared preoccupation with the changes of the society. What distinguished both feminists and the social sciences from the academy, and made them uniquely central agents in the process of feminist scholarship, is the fact that their presence in the academy and their methods of exploring sex differences were relatively radical. Feminists and social science were joining and changing the academic scene.

What *unified* feminists' concerns during this period were the limitations imposed by male control of the universities. Overcoming the notion that "women are weaker" was the central issue; gaining equal access was the main task. For those feminists who overcame the limitations of both, changing research directions (or disciplinary content) was the shared goal.

Feminists' efforts in breaking down the boundaries established by sexual stereotyping were clearly historically important and undoubtedly professionally fulfilling. Of equal historical importance are the institutional, disciplinary and private/public barriers which prevented them from eliminating that dividing line, and to some extent questioning its very purpose.

The institutional barriers created by the university severely circumscribed both women's academic work and their lives. Moreover, the academy itself, in this eventual efforts to professionalize, formed particular types of organization which largely excluded women. In the process of integration with the "profession", feminist scholars were cut off from the community of women social reformers and activists. And in concentrating on gaining access to a "public" which was male-defined they inevitably used those male definitions of their "private" relegation. In identifying themselves more as "professionals", feminists scholars lost the values of their feminism. In identifying themselves in the terms with which they were culturally subordinated, they lost the values of their personal need that informed their feminism.

The barriers to their scholarship were prohibitive in that feminists faced continous struggle. Nevertheless, within the parameters of those barriers, feminists managed to forge a social science tradition and an academic legacy which we can call upon to re-evaluate current traditions. Finally, the *historical contradictions* which transformed feminists scholars and which in turn led them to transform, are similar to the contradictions which hamper present feminist scholarship. In the process of writing this chapter, it became clear that feminist scholars are today in a living relationship with the past. But that relationship is not linear nor smooth. *Like* the feminist scholarship in the late nineteenth and early twentieth century, the Second Stage (1960s) of feminist scholarship arose out of larger social and political movements; they were "enlightened" by them and ultimately limited by them. *Unlike* the First Stage, however, the Second Stage attempted to reconcile or at least bring the personal to the forefront of their political concerns. *Unlike* the First Stage, the Second Stage saw the importance of gaining access to the university, but did not assume that the university's actual practices and organization were unproblematic. It is to the Second Stage that we now turn.

3

THE SECOND STAGE:
THE 'PERSONAL IS POLITICAL'

The demands of the women's liberation movement include equality in jobs and education, beginning with the *same* opportunities as men for
admission to schools and colleges, the chance to
work at challenging jobs, and the opportunity to
receive the same pay as men who do the same
work

Lucy Kosimar.

How did the social context of the late 1960's and early 1970's affect
the feminist dissenting arm of the academic world? It affected two
institutions: the growth and composition of the universities
changed to include more middle class and many more women; industry was booming and the percentage of women working outside
the home was rapidly rising (Hole and Levine, 1971). Those women
who came to the university with a feminist consciousness, focused
their critique of academe on the problems posed by the discriminatory institutional policies of the university. Like their nineteenth
century counterparts, the feminists in this period were aware of
other barriers and obstacles to their presence in academe, especially
the constraints of the private/public ideology which had largely
defined the politics of the wider women's movement outside the
university. While the women's movement was suffering the on-
slaught of male members of the sectarian Left, feminists were grop-
ing for some kind of synthesis of the personal and political (Rowbotham, 1979). Feminists on campus (with direct or indirect ties to
the women's movement) reverberated this struggle, during the time

they were fighting for equality of opportunity. The concern for equal opportunity was catalyzed by the invisibility of women as faculty and by the policies which supported that absence.

This chapter will present a brief overview of this perspective. Internally the Second Stage is complex, so without attempting to make a definitive or conclusive statement, particular issues are examined, which through the lens of the period's literature as well as recent accounts appear to have been the crucible for further developments in contemporary feminist scholarship. Finally, the reader should be reminded that the concern of this section, is with the feminist *ideas* of the late 1960's - mid 1970's. The Second Stage in this sense, is more distinguishable by the *response* of the feminist dissent to the social context of the university, than to the general 1960's social milieu, though in actual fact the two cannot be separated from each other.

A. The Setting

The changing academic system was central to the process of the Second Stage dissent's emergence. Karabel and Halsey (1977) assert that in a general sense, the conflict between the scientific and technological orientation of the society and people's personal and collective search for identity, was most manifest in the education system.[1] Students for instance, were not only trained to become the "new mandarins" of whom Chomsky (1967) speaks, but they also became accustomed to finding within the university, a production and training apparatus functioning as a corporation.[2]

Because the production of knowledge was a more important factor of social/economic development, the university's political arena could not avoid experiencing the tensions which accrued from its role in scientific production on one hand, and the critique of such production's personal effects on the other. As a result, the mid to late 1960's saw an increased politicization of both faculty members and students. Many, for example, who started in the Civil Rights movement became later involved in the Free Speech movement and in the Students for a Democratic Society (Freeman, 1973; Piercy, 1978). Also, the Anti-War movement joined forces with other radical groups to make organizing and resistance a way of life on numerous campuses. Howe (1975) believes that the spectacular growth of these movements led to the emergence of the "New

Left" and with it a critique of the alienating nature of science and technology. From this broad analysis, the "New Left" turned its focus inward to indicate how the university symbolized the "society's wrongs" of which Theodore Rostak (1967) speaks. Significantly, such an analysis was coincident with the tremendous growth and expansion of the academic system.

The "New Left" protested the alienation of humans and their labor, the de-humanization of an automated, technocratic society and the appropriation of identity by mass consumerism and the world of the corporate elite (Marcuse, 1972).[3] Coupled with these issues was a concern for idenity and freedom which became reflected in a criticism of social structures. In the emergence of these political struggles, the question of human nature was central. In short, 'the personal became political'. Radical groups argued that the restriction of radical political activity to a separate and narrow political sphere or an equally narrow work place was impossible.

Within the context of these struggles, feminist radicalism emerged (Hole and Levine, 1971). For feminists, the question of male dominance and an essentially masculine 'humanity' was opened up. The literature of the period however shows very clearly that the establishment of autonomous women's groups cannot be adequately understood as simply a reaction against sexism on the left. Sexist practices were a powerful immediate cause of women's anger and disillusionment. But women's critique went well beyond that. They saw their subordinate position as indicative of a general failure to create an independent statement about women.

Concurrent with the political movements that led women to begin once again to challenge patriarchal society, were the political movements that challenged hierarchies of academe, demystifying the illusion that the university as an institution could be isolated from the mainstream of national power. From the male left, Chomsky (1967) Marcuse (1968) and others, scathingly attacked "elitist" education sociologists in the "New" wing similarly connected problems of education on all levels to the perpetuation of social class hierarchy. For many students and faculty, although not *all* the ivory tower of academe reflected the interests of governments, corporations, and military political machines. Those academics most clearly discontented were those who had direct or indirect ties with the New Left, and/or the Women's Movement.

"The first women's campus groups to emerge in late 1968 and

1969 were composed primarily of undergraduates who had some relationship to various New Left organizations" (Freeman, 1973, p. 28). Beginning in 1968 and 1969, faculty women responded to the ivory tower and to the discrimination they experienced by forming cuacuses in academic professional organizations. Supported and sometimes led by feminist students, staff, or community women, these innovators were often political activists who sought first to understand and later to confront the sexism they had experienced in movements for the liberation of other oppressed groups. Their efforts at organization and course development were inspired by both the Free-university movement and the Civil Rights movement, which provided the model of Black Studies' courses and program. But we do know that the dissent comprised a multifarious group, some of whom were attacked to the New Left, some of whom belonged to liberal organizations such as the National Organization of women, and finally, some whose feminist work began after exposure to the dissent.

Hence the second stage of feminism in universities emerged within the context of larger radical debates which argued against the status quo. These wider movements protested the alienation of humanity in the midst of corporate, government and military proliferation. And many within these groups were part of the university community. The context provided feminists with a framework within which to protest their own alienation as women. Many of those women were already involved with the university many were not. For those who were, they organized on campuses around issues of concern to women — issues which were of pragmatic immediacy and which reflected the grass roots concerns of the movement: i.e., health collectives, rape crisis centers, day care centers, employment referral services. Other kinds of associations were formed which were related more directly to the specific concerns of faculty women such as Women's Studies and, affirmative action. These various groups were not necessarily isolated from each other. For example, faculty women were and still are often involved in community organizations, and community women similarly provided input about the roles of universities and their responsibilities to the community of which they were a part. In some cases, feminists from the community have initiated courses of study primarily *for* community women, but within the legitimization of academe.[4] Despite the complicated and tangled roots of feminist presence on campus, it is clear that in several senses, the wider feminist movement had given it its *genesis*, and to some extent its *support*.

B. The Barriers to Feminist Scholarship

In this section nine clusters of barriers faced by feminists in academe are described as is their assessments of the various modes of male power inherent in the barriers, and their preferred strategies for changing the status of academic feminists.

In juxtaposition to the First Stage, the unifying theme in the Second is the overarching limitations imposed by male control of universities. In this instance however, overcoming the sexism of institutions is the fundamental issue; changing the institution's sexist practices is the fundamental task. The main tactics employed at the time or suggested were legal action, direct action and moral pressure and skill building.

Finally, it should be noted that despite temporal categorization of Second Stage work such analyses are presently ongoing. As we see in the Third Stage, the tenacious hold which these problems have on systematic learning remains the same though different in form and degree. Because of this difference in context I separate the response into second and Third while reminding the reader of the process-like nature of both problems and dissent.

C. The Percentage of Women Faculty: Hiring, Promotion, Salaries, Tenure

Feminists in the Second Stage accumulated considerable evidence which showed that women faculty are systematically discriminated against with regard to hiring, promotion, and salaries (Harris, 1974; Roby, 1972; etc.).

Second Stage literature specifically made evident the fact that the academic system had been detrimental and unjust to women on may accounts (See for example: Astin, 1971; Bernard, 1973; Roby, 1972). Women tend to teach more and have less time for research (Howe, 1975). They are channelled into fields that are not particularly well-paid (Astin and Bayer, 1973). Women faculty have not been as readily accepted at selective, affluent, and large institutions (Graham, 1972). They have not been promoted to or asked to assume administrative leadership (Bernard, 1973). Feminists concluded that the present system, as it is structured and as it allocates rewards, "... has discriminated against women and is in need of change" (Astin and Bayer, 1973, p. 355).

Hawkins (1975), Hopkins (1975), Janeway (1975), and Rossi (1972) delineated academia as, "... getting on without half the research talent and teaching skill it might have laid claim to just be ignoring women" (Janeway, 1975, p. 13). At the time, Hawkins predicted that the gap between women and men would widen, "... since women have gained scarcely 20 percent of the available places during the greatest expansion of higher education in this country" (p. 31).

Hawkins' analysis demonstrated that declining percentages of women faculty members, "... reflects academic quotas on women, higher standards of admission for women, denial of loans and fellowships, discouragement of part-time study, and course scheduling and other procedures geared to the service of men" (p. 29). The results of Gillett's (1975) study indicated as well, that the "percentage of female teachers is highest at the lowest ranks of the academic scale (i.e., lecturer and instructor) and declines progressively through the assistant and associate ranks to full professor" (p. 70). It seems, feminists argued, that women have difficulty in being hired above the lowest ranks, regardless of their academic qualifications or abilities.

Criticizing the marginal status of women in academia, Harris (1974) pointed out that part-time teaching is one area of employment where the percentage of women often surpasses the nineteen percent average of women employed at all levels. For example, Canadian universities include contingents of part-time faculty or sessional lecturers and most of the individuals are women (Vickers and Adams, 1977). Positions in this area do not have the status or fringe benefits of full-time positions and are thus comparatively poorly paid. "They also are rarely tenured" (Harris, 1974, p. 309). When men hold such positions, "... it is nearly always because they have another full-time job. Such arrangements permit the university to invite men who may have unusual expertise in some relevant area to teach one or two courses a year in that specialty" (p. 310). Women in part-time positions, however, often do not have other full-time jobs, although some have other part-time jobs. Vickers and Adam in 1977, pointed out that women who wish to teach full-time are often precluded from doing so because of "private-life concerns, or because their husbands are also employed by a university which maintains a so-called anti-nepotism regulation" (p. 108).

Studies showed that as faculty and administrators, women are underrepresented in proportion to those eligible in their respective fields; where they are employed, they are typically in the lower ranks or among part-time personnel. These issues are related to the mechanisms by which promotions, salaries and tenure are used to discriminate against academic women and which serve to perpetuate the lower percentage of women as faculty members. These processes we have seen, have an historical linkage, dating back to the establishment and the admission of women to higher education in the nineteenth century. Like their nineteenth century counterparts, we can say with some measure of certainty that feminists in the early 1970's saw change in a way which did not threaten to dismantle the underlying structures of universities. They argued initially that women needed to be seen as equal/the same in order to have equal rights and to receive the same treatment as men.

D. Hiring

Among the problems that confront women once they have received their credentials is that of restricted access to professions which have been predominantly male (Armstrong and Armstrong, 1978; Connelly, 1978). The predominance of male faculty in universities, and the underrepresentation of females proportionary speaking, belies the structural mechanisms which keep women *out* of faculty jobs. The problem can necessarily be traced to the hiring practices of the particular university (Bernard, 1964; Smith, 1975; Vickers and Adams, 1977). The term "discrimination" has several dimensions. Hopkins (1975) suggested that discrimination can be implicit as well as explicit, inadvertant rather than blatant, and institutional rather than individual if policies, however "objectively" applied, produce differential results. On the other hand, Bienen et al. (1977) and Weitzman (1973) argued that anti-discriminatory policies are problematic because the task of rectifying discrimination has been left essentially in the hands of those who have been in charge in the past. Two assumptions lie beneath discriminatory policies, neither of which have been substantiated by concrete evidence. The first problematic assumption is that colleges and universities "are eager to hire, promote and pay appropriate salaries to qualified women if they can find them; this point is argued by assertion" (Bienen, 1977, p. 371). The second is that[11] the supply or "pool" of women candidates for positions is relatively inferior in quality as well as in numbers to the pool of male candidates; "this is argued largely by innuendo" (p. 371). Rooted in these sorts of assumptions, are policies which portray idealized pictures of decisions on hiring. The notion that these policies are objective is simply not true however. As Bienen suggested, objectivity in hiring is not a banal rationale: it can be and frequently is used to support patronage and nepotism in the most covert ways.

E. Promotions, Salaries and Tenure

Once women *are* hired for faculty positions the dissent insisted, they face similar discrimination with regard to promotion, wages and securing tenure (Astin and Bayer, 1973; Gillett, 1975; Graham, 1972; Rossi, 1973; Vickers and Adams, 1977).

Vickers and Adams' (1977) research findings coincided with Gillett's (1975) work. They argued in their widely read monologue entitled, *But can you Type?* that the women who "make it"; that is, who get a job in a university on a full-time basis, encounter "... lower salaries, slower advancement, less likelihood of being granted tenure and, in may cases, heavier workloads restricted to the undergraduate level" (p. 106). In 1970 for example, less than one-fifth of all full-time teaching positions in Canadian universities were held by women. These women are distributed very unevenly within the university with regard to field" (p. 107). They were concentrated in the lower ranks and were paid lower salaries than their male counterparts at every level.

In many academic institutions, the hurdles that had to be overcome in order to achieve tenure were considerable (Astin and Bayer, 1973; Graham, 1972; Vickers and Adams, 1977). The situation for women was be described as follows:

> It is now standard in may fields to receive a Ph.D.
> when one is in one's late twenties. If the new
> Ph.D. accepts a teaching appointment at the assistant professor level, then ordinarily within six or
> seven years the tenure decision is made. In may
> universities this means that the dissertation must

have been converted to a publishable manuscript, and that some other scholarly research, ideally another book, has been completed. The six or seven-year period coincides with a woman's childbearing years, and, if one assumes that the couple wants two children, both are ordinarily born before a woman is thirty-five. Therefore, the greatest pressures ... coalesce in these years between the ages of twenty-eight and thirty-five (Vickers and Adams, 1977, p. 272).

In juxtaposition, tenure has helped to "sustain the under-representation of women in university faculties" (Groarke, 1983, p. 20). According to Groarke, it has done this by keeping many positions in the hands of men who were awarded their posts in times when sexual biases did not even allow women to qualify and compete for university appointments. "The lack of new positions ensures that the male status quo which occupies university faculties will continue to occupy a disporportionate number of positions in the forseeable future" (p. 20). The barriers of hiring practices, salaries, promotion and tenuring then, according to the Second Stage dissent, appear to form an enclosed vicious circle or a closed in-house system: if women managed to get hired, they were paid less than their male counterparts with equal qualifications and were less likely than males to become appointed to higher positions. In order to get tenure, the qualifications and indices of merit required (such as holding a certain position) were considered problematic for women because of the above issue. Centrally, such mechanisms ensured that women were treated as "secondary labor" participants.

These feminist analyses shared the view that eliminating discriminatory hiring and reward system practices would bring about "equal opportunity" for women in the academic system. The assumption was that the university as a social institution must be *modified* to permit women equal representation and equal decision-making power.

F. The Male Hierarchy

The male hierarchy was viewed in the 1970's as a more implicit, less overt hurdle in the university (Rich, 1975; Wood, 1977).

Webb (1974) argued that the purpose of education historically was to create a more sophisticated manner of intellectual rule and psychological indoctrination. (We might add here that the development of the research academy had similar purposes; not only was there the establishment of an elitist hierarchy, but also the building of a *male-dominated* hierarchy.) To this purpose today has been added the need for a "technically knowledgeable working class" (p. 416). Because of this the university has always been conducted in the style of hierarchical rule. The feminist vision, in contrast, is based on the elimination of all domination/submission relationships, inherent in a class-based society. Webb envisions feminism as a means to eradicate *class-based* elitism, particularly within the education setting:

> the teacher is faced with a double job: helping people to understand the seriousness of a feminist philosophy and teaching so that students feel a strength of collective learning rather than historical control (p.417).

Webb believes that one of the goals of a "Feminist Studies" program should be for each woman to learn as deeply and broadly as possible the historical, literary, biological, and psychological roots of our "collective colonization" and to formulate theoretical perspectives of what female nature is and could be. At this point, the reader will note the first suggestion towards building *alternative* modes of institutional structure. The use of egalitarian methods however,

> is precisely the antithesis of what universities are all about. Rather than building collectively, they divide by competitiveness and grade hierarchies. Rather than creating group solidarity, they create an intellectual; elite whose social status, but not real power, is meant to be above those who have never received a higher education (p. 411).

Rich (1975) and Howe (1975) agree but go further. Rich condemns the university for fragmenting *women* who work in a university setting. This fragmentation is merely an outcome of the outer society's imposition. The hidden assumptions on which the university is built comprise a system whereby "each woman in the university is defined by her relationship to the men in power instead of her relationship to other women up and sown the scale" (p. 27).

Clearly, one has to question whether it might not be an ultimate defeat for women to define themselves and their goals in terms of a masculine construction of experience. Yet this is implicit in many Second Stage diagnoses of "the problem" as one of subjugation, and in the recommended remedies which (in demanding no differentiation of sex roles in academic work) would reject intrinsically feminine modes of operating. Rich prescribes particular reforms which she believes if put in place, would expedite the deconstruction of academe's present form. These reforms, Rich admits, would not, in themselves, disconnect certain underlying, assumptions which lie existentially embedded in the *thinking* of those who perpetuate academia's pyramid.

From Daniels' (1975) perspective, the essential problem is: Can those who are located *inside* the centers of power overcome their own position which in turn comes from the limits or perspective of their own location in society?

Smith demonstrates that the perspectives and concepts of sociology are indeed determined by a dominant class position and interest (as Rich (1975) has said), but adds a further element in making the fundamental case about the exclusion of women:

> Women are outside, subservient to, and silent in the social organization that subtends the sociological discourse and structures its concerns and concepts. The various actualities of women's existence in contemporary society cannot be described or analyzed adequately by a discipline whose themes and domains are largely organized around what goes on in the working contexts and relations of those who organize and control the society and who are men (p. 18).

The phenomenon has been similarly recounted in psychology (Carlson, 1972; Vaughter, 1976; Wood, 1977). To work cooperatively rather than competitively, to value teaching as well as research, and to concern ourselves with self-growth and self-awareness in the context of our research, argues Vaughter (1976), goes against our training as scientists and the atmosphere of most departments and laboratories. Furthermore, "self-examination goes against the masculine model of the scientist" (p. 148).

Most feminists agree on what the basic problem is: "There is little doubt that Canadian universities are not neutral in this matter" (p. 131). Perhaps this is where agreement ends and differences over strategy appear. Vickers and Adams (1977), argue that "... women within the academic profession must be prepared to actively force their way into the positions and structures which control universities" (p. 142).

While there is continuing debate about how to eliminate such discrimination, feminists agree that the solutions to the problem will be some time in coming. For if in fact feminism stands fundamentally opposed to the overall hierarchical structuring of academe, the solution would seem to indicate the necessity of going beyond "adding women and stirring", to radically reorganizing the whole internal structure of universities. In the latter parts of the Second Stage for instance, the feminist development of different pedagogical styles reflects perhaps the most important innovation which rejects hierarchical institutional practices and which exists autonomously within the university. This development has gone a long way toward bridging the gap left by an exclusionary male hierarchy and the lack of support systems for women in the university.

G. The Lack of Support Systems or the "Old Boy's Network" Syndrome

Dorothy Smith (1978) has described women's exclusion from formal/informal networks as a "circle effect" which denotes a process whereby men attend to and treat as significant only what men say, with the result that women have been: "... largely excluded from the work of producing the forms of thought and the images and symbols in which thought is expressed and ordered" (p. 281).

This exclusion is grounded historically in varying discriminatory hiring and promotion practices which prevented women from producing research (knowledge) in the first place and which currently continue to exclude women. The result of this "circle effect" suggests Smith (1978), is that informal/formal mechanisms of knowledge production perpetuate gender production as males define what knowledge *is* how it is denoted, through which symbols and for whom.

How does the Old Boy's Network concretely impede the work of feminists academics? White (1972) suggests that during the course of a woman's career in academe she must learn "... to behave in ways which other people in the field regard as professional" (p. 361). Professional socialization of identity/formation, in other words, involves learning the roles, attitudes, and expectations which are an important part of real professional life. This period of role learning is extremely important, not only in terms of the social, but also in terms of becoming "... knowledgeable about many aspects of institutions, journals, professional meetings, methods of obtaining source materials, and funding grant applications" (p. 362). Knowing how to command these institutional facilities, feminists argue, requires numerous skills, many social, many unanticipated by new women faculty members and is, as White explains, kind of learning we speak of as "caught", not "taught", ... a valued by-product of acceptance and challenging association with other professionals".

"Learning" professionalism in the academic world frequently eludes official policy or for that matter, explicit delineation. Instead, it entails, an implicit understanding (unofficial and unarticulated) about what constitutes appropriate academic behavior and in particular, about the conditions (norms, beliefs, ideological affinities) of admission into the group. Academic socialization in this regard, is not unlike other types of socialization and the stock of knowledge which accompanies them. Some learn the rules more quickly or appear more clever but generally speaking everyone has basic sense of the rules of the institution and of the code of behavior set down by the group.

Historically, the academic world developed forms of group life for the fundamental purpose of carving out an identity. Each group grew autonomously, though not completely separate, and adopted a mode of conduct, a code of principles and a linguistic paradigm that would characterize that group and would bear its stamp. It is not my intent here to discuss the considerable efforts that various learned societies have gone to naturalize the claimed intellectual superiority of one or another discipline. But it is pertinent to note that in the process of establishing group identities, the academic disciplines developed a set of criteria for admission which tended to exclude those who were not white, upper class males (Touraine, 1974). Social selection is presently expressed in a more diffused, though equally prejudicial way through the existence of professional groups whose opinions often determine which academic receives, sponsorship and support. Whether it be for hiring, a promotion or tenure, women are less likely to get sponsored than men in the same position. One reason for this is that the majority of those in positions with the authority to sponsor are men and they predominantly sponsor other men. At this point women cannot become admitted to the academic group and cannot therefore, provide support for other women. The circle is complete; women remain on the periphery, and as White maintains, whether a woman is "sponsored" ... will partially determine who reads her work, listens to her reports, or even offers friendly comments on the draft of a paper (p. 363).

The issue then is not always the *kind* of academic socialization women receive. Rather it is that they are frequently denied access to the relationships that are necessary to acquire the "tricks of the trade." This in itself is a form of alienation, and indifference and it is itself the most neglected issue between feminists and academe.

Another less open and in some ways the most problematical form of gender alienation is the psychological expropriation of women's confidence and academic motivation. The much-talked about problem of women's "achievement motivation" or more accurately perhaps, women's lack of it, is the topic of another section in this chapter and has no bearing on what I am referring to here. What I mean here is the loss of confidence that comes when an individual realizes that their acquisition of credentials, their appropriate their performance ratings and their high levels of energy, sacrifice, and dedication, have been precluded by their gender. And indeed it is the case, as feminists demonstrate in the late 60's - early 70's, that women's exclusion seems to be something that women themselves feel lethargic about. According to White, women don't protest their being left out, and therefore seem powerless to change the situation. She points this out with caution, and rightfully so I think. It becomes very easy to fall into the trap of "blaming the victim" which is how many early feminist analyses were rendered. The cure, argued feminists in the mid 70's, is not necessarily more individual boldness nor overcoming individual apathy.

It must include new institutional arrangements and programs which do not depend on individual initiative; and therefore do not insinuate that the issue at stake is an individual problems with an individual/attitudinal solution. She says that;

> there have been lone individuals who have flourished on society's neglect and produced great ideas or masterpieces, but this is not characteristic of those in the professions or the majority of people. It is acceptance and interaction which are often denied, both professionally and inadvertently, to women, whether they participate full-time or on a flexible schedule, whether they remain continuously in the field or seek reentry (White, 1972, p. 364).

From White's perspective, a major hindrance to the development of sponsorship relationships in women's life patterns is the dual commitment to family and career, to the public and private. Many women seek "... an occupational or professional identity which recognizes and takes into account this dual commitment" (p. 364). Because the "Old Boy's Network" implicitly assumes that women's "proper sphere" is in the home, it excluded women from its membership, but also actively reinforces policies which militate against provisions for needs in which women are full-time university employees. The "Old Boys Network" is thus concretely connected to the lack of day care centers, health and psychological services, rape crisis intervention organizations. financial advisors and legal supports. This point speaks to the division of public and private spheres, and suggests that the maintenance of women's marginal position in academe is interdependent with the separation of private/public spheres.

More recent research has approached the problem of lack of support systems somewhat differently, while relying on the insights of others. For example, Sherman and Beck (1977) in their anthology have discussed the lack of communication between women working in different fields and state that the original impetus for the planning of *The Prism of Sex: Essays in the Sociology of Knowledge* arose from the recognition that an instrument of communication was needed amongst women scholars — instruments that are difficult and/or impossible to develop on campus. At the same time, organizations *on* campus arose during the Second Stage with precisely this aim in mind, such as women faculty associations. Similarly, a number of anthologies, in psychology, philosophy, sociology and history, etc., have been produced with precisely this aim. Volumes and journals have also emerged which are solely committed to providing cross-disciplinary and inter-disciplinary communication amongst women.

In a perhaps more radical leap, other feminist writers such as Daly (1973), Howe (1975), and Rich (1975), remind us of the implicit trap of accepting the premise that advancement and security — even the chance to do one's best work — "lie in propitiating and identifying with men who have some power". Rich (1975) says that as women, "we have always found ourselves in competition with each other and blinded to our common struggles" (p. 26). The problem is exacerbated by the fact that for their own survival women have learned to "... vote against other women, absorb the masculine adversary style of discourse, and carefully avoid any style or method that could be condemned as "irrational" or "emotionally charged" (p. 27). Employing survival techniques are both necessary for legitimation and for acceptance in the academic world though. Some women see the compromise as a "no-win" situation. For feminists such as Adrienne Rich, the solution involves much more that strengthening women's support systems within the *existing* university. In her terms it means building a "women-centered" university: The idea of creating an entirely different learning institution premised on female values is one shared by many feminist scholars. As the idea caught on and gained momentum, the whole thrust of the problem of sexism in academe changed direction as has the theoretical slant of the dissent's explication of the problem. To oversimplify the case perhaps, the late 70's - early 80's ushered in a shift from "reformist" solutions within an integrationist approach to a transformist solution within a separatist approach. However it is not clear how such a "woman-centered" university could function in a patriarchal society, or where the processes would begin through which individuals would work towards its support. Pragmatically, one can ask where financing would come from; how it would stay viable; who would dictate its agenda and how it would respond to the demands of the labor market. These questions are complex, but the concept of a separate academy has had appeal since the rise of single-sex colleges in the early nineteenth century.

H. Disciplinary Divisions

We have seen that the lack of communication between women working in different fields has arisen mainly through the boundaries imposed by disciplinary divisions. This fourth set of barrier clusters specifically around the fragmentation of knowledge into academic disciplines. The division of disciplines imposes a separation between those people who produce the knowledge in one field and those who produce the knowledge in other. This division was historically established in the late nineteenth - early twentieth century. The major problem it posed then for feminists was twofold: first, it served to separate feminists who were forced to work in isolation from vital support systems and second, it established the subsequent specialization attached to professionalized areas of knowledge which worked as an exclusionary device for those women who had been unable to attain professional legitimization by the university. This fragmentation exists in a similar fashion today, and is interrelated with the perpetuation of the male hierarchy. It works against developing feminist support systems; women remain isolated in numbers and are divided intellectually along disciplinary lines. It forces women moreover, to identify their loyalties with their discipline and to see their feminism as a secondary concern.

Disciplinary barriers also impose limits on what we can *know*. Feminists argue that disciplinary barriers hamper their understanding and analysis of the world in which they live in and study. "The artificial categorizing of women's experience into various abstractions is limiting our understanding of women's total situation and experience" (Malmo, 1979, p. 14). The traditional organization of academe has been attacked on many fronts, but as Rich (1975) allows: ... like an old and condemned building, we may want to photograph these for posterity and tear them down; some may be reconstructed along different lines; some we may continue to live in and use. But a radical reinvention of subject, lines of inquiry, and method will be required" (pp. 30-31). By "some", Rich is referring to the actual disciplinary frameworks themselves, and the constrictions which ultimately result from their imposition. She and Daly (1973), believe that "the tyranny of methodolatry hinders new discoveries. It prevents us from raising questions never asked before and from being (illuminated) by ideas that do not fit into pre-established boxes and forms..." (pp. 11-12).

From the early 70's on, feminist theorists argued that insights into elements of women's lives do not sensibly divide into the academic disciplines; they "cut across all modes of inquiry" (Tobias, 1980, p. 15). For example, understanding how the concept "human nature" is distorted by the omission of women from the particular subject area requires sophisticated knowledge of history, sociology, psychology, linguistics, philosophy and other fields. "Feminist analysis requires global knowledge" (Ruth, 1980, p. 68).

Drawing on their own research many feminists went on to challenge entire departmental or disciplinary structures as they exist. Some even suggested that the division of knowledge into neat, compact little areas with boundaries that ought not to be crossed is analogous to (and possibly derivative of) the warrior behaviour of separating land into territories that then must be justified and guarded (see for example Rosaldo, 1975). Intellectual boundaries, feminists argue, are not only artificial; they are destructive.

Because of the severe constraints imposed by disciplinary boundaries, feminists have been philosophically commited to interdisciplinarity from the very beginning of the Second Stage. Generally speaking, they have, in their own research attempted to be interdisciplinary in their theory and practice. Malmo (1979) for example elaborates her concern for interdisciplinary feminist research in the following. She strongly urged that,

> A broader, more sophisticated understanding will come only when we transcend our belief, sometimes held with religious fervor, that our discipline has *the* answer. In my opinion, we are limiting both our understanding and our progress if we do not make every effort to go beyond the narrow scopes of our disciplines and begin communicating with each other. We have so much to learn (p. 14).

In her critique of disciplinary divisions, Malmo mentions a number of feminists works which have gone beyond the narrow specialization of a single disciplinary framework, to necessarily alter simplistic theories. For example, she shows how Bloch's (1978) *Untangling the Roots of Modern Sex Roles: A Survey of Four Centuries of Change* analyzes the historical development of psychological theories, in the attempt to demonstrate that psychological theories of women reflect the social and religious attitudes of the time. She believes that the conclusion reached does represent a radical departure from the established North American behaviourist orientation in psychology which assumes history to be irrelevant and science to be objective and neutral" (p. 15). Similarly, Laidlaw (1978) in her doctoral dissertation entitled, *Concepts of Femininity 1880-1930: Reflections of Cultural Attitudes in Psychological Theories* unlock the myths of psychological theory and shows the significance of history in revealing this and the banality of the scientific objective stance in supporting it. In her research the author utilizes history, psychology and drama, to demonstrate that psychological theories of femininity continually reinforced the changing attitudes and beliefs of patriarchal society. Concluding that, "The definition of the feminine remained a patriarchal definition with the playwrights reflecting it, the feminists eventually succumbing to it and the spsychologists reinforcing it by providing it with scientific credibility" (p. 180). Such a conclusion is indeed a radical departure from the assumptions of established North American psychology though as a whole, feminist research in itself represents a radical departure from traditional research models.

The structure of the academy, through its packaging of knowledge has impeded to a large extent the work of feminists, but "... by asking questions in terms of *women* (and not in terms of a particular framework such as psychology or history, for example), feminists moved beyond some of the limitations which are imposed by compartmentalization; they reconceptualized the existence of women and began to encode knowledge in a radically new way" (Spender, 1981, p. 2) (emphasis mine). And, as Spender continues: "... feminists began to establish that this omission was not a peculiar development within a particular discipline but a problem common to many disciplines. It was the problem of male dominance in the construction of knowledge and it manifested itself across disciplines" (p. 2).

Feminism, in other words, is considered a philosophy of knowledge, a way of seeing and knowing the world and an experience that is both, simultaneously, personal and political, private and public. While the subject matter of feminist research is women, feminists insist that women's "knowing" and experience does not live in a vacuum: "they are located in a social context which includes the study of men (and children) as well as the natural and the "man-made" (sic) environment" (Duelli Klein, 1984, p. 226). Feminists research therefore, is not limited to specific issues and has rejected the compartmentalization of knowledge. This has led feminists' to adopt what some call "interdisciplinary" knowledge, but which may be more accurately coined "transdisciplinary" research.

I. Subject Matter

> women cannot simply be added to the subject
> matter of existing .. theory, for the works of our
> ... heritage are to a very great extent built on the
> assumption of the inequality of the sexes .. (Okin,
> 1979, p. 10).

Feminists in the Second Stage critiqued the barriers imposed by the disciplines first in terms of the divisions between knowledge areas and second looked inward at the *subject matter* of those areas. Generally, the dissent argued that women as a topic of research were excluded altogether, or if they were included, they were either (a) "confined to a special section" (Mackie, 1983, p. 15) or (b) "appeared in male-related roles: family sociologists studied dating, mating, and domestic interaction; students of deviance/criminology investigated prostitution or sex delinquency; demographers studied birth, death, migration and divorce. In explorations of economic, political, and religious institutions *in sociology* (for example) women were invisible" (Huber, 1976, p. 685) (emphasis mine). Huber (1976) notes that after 1970 new trends appeared.

Earlier critiques of social science were concerned with *including* women in academic areas which had previously ignored them. Disciplines thus have a "before" and "after" look — before the "discovery of women". This is part of an evolution, both in feminist scholarship and in academic content matter.

The exclusion of women in social science research is widely documented. Beginning in the early 70's, feminists in disciplines such as philosophy, psychology, history and anthropology, followed somewhat later by women working in biology, physics and literature, exposed how traditional research focused exclusively on male activities, often excluding women altogether, and consistently viewed men as more advanced than women, crediting men as being the norm and women, the derivation, the deviant of human kind.[5] It is further evident from feminist accounts that male scientists/social scientists, while claiming to observe social reality in a "neutral" and "objective" manner, were extremely androcentric if not downright misogynist. It was learned that interwoven throughout mainstream research lurked assumptions about women's "proper place" and women are not even studied directly (See for example: Daniels, 1975; Rosaldo, 1974).

Central to the feminist critique of the academic disciplines then, was and is the argument that in theory and research the male has been regarded as the prototype of humanity and the female, if considered at all, considered in relationship to him. The "male-as-prototype pattern" feminists make clear is particularly incidious in the way it has meant leaving women out of the research altogether. On another level, women's empirical or theoretical omission exacerbates the fact that across disciplines gender has simply not been addressed as a social fact.

In history for example, feminist historians have criticized traditional history for its failure to understand women's situation, its adequate treatment of women, and its consistent focusing on the activities of men: "Traditional history lacks an understanding of women's situation because it has considered civilization to be making ware, wealth, laws, government, art, and science, all activities that women have been largely excused from" (Kelly-Gadol, 1976, p. 810). Women's omission, people like Kelly-Gadol argued, reveal central distortions in our historical knowledge and theory (See also: Lerner, 1975; 1976a; 1977; Smith-Rosenberg, 1975). The male orientation of what is considered historically significant and significantly knowable about the past, stems from male historians themselves, as a male perspective has denied knowledge of women's historical experience claiming it by subsuming it under the rubric, "the history of man". All in all, it is men who have conceptualized, categorized and given themselves parentage to the historical record and the cultural process. "Their categories and periodization have been masculine by definition, for they have defined significance primarily by power, influence and visible activity in the work of political and economic affairs" (Gordon, Buble and Dye, 1976, p. 27).

In psychology the impact of new scholarship of women, for women has also been profound. One notably visible area where women have been rendered invisible and then cast as inferior, partly because of this invisibility, has been the equation of male psychological development with the healthy norm, especially in the theories of Sigmund Freud, and later, Jean Piaget, Erik Erikson and Lawrence Kohlberg. Specifically developmental theories of psychosocial, psychosexual and moral maturation have deemed women inferior because of their, lack of assertiveness, indivduation, rationality, and "objective" standard of moral judgement.

Aside from the more troublesome questions of bias, in psychological theory, or perhaps it is more correct to say, before the analyses of sexism in theory, feminists critiqued the male - centeredness of psychology noting how males were studied more often; how male psychologists perpetuated what Naomi Weisstein (1971) scathingly referred to as a "male fantasy life"; how orthodox methods of studying and interpreting sex differences (a topic of some longevity in the history of psychology) were capable of delivering erroneous conclusions and finally; how sexist assumptions about the individual lie beneath the diversity of psychological theories and their associated procedures. These problems persist despite the fact that demonstrations of bias, some dating to the earliest days in the history of the discipline, were documented and disseminated by women such as Mary Calkins, Helen Thompson Woolley and Mary Putnam Jacobi.[6] Second Stage dissenters insisted because of this, that it was not simply that there were not enough women in psychology. Clearly there is "something in psychology's assumptions and working practices that also needs attention" (Wood Sherif, 1977, p. 94).

The assumption that it is unproblematic to ignore women, led feminists to begin adding women to psychology's agenda.

In fact, psychological research conducted in the early to mid 1970's seems to have focused solely on the presentation of "new" data, meaning data about women. Parlee (1975) believes that the fundamental aim of providing this new data was to contribute information about women to already existing subject/topic areas such as personality, motivation, anxiety, interpersonal interaction, learning theory, social roles, intelligence and achievement, etc. For example, Julia Sherman's (1971) *On the Psychology of Women* and Hochschild's (1973) "A Review of Sex Role Research" provided

commentaries, discussions, and references on psychologically selected topics covering psychological studies of sex roles, achievement motivation in women, and women and psychotherapy. The
latter topic was the subject of Phyllis Chesler's (1972) *Women and
Madness*. As well, Bardwick's (1971) *Psychology of Women*, and
Eleanor Maccoby and Carol Jacklin's (1974) *The Psychology of Sex
Differences* illustrated the empirical development that had occurred in the previous ten years in psychological studies of sex
differences. This work contained extremely comprehensive sum-
maries/reviews of psychological studies on selected topics — again
traditional topics that would now *include*, rather than preclude
women.

Other directions in psychology included the establishment of a
"psychology for women" which was to move beyond correcting lacu-
nae caused by psychology's past record of omitting women as subjects. First and foremost, "a/the" psychology for women can be
"characterized as pointing out "new" phenomena", asserted Parlee
(1975). "The "new" phenomena and "new" realms of data are, of
course, new only to the psychological literature. They represent
some of the psychological experiences that have long been real for
women but which have been ignored by traditional psychologists"
(p. 131).

As a result of the feminist research on women Parlee predicted
that "women, at least as a topic of research, are unlikely ever again
to be excluded with the same efficient thoroughness as they have in
the past" (p. 119). She nonetheless had caveats when she warned of
the problems that lie ahead "... for the development of a research
tradition within psychology that is relevant to women — relevant,
that is, to the scientific understanding of human behavior and experience, not just to that of males" (p. 120).

Apart from the difficulties posed by the rubric "psychology of
women", feminists like Parlee (1975) and Carlson (1972) argued that
it would at least attempt to broaden the scope of subject matter and
methodological inadequacies of individual studies.[7]

If we look hard at the "themes of relevance" of sociology it
becomes apparent how equally ubiquitous the problem of women's
absence is.[8] Exposing the male bias in sociology has yielded the
discovery that the topics of inquiry have been *male* sociologists'
defined topics of interest. These topics of interest (as in psychology) are constitutive of the discipline itself — defining its very

existence.[9]

A discipline that touches closer to home is the field of Education where the discussion of gender bias in subject matter has taken on astronomical proportions. Briefly the scale on which women have been ignored is massive. For instance, Acker's (1980) survey (cited in Spender's (1981) article) of British Sociology of Education indicated that the study of women has been minimal, "for while 58% of the articles purported to be studying both sexes, 37% had all male samples and only 5% all female samples" (Spender 1981: 161). Other feminist researchers have demonstrated that traditional educational research focuses almost exclusively on male activities (see for example: Arnot 1981; Astin and Bayer 1973; David 1978; Deem 1980; 1981; Eichler 1977; Gaskell 1981; Janeway 1971; O'Brien 1984).

Feminists in educational psychology, like their counterparts in sociology of education, have shown that a male perspective prevails and a male presence predominates. Existing subject areas such as personality, motivation, anxiety, interpersonal interaction, learning theory, social roles, intelligence and achievement, have been topics that have been conceptualized in male forms and as such, have had little relevance to women's experience (See for example: Sadker and Frazier 1976; Vaughter 1976).

In the case of the history of education, feminists have shown how traditional accounts of the historical development of education institutions have continued to overlook women (Pierson and Prentice, 1982). To mainstream historians, the evolution of educational systems, for example, impacted on and involved only males. One illustration of this can be found in classic examinations of working class educational patterns, which often provide brilliant analyses of young *boy's* educational experience and the way that experience is shaped by their social class definitions. "Thus it is the feminist perspective that has exposed the preoccupation with men in, and the general absence of women from, most official, published and academically respectable history" (Pierson and Prentice 1982: p. 109).

Studies of contemporary schooling that deal with questions of school policy, school processes, teacher/student interaction, and curriculum design are conspicuously devoid of any mention of gender (Clarricoates 1980; Deem 1980; Roberts 1976; Spender 1982). Serious gaps as well, can be found in research on teacher training, the teaching profession, higher education, sports and science education, educational policy and administration and the school/labour force connection (See for example: Arnot, 1981; David, 1978; Thibault, 1986). Each of these areas in education - e.g. history, sociology, psychology, etc. - reveal the absence of women.

Characteristically, the research conducted in education's numerous subfields has been quite conservative in nature, using 'structural-functionalist' methodologies to support, rather than question existing educational ideologies. This has been the case until well into the 1950's though much less so since the 1960's. With the exceptions of certain fields that have overwhelmingly been radical in posture; studies of schooling, learning, motivation etc. have tended to shy away from any sort of criticism of educational structures. Educational practices were essentially seen in these studies, as performing a necessary function (and a necessarily benevolent one) in the society (Karabel and Halsey, 1977). Hence, such studies were not easily attracted to critical theory and on the whole, were resistent to envisioning education as anything other than a necessary "evil". From this perspective, it is understandable (to some degree) how feminist ideas would be dismissed out of hand. The adherence to conservative frameworks in education, however, was a temporal phenomenon and beginning roughly in the early to mid 1960's a few educationalists emerged on the academic scene with incisive criticisms of the educational enterprise. many of these now classic writings went a long way in influencing the direction of educational research. And many of these analyses were to lay the vital groundwork for later feminist criticisms of education. But even the classic, critical works which were and are highly critical of educational systems and of mainstream educational research - have paradoxically enough, excused any mention of gender.

From a humanist bent, in North American Sociology of Education for instance, germinal pieces such as: Erikson's (1963) *Childhood and Society*; Friedenberg's (1965) *The Dignity of Youth and Other Activisms* and his (1970) *Vanishing Adolescent*; Holt's (1967) *How Children Fail* and his (1968) *How Children Learn*; Illich's (1970) *Deschooling Society*; Hickerson's (1966) *Education for Alienation*; and Silberman's (1970) *Crisis in the Classroom* all in different ways, contended that preoccupation with order is the most important characteristic schools share. The means of socialization used by schools are neither innocuous nor banal. Rather, as

Silberman pointed out, schools discourage students from developing the capacity to learn by and for themselves (something John Holt favours). They are structured in such a way as to make students dependent on teachers and other "authority personnel". At the same time, teachers have had the use of the "hidden curriculum" (which describes the process of transmission of implicit norms, values and beliefs through the written curriculum's underlying structure) and the "overt curriculum" (or the articulated, written agenda of schooling) to achieve their desired effect. In Friedenberg's (1970) elliptical social-psychological study of adolescent character, he brilliantly attacks the school not only because he sees it as "a sorting station for academic aptitude, but a monitor for conduct and personality as well" (Riesman 1970, p. 13).

The insights of Friedenberg's and others' were instrumental in destroying myths about the supposed social and political neutrality of schools. They were equally effective in displaying how educational knowledge is a "social invention, reflecting conscious or unconscious cultural choices that (accord) with the values and beliefs of dominant groups." (Whitty 1985:8).

Various critical inquiries sprung from the early pieces of such people as Silberman, Illich, and Holt. In later research, analyses of "cultural deprivation", "the disadvantaged child" were seen in a radically changed light as were issues of the educational status of language differences (Bernstein, 1977). Willinsky's (1984) book, *The Well-Tempered Tongue* follows in this critical tradition, though in Willinsky's case, the work is exceptional in its inclusion of gender.[10] With regards to language, the earlier critique also prompted the exposure of linguistic prejudice and cultural imperialism in conservative research and catalyzed a virtual proliferation of differing viewpoints on the equality of educational opportunity debate.

The critical theories of humanists, in other words, made an immeasurable dint in the direction and focus of sociological and psychological research in education, and they continue to affect the discipline as a whole. However, the explications did not discuss and evidently did not see as pertinent the processes through which gender is ordered, controlled, and maintained in educational praxis. As Riesman (1970) found significant to state about Friedenberg's book; the study was consciously more concerned with boys' experience of alienation than with girls'. Friedenberg's study was the rule, not the exception. I all cases, issues of school practice, teacher/student in-

teraction, differential treatments and analyses of the "hidden curriculum" were conceptualized exclusively in terms of their impact
on males. The means by which teacher/student interchange and
differential treatments operate in relation to the sexes, are inquiries
that have been left to feminists to analyze. Similarly, the fact that
the "hidden curriculum" actually intends and accomplishes very
distinct things along gender-divided levels, is only academically
knowledgeable because of feminists' efforts in this area. Finally,
the fact that the "non-hidden" curriculum is blatantly more ideological in its philosophic and practical execution of gender reproduction, is only now become part of the academic knowledge because
of feminists' insistence on including gender in educational research.

Like the humanists, the radical sociologists in the "new Sociology of Education" deliberated over the role of social and political
forces in the school curriculum. Like the humanists, they explicated
the curriculum as an ideological practice and like the humanists,
there was no mention of gender in the research. Certainly as
Spender (1980; 1981; 1981a; 1982) and others have repeatedly made
clear, school knowledge *is* a social/cultural artifact. However questions about the nature of knowledge that is produced and legitimated *vis a vis* school policy, and how it is used, from a feminist
perspective, take understandings of that knowledge in entirely new
directions. One direction points to the fact that "if sexism were to
be removed from the curriculum there would be virtually nothing
left to teach because our society knows so little that isn't sexist"
(Spender 1982: 3). The reason for this, Spender contends, is that "the
interests of men are pursued; knowledge is produced about men's
interests and fed into the whole society, while the questions that
may interest women too frequently "evaporate" when men are in
control" (p. 3). From this standpoint, it is apparent that both the
radical sociologists and the humanists' critique of education is consistent with and shaped by their male interests. In fact, the critique
itself is a part of the same process that legitimates and conceals
ideological dimensions of educational research. It also seems clear
(and ironic) that male critical theorists could use their own theories
to illuminate their own roles in perpetuating a particular kind of
knowledge that speaks to humanity through the lens of a male perspective.

These are but a few samples of the studies which have left
women out of the educational account. Spender's contention that

male interests are pursued in academic research holds true here. The subject matter of education has reflected and reflects male interests at the expense of women's interests. Women are both excluded from and marginalized by research and this exclusion is constitutive of the discipline itself. But when I say that women's exclusion is constitutive of the discipline itself, making education's topics of inquiry neither unique in their patriarchal posture nor isolated in their mistreatment or nontreatment of women.

Having completed the exposition of bias, feminists turned to the "reconstructive" part of their project; namely, they began making women the topic of inquiry. In sociology topics were expanded to take into account both women's interest and the role of gender. For example, feminists redefined women's locations in the social structure (work, family, education, etc.) as problematic, and analyzed how these locations are maintained and perpetuated in the home and workplace (Arnot, 1981; David, 1978; Deem, 1978; Gaskell).

Within the context of the sociology of education, for instance, feminist research responded by taking up home and family as social sites revealing the interconnection between the school and the family in maintaining women's subordinate status (David, 1978). Huber (1976), Lapata (1976), and Smith (1974); 1975; 1977b; 1979b) contended that it is evident that an extensive revamping of sociology must take place in order that the interests and experiences of women be properly included. In 1976 Lapata said that, "The recent research and reanalysis in the sociology of the family, of work, of socialization and identity, and of social structure have opened up new perspectives and questions. However "consciousness raising" in a scientific discipline may mean reexamination of the whole paradigm and the store of knowledge which form the foundation for our construction of reality" (p. 176).

Feminist after feminist emphasized the need to go beyond fitting women into male subject areas. Despite their diversity, psychology and sociology (as well as other academic disciplines) share a constraining element. They have all constrained feminists' research by essentially giving them no place to *begin*. In all disciplines, content-area/subject matter has been male-defined. Earlier feminist scholarship made women and their experience visible in these ares, while providing new insights into those "subject-areas" themselves. Perhaps Smith (1977b) spoke for feminists in all disciplines when she explained that in order to eliminate of break out of the confines of "subject" boundaries, we must make women subjects of our focus. In a nicely articulated piece she spoke to all feminists when she said that,

> we must begin with knowledge of women's everyday worlds and of their experience. This means, in the first place, learning *from* them (my emphasis). Much of our work in the field now begins from the framework, concepts, and perhaps even more importantly, the organization of subject matter that sets up description as an objective account ... . The experience we must begin from, however, is that of those who live it rather than those who merely observe for the purposes of entering into the .. discourse. I am suggesting that the world within the experience of actual individuals should become the place where inquiry begins (p. 23).

Feminist work which earlier examined the problem of women getting published dealt with women's difficulties of finding *time* to write. The dual responsibilities of family and career, coupled with women's socialization, (which dictates that women give primary attention to their families and only secondary attention to their waged work) led to women's dilemma of having virtually no *time* for research and publication (Graham, 1972). From this perspective, publishing as a barrier was seen in terms of women's individual inability to cope with the excessive demands of academic life.

Later work however, more clearly explored the actual problematic institutional *processes* which are instrumental in determining who or what research gets reported, or published (See for instance: Ardener, 1975; Smith, 1978; Spender, 1981). The discussion of the processes of publishing is one which has necessarily followed form feminists' explications of the construction of knowledge and these explications have come in the latter periods of the Second Stage. This literature is more contemporarily located in a critique which moves beyond documenting the biases that have been encoded against women and which argues that built-in mechanisms of publishing militate against women getting published (Roberts, 1981).

Spender's (1981) analysis in particular, dealt with the social construction of publication.

Spender has argued that it is men who are in positions to determine what gets published and what does not (those whom Smith (1978) calls "gatekeepers" in the academic community). She raises four issues that bear directly on women's problems in getting published: the significance of publication in academe; the role of publication in shaping disciplines; the criteria used for determining "scholarly excellence"; and the problem of male dominance in the processes and practices of publishing. The cohering theme is that it is considered "best" if women do not write at all (even as they expected to fulfill academic requirements), but if they do then there are ways of discrediting their words and making them invisible.

We have already seen how this process began in the nineteenth century when new research universities established research (and hence publishing) as a fundamental criterion for gaining professorship. Women who *did* publish had to submit work to male publishers, precisely those people who decided which *knowledge* is disseminated, and such an historical process facilitated keeping women (academic) writers a muted group.

Similarly, today, it is males of a particular class, according to Spender, who have decreed what constitutes good writing and they have done so without reference to females of any class. She draws on Smith's (1978) comment, which outlines the role that males have played in the construction of our culture and which emphasizes:

> that the forms of thought we make use of to think of ourselves and our society originate in special positions of dominance occupied almost exclusively by men, and this means that our forms of thought put together a view of the world from a place women do not occupy. Hence, the means that women have had available to them to think, image and make actionable their experience have been made for us and not by us (Smith, 1978, p. 282).

Smith believes it is the dominant group "that has decreed and promulgated the ideologically sanctioned form of social relations; that has developed the criteria of "authoritative ideological sources (what kinds of books, newspapers, etc., to credit, what to discredit, who are the authoritative writers or speakers and who are not)" (pp. 286-287). It is primarily men who have determined whether or not women have "passed the test" and it is usually men who have operated from the underlining premise that women should not be in the framework anyway.

Spender warns that we cannot take as evidence of women's emancipation from male control the fact that some women occupy influential positions as publishers, editors or critics because what we know of as praiseworthy has been standardized by men and institutionalized by a system of patriarchy. Women writers themselves have often felt betrayed by women publishers, in some cases because the standards of evaluation are felt to be male ones. Spender says that "... this behaviour is to be expected, although not condoned, ... anyone who expects otherwise is ignoring the basic power configurations of our society: women are muted — by their publishers, editors, critics or writers! And as a muted group they have frequently made decisions which support the dominance of men" (Spender, 1980, p. 201).

For women writers (academic and other) the problems of becoming "published" are very different from the problems experienced by men: "Men ... operate from a basis of shared subjectivity with publishers, editors and critics which women do not; they are encouraged and made confident which women are not; they have linguistic resources which enhance their image and support their values which women do not; they can write for men without jeopardizing their human — 'masculine' — identity while women cannot without jeopardizing their human — 'feminine' — identity" (p. 201).

Finally, Collins' (1975) review on the activities of the Feminist Press supports Spender's, Smith's, and Eichler's (1981) shared belief that feminists must develop their own publication support systems. In fact, she intimates that developing autonomous literary processes of publication may be the only solution.

J. Pedagogy

Among the many structures criticized by feminist in higher education, classroom activity - both teaching and learning - has evoked overwhelming resistance by the dissent. In general terms, feminists have first mapped out the problems and second actively worked to undermine the deeply held and powerful sets of distinctions drawn in North American intellectual thought and society. These distinctions epitomize the teaching/learning enterprise and are redolent of a separation of the personal, subjective or private, from the public, objective or impersonal. Traditional academic pedagogy leans toward the detachment of teacher and learner: it shuns the introduction of the personal/subjective in this functioning; it promotes a hierarchical arrangement in the classroom; it dismisses the personal/subjective experience of teacher and taught as contaminating and it disguises the power relations through which it operates. In a word, the difficulties posed by these practices have feminist scholars to reject them and have fashioned what can be called for lack of a better term, "feminist pedagogy".

One of the best definitions of feminist pedagogy I have come across, is Culley and Portuges' (1985):, "The phrase 'feminist pedagogy couples the contemporary and the traditional, joining current political movements with a concern for the transmission of knowledge more ancient than the Greek word for teaching (p. 1). In their excellent book, *Gendered Subjects: The Dynamics of Feminist Teaching*, they explain that feminist pedagogy arose as an alternative to traditional methods of teaching. Feminists realized that in order to transform the content (or what we teach) of the curriculum, there must also be changes made in how that content is taught.

From this starting point, the authors contend that feminist pedagogy is distinctive in that it is predicated on two interconnected sets of concerns. "First, it practioners define themselves as feminists and implement that self-definition through work that challenges the economic, socio-political, cultural and psychological imperatives based on gender" (p. 2). Simply stated, when teaching in the university, feminists tend to apply feminist principles to their practice in the classroom. Admittedly, the term pedagogy (singular) may be a misnomer because in fact there are an entire range of teaching styles, each of them an expression of the individual feminist.

From the beginning however and what *was* clearly revealed were a number of fundamental problems inherent in the traditional academic curriculum. In turn, *teaching* the traditional curriculum through the use of traditional styles of pedagogy, was seen as problematic. These common perceptions among feminists led to a common commitment to first restructure the classroom experience of students and faculty. "Circular arrangements of chairs, periodic small-group sessions, use of first names for instructors as well as students, assignments that required journal keeping ... collective modes of teaching ... all sought to transfer to women's studies the contemporary feminist criticism of authority and the validation of every women's experience" (Boxer, p. 243).

The general critique of academe's *institutional organization* and the specific critique of mainstream teaching techniques were not purely feminist discoveries. The 1960s, and 1970's were periods in which the legitimacy of most societal institutions were questioned (Hurn, 1978). The question of how universities should be responsive to the needs of their "clients", and less "coercive", "inhumane" and "authoritarian" attracted a wide and diverse audience. Critiques of higher education and cohort expositions led to the rise of alternative education movements: the "free school" movement, "open classrooms", the deschooling movement, the open university concept, etc. These groups shared a common commitment to shifting the role and practice of pedagogy. Overall, the distinctive features of radicalized pedagogy were the move to change classroom organization and the rejection of traditional student-teacher interaction patterns. The latter suggested that a redefinition f roles of both students and teachers was imperative for fundamental changes in the social order of universities.

Hence, feminists used these practices to provide alternatives to traditional forms of pedagogy, and to provide women with support systems.

Feminist faculty frequently diverge and continue to diverge from their colleagues in attitudes, experience, or methods:

> Many of us have come to academe from the learning laboratories of social action outside the university — from counter-culture organizations, from consciousness-raising groups and feminist groups, from political parties and equal rights agencies. Out of these experiences, we have learned the strength of the entrenched power structures. Others of us, having lived within the established system and have tried its regular channels and found them resistant, have learned the same lesson in another way (Ruth, 1980, p.

14).

In the mid seventies, there were no formal credentials *in* Women's Studies broadly speaking. Writing about the period, Janeway (1975) suggested that "one enters this field as thinkers entered any field centuries ago –– through experience and self-directed research. We have no models after which to style our activities. The criterion for our methods is productivity" (p. 27).

Feminists agree that feminist pedagogy is a highly innovative, and spontaneous, alternative form of teaching (See for example: Abel and Abel, 1983; Eichler, 1978; Freeman, 1970; Gaskell, 1978; Howe, 1975; Rich, 1975; Roberts, 1976; Sherman and Beck, 1977; Smith, 1974; Spender, 1981; Wine, 1983). Noticeable in a feminist classroom are tow factors not typical in college classrooms: "an acceptance of, and even emphasis on, the personal/affective element in learning; and a warm human relationship among persons in the class, students and teachers" (Tobias, 1980, p. 15). Having rejected the commitment to inappropriate or unnecessary reserve, feminist teachers are no longer at pains to maintain the authoritative aura of distance — from their work or from one another. Recognizing too that hierarchical structures believe the commonality of female experience as well as the commonality of human purpose, feminist faculty often seek alternatives to the traditional student/teacher dichotomy (Mackie, 1983; Malmo, 1979; Oakley, 1974; Smith, 1977; Spender, 1981). All and all, feminist pedagogy is one strategy for deconstructing the hierarchical structures of academe.

Understanding this central commitment to feminist pedagogy, most feminist teachers have experienced the extent to which it is both antithetical to traditional pedagogy and impeded by traditional academic policy. And here I want to draw exclusively on the analyses of Webb and Rich (1975) firstly for their assertions that, "what has come to be considered the operating assumptions of universities seems greatly divergent from the aims of a feminist movement, although this means more of a necessity for consciousness of our own situation than for splitting with the universities right now" (Webb, p. 400) and secondly, for their parallel outlines of the barriers to practicing feminist pedagogy. Webb for instance, divides her critique into two equally important sections: what do we teach? and how do we teach?

The working premise is most universities seems to be that it is legitimate to know certain bodies of knowledge. "Therefore we find that most college students learn by rote what they promptly forget, sometimes even before the ink dries on their B.A.'s" (Webb, p. 415). But as feminists, it is not this skill, or the "sterile" body of information we are trying to teach. In Webb's words she says, "I think all that we teach should have intrinsic to it an understanding of the power dynamic of patriarchy, and a purpose that is constantly up front about action against this dynamic. I mean it's more how we look at whatever body of information we have ..." (p. 416).

The difficulties are visible when one examines the methods of feminist pedagogy and sees how these strategies and methods stand in contradiction to traditional teaching methods. Webb outlines these methods" (1) feminists attempt to teach without imposing authoritarian structures; (2) feminists attempt to build a "... consciousness of an alternative, e.g., collective learning and action" (p. 417) rather than individual isolation and competitive striving; (3) feminists are faced with a double job: "helping people to understand the seriousness of a feminist philosophy and teaching so that students feel a strength of collective learning rather than hierarchical control" (p. 417); (4) feminist classes try to be different from traditional classes in that they try to included "actual experiences of what we are talking about in our teaching so that real conclusions can be made (not unthought-out acceptance of ideas)" (p. 417); (5) feminists the whole, agree that, "... the most learning occurs in reflecting about what was happening in the real world as opposed to the school world of pure ideas" and is therefore largely experiential in nature (p. 418).

Here one can view *feminist* pedagogy as a response by feminists to the barriers they find inherent in traditional pedagogy. The notion that learning is necessarily *experiential* relates directly to the feminist argument in this stage, that the "personal is political" and to divide the two does not apply to the experience of women.

Howe (1975) also sees fundamental divergencies between feminist methods of teaching and course development and so-called established curriculum and pedagogy. She asserts that feminist teaching strategies are as *politically* significant as the curricular innovations. They are "responses to adaptations of the movement's consciousness — raising groups, and include an emphasis on sisterhood and on action" (p. 155). Howe believes that the feminist classroom is very different, from other types and sees the educational arm of the women's movement as having three particular tasks to accomplish, two of which are clearly under way:

> In an institutional setting that has been tradition-
> ally careless of or hostile to women, the women's
> studies teacher has led the development of
> courses and teaching strategies aimed at changing
> the consciousness of women ... and at adding new
> knowledge to their kin. Equipped thus with con-
> sciousness and knowledge, their students have
> brought fresh leadership to ongoing movements
> for change on campus and off. Second ... teachers
> ... have added significantly to areas of knowledge
> and new research developments in such fields as
> sex-role socialization and gender identity ... The
> third task, dependent on the first two, is more
> elusive: to change the male -centered college cur-
> riculum, with regard to women ... (pp. 157-158).

In conclusion, precisely *because* the methods, practices and procedures of feminist pedagogy imply rejection of mainstream methods, feminist approaches to teaching can be seen as a problem in terms of the institutional structures which impede its existence. Feminists, begin first and foremost by insisting that women matter, and by insisting on the importance of women's experience and the validation of their personal experience, they pose a challenge to a male-defined curriculum which has typically obscured women and their experience altogether. But such a commitment has meant more. The commitments which underlie feminist pedagogy are intertwined with a prohibitive set of practices, which have made the achievement of feminist methods a difficult, yet powerful goal.

From this vantage point what exactly does feminist pedagogy involve? Predominantly it involves seeking strategies which attempt to define a female way of doing things. Feminists insist on multiplicity and acknowledge the uncertainties implicit in an approach which values the personal, the subjective and the experiential. These two explicit commitments place demands on feminists, which suggest that feminist pedagogy is as taxing on a personal level as it is vital on a political level. Herein lies the most *profound* insight about the unique position of feminists in the academy. The modes of operation of feminists present a mirrored image of the problems of existing in a patriarchal university. The germ of contradiction lies within the feminist agenda of changing teaching, and changing research, the curriculum and knowledge itself.

K. Achievement Motivation

The "achievement-motivation" paradigm, (heralded in the late 1960's and early 1970's as an explanatory tool for understanding women's *psychological* experience of conflict in nontraditional roles) was context-specific and later seen to be problematic - both because of its inherent assumptions about sexism and because of the way in which it considered women's role in thwarting their own success. The very use of the term "success" was as well fraught with contradictions and these difficulties in the model will be discussed later on. Nonetheless, the theory, generally associated with the maverick studies of Matina Horner (1968; 1972), had and continues to have its merits particularly in its validation of the tensions women do feel between their own and society's definitions of femininity. Equally important, was the focus of achievement-motivation on the psychologic dynamics of that tension. Previously, research centered on women's *reaction* to structural discrimination and little or nothing was asked about how reactions and responses were underscored by deep internal conflict. Achievement-motivation theory attempted to redress that balance by bringing to the fore, the issue of what it is women experience when faced with the potentially frightening possibility of achieving in ways not considered appropriate or proper for women. And it did so at a time when women's psychological make-up was rarely acknowledged and virtually never taken into account. In this sense, the second stage development of the paradigm was as timely as it was necessary.

Hence the Second Stage focussed concern on women's achievement in terms of a *psychological* barrier to success (Horner, 1971; Kipnis, 1974, O'Leary and Hammack, 1975; Stein and Bailey, 1973; Veroff, 1976). Much of the research in achievement motivation attempted to make connections between different socialization patterns and later achievement patterns in women (Graham, 1972; Mednick and Tangri, 1972). For example, Sherman (1971) argued that most summaries of psychological sex differences (i.e., dependency, fearfulness, empathy, passivity, etc.) reproduce the main features of the female stereotype, and none of these characteristics are associated with intellectual achievement. Such socialized sex-differences, leave women at a disadvantage within the present aggressive-competitive structure for intellectual and other kinds of achievement (Maccoby, 1966). Traditional institutional structures reward competition, and aggression, traits which are part and parcel of the masculine stereotype and primary to the socialization agenda for boys. Because of this, traditional definitions of women's "role" are often underpinning various jobs designated as "female" (Tangri, 1972).

Models of achievement motivation in the late 1960's - early 1970's gave insight into the different internal experiences of women in academe. The conflicts and internal tensions described by women in a traditional "male" domain, subtlely suggested that the "fear of success" (a concept developed by Horner (1968)) was integrally tied to the larger tension imposed by the private/public dichotomy. Feminists argued that because of sex labelling of occupations and gender role prescriptions, academic women were required to maintain a high degree of autonomy to manage emotionally being reacted to as deviant. Feminists in the Second Stage also argued that biases in *composition* or *treatment* of both students and faculty affect the achievement opportunities of large numbers of women (Astin and Bayer, 1973).

From these kinds of analyses, other literatures developed, often building on or elaborating the earlier work. Graham (1972), for example, maintained that internal ambivalences are especially acute "... in the years between eighteen and twenty-five years which, in this society, men generally devote to intense preparation for a career" (p. 264). For women these years are likely to be a time in which they seek, "... affirmation of their femininity, an activity likely to be at variance with serious vacational commitment. These activities are certainly not the only ones young people engage in, but they are likely to be the ones invested with the greatest psychic energy" (p. 264).

Some young women are able to do graduate work, Graham pointed out, and do it well in these years, "... but few pass through this period without severe qualms about the desirability of planning for a demanding professional life". men, too, are beset by a variety of doubts during these years, but for the majority of them, at least, "academic success does not bring substantial psychic problems as it does for women". Quoting Horner (1971) who concluded that the *desire* to achieve is often contaminated by "what I will call the motive to avoid success" (p. 62); Graham (1972) argued that the problems of aspiration and expectations are acute, and lead to a "motive to avoid success".

Finally, work on achievement motivation attempted to deal specifically with the larger conflict women academics faced when trying to reconcile and juggle their home and work life responsibilities (Epstein, 1971; Simon et al. 1972; Smith, 1978; White, 1972).

While the ideological undergirding of this conflict was not fully explicated in the late 1960's - early 1970's, the tensions feminists identified were both materially and conceptually indicative of the conflicts inflicted by the separate spheres ideology. In this light, what feminists then described as lack of achievement motivation may be interpreted as the psychological conflict imposed by the ideological construction and division of women's lives. Feminists saw the conflict developing over the span of an individual's life, through processes like socialization.

Very briefly, this literature stressed that commitment and participation in academe are not merely a function of an individual's competence or excellence, but are a product of the social environment as well. Acceptance and recognition from significant others (one's peers, family, etc.) and opportunities for stimulating and challenging interaction are essential for developing a strong occupational or professional identity (without losing identity as women), and for creating the inner sense of role competence which can lead to greater commitment and productivity in professional work. Unfortunately, women — especially those who have experienced interrupted or discontinuous careers — find such opportunities and acceptance difficulty to obtain. More often than not, women have internalized societal expectations of proper "feminine" roles — roles which do not include those activities associated with "success".

Thus the way that women see themselves has important consequences for their participation in academia, and women have been taught since birth to see themselves and their lives as societal norms would have them. The contradictions inherent in such a situation are clear.

The impetus for this concern with socialization arose from the woman's movement because it "offered glimpses of what might happen by showing that the "raising" of one's consciousness as a woman required rejection of others' definitions of self coupled with an understanding of the relationships in which women became enmeshed" (Wood Sherif, 1977, p. 126). From the perspective of feminists, what women required was a renewed self-definition, but the rest of society changes more slowly than the new awareness of self, and parts of both resist changes or simply stay the same. Again the contradictions are clear.

Hence the topic of achievement motivation arose largely from the work of feminist *psychologists* who were concerned to explain why *women* did not "succeed" in particular fields — in this case in academe. It was an early attempt to psychologically explicate women's *internal* barriers. Women's psychological internment, these feminists argued, has precluded them from achieving high status jobs. The emphasis on the role of internal conflict was extremely important, but in focusing solely on subjective feeling in isolation from its environment, analyses remained at the level of describing an "individual problem" that required an "individual solution". This work nonetheless provided the essential groundwork for deeper, more full analyses in the Third Stage, and equally provided feminists with the first attempt to make the psychological primary.

L. Private/Public Spheres

At every level of the institutional and ideological barriers we have examined for both the nineteenth - early twentieth centuries and in the late 1960's - early 1970's, one can see the ways in which feminists have been forced to confront the private/public dichotomy. Explanations of this barrier play a more central role in feminists' work in the Second Stage. The barrier gets de-closeted and upon examination, analyzed.

The original and important feminist extension of the analyses of private/public spheres lay in their awareness and in their articulation of the fact that the spheres of personal and private life are not just subject to the power relations from outside but that these relations of domination are integral to personal life and identity. Because personal life itself, concretely, reinforces and strengthens social relations of domination, the "personal *is* political". The clearest expression of this motif in the Second Stage, is perhaps found in the development of a distinctive feminist pedagogy, which began with the premise that we begin with women's *subjective* experience of the world in order to grasp the structural means through which it is objectified.

Those feminists in the late 1960's, who came to the academy from the larger women's movement brought with them a fundamental *feminist* criticism of the ideology of a private/public split and its implications for women. This is not always explicit in their analyses, but what we can see is their implicit awareness that the private/public construction has reflected and reinforced the male claim to occupancy of the public or academic realm, and in turn served to keep women excluded or peripheral.

This exclusion is reflected and ideologically interconnects in the seven sets of barriers just described: 1) Achievement motivation reveals the internal conflicts produced by the dualism; 2) the ubiquity of the notion of a private/public split is evidenced in university hiring practices and in the processes of granting tenure or promotion to women; here the private/public split takes on an economic function and is materially visible through women's relative invisibility as faculty or through their salary or rank differential; 3) The male hierarchy is another one of the split's side effects, simultaneously serving to reinforce the ideology of separate spheres and ensuring the lack of support systems for feminists; 4) disciplinary divisions symbolize the dualism: divisions between disciplines often denote different graduations of what is considered more or less important knowledge areas, while the *truncation* of knowledge into "objective" and "subjective" realms is part of the *truncation* of life into two spheres and similarly; 5) the selective processes at work in publication are part and parcel of the university's institutional procedures which hold the assumption that because women "belong" in the "private", they do not fit into the "public world" of publication. Not only are each of the barriers in and of themselves evidence of the private/public split, but they are interconnected through it.

Perhaps the most significant point to be made here is that while the private and public spheres have distinctive features, they cannot be intellectually separated. As we have seen, the experiences of feminists in both historical periods speak poignantly to the interconnections of the private and public. And in both periods, feminists experience the patriarchal formulation of the dichotomy in their private lives and in their public lives.

In other words, in perpetuating the notion that women belong "naturally" in the home, the universities of our culture have knowingly supported cultural constructions of femininity and of women's subordinance within the parameters of those constructs. This ideology has been reinforced by, and been an integral part of, the modern division between the private and public spheres. Finally within that division, the construction of femininity is used to rationalize and justify "... circumscribing women into the domestic realm, or insofar as they are drawn into the public domain, relegating them to menial and low status positions" (Pierson and Prentice, 1982, p. 106). Within the academic context, this means that women have been considered to rightfully belong at home; that they have been treated as secondary in their faculty status; and that they have not been considered worthy of academic study.

How did the private/public ideology appear in feminist writings in the 1960's and early 1970's? Feminists asserted that the compartmentalization or fragmentation life into two "places" has necessitated the notion and indeed the official sanction that in different spheres one behaves according to different rules. Further these spheres have come to be defined as "male-dominated", or "female-dominated", depending on which sphere one is examining (Antler, 1981; Janeway, 1975; Smith, 1977). Feminists have been particularly concerned with the separation of the personal from the political, but this distinction is simply one of the many compartmentalizations that divide the world into disparate spheres: the public is separated from the private; "academic" judgements from human ones; the world of so-called "facts" from that of values (or "objective" versus "subjective" as it is better known).

This same fragmentation moreover has given rise to the appearance of a separation of personal life (as an area of fulfillment) form *outside* work or public life. As a general organizing principle of the late twentieth century western culture, the separation of the sphere of work from the privatized sphere of the home, and the designation of those realms to men and women respectively, has meant that women are at one stage primarily located within the home performing domestic labor and child care. If they are not, "they are expected to be" (Oakley, 1974). What is perhaps the most detrimental facet of this schema is that the "private" world of home and family is considered "feminine". While women's increased labor force participation has helped weaken the doctrine of spheres:

"Women, except under special circumstances, toil in the private world. If secondary in the public world, they are primary in the private world — as faithful wives, as lovers, as mothers. The pressure of a conservative fear of any real change in such domestic arrangements — a fear the powerful and the powerless share — circles back to reinforce the unequal distribution of power and the genderizing of labor ..." (Stimpson, 1979, p. 71).

Short of calling for the complete abolition of this ideology, Hochschild (1975) asserted that several alternatives seem possible and just. She suggested that, "women might adopt a relation to home and family indistinguishable from that of their male competitors. Women could marry househusbands if they can find them, or hire a substitute wife-mother in their absence. Academic women could thereby establish a two-roled life for another person (a husband) or divide such roles between husband and housekeeper ... . But neither a housekeeper nor a child-care center would solve the problem completely ..." (p. 73). The "problem" she refers to has to do with the very 'clock-work of a career system' that seems to eliminate women, "not so much through malevolent disobedience to good rules, but through making up rules to suit half the population in the first place".

The dilemma (of having the responsibilities of child-care, domestic labor etc.) is often perceived as a "woman's problem", *her* role conflict, as if that conflict were detachable from the career system itself. "it is her problem to choose between a few prepackaged options: being a housewife, or professor, or trying to piece together a collage of wife, mother, and traditional career" (Hochschild, p. 68).

Given the academic career and the university setting as it is now, "... women can only improvise one or another practical solutions for fitting their families to their careers" (p. 68). In most cases, 'fitting families to careers' means having no families. "It is one thing for a woman to freely decide against marriage or children as issues on their merits. But it is quite another matter to be forced into the choice because the choice is shaped for and by the man with a family who is family-free" (pp. 69-70).

Erkut (1982) and Schwartz and Lever (1973) describe the "double-bind" of women scholars who worry with justification about how they can commit themselves to be academic and reconcile it with marriage and family; many do not want to do "injustice" to one or the other or both. Many women they argue, are afraid to choose an academic profession that might conflict with their own and their peers' definition of femininity. They are afraid of the implications of professionalism particular in light of the choices which women are forced to make and the decisions which are ultimately left to fall on women's shoulders.

In the final portion of her discussion Rossi submits that for too long it has been assumed that personal and family circumstances have both theoretical and practical significance for women only. Academic pressures also provide a nice excuse for junior male faculty to be unable to help with domestic work, thus further trapping their wives and increasing the split between academic wives and academic women. She states that "a decade of research on women clearly substantiates that personality, marriage, and family status are indeed determinants of women's career development. But until more research has been conducted on the work and family roles of men, there is little evidence to support the observation of many women that family factors affect the work careers of men as well as women" (p. 521). This analysis can be found problematic on several levels, but it is the central omission of the *ideological* connection between the family and career lives of women that stands gapingly missing and that tends to overlook the fact that women are treated similarly in both sites. Again Rossi assumes an unproblematic structuring of life into two spheres and overlooks the ideological structuring of women's lives around the "private sphere".

In this sense Erkut's (1982) explanation of academic women's relation to the private/public is vastly divergent from Rossi's (1973). She argues, quite rightly that the barriers to women in academe are at once "a part and reflection of the total social order" (p. 413). Any social change toward achieving educational equity for women will necessitate changes in other parts of the total social system. Erkut places the works of Rossi, Austin and Bayer, and others within the context of the early 1970's when the issue was identified as the "career-versus-family dilemma". She suggests that one of the predominant solutions proposed was to recognize this dilemma as an insurmountable barrier and to opt for a career. "It is no coincidence that many of the achieving women of this century have been single women (unmarried, divorced, or widowed) or women who married later in life" (p. 413). The major point, is that because women have been socially defined in the private sphere, a complete and radical transformation of the society is needed before the conflicts and associated problems in reconciling private/professional lives are eradicated.

Feminists in the Second Stage did not analyze the *ideological* character of the private/public dichotomy as more recent feminists do. In this period (1960's-1970's) some feminists, brought the relevance of the private/public split to bear on women's "secondary status" as scholars. Further, in arguing the problems inherent in attempting to juggle priorities between the two spheres, their explanations of the split frequently reveal their uncritical acceptance of the categorical separation of the private and public. It is not until later, in the 1980's, that we see feminist explanations which attempt to collapse the *analytical* divisions between the "private" and the "public". However, despite the fact that feminists have only recently begun to analyze the private/public split as ideological, as a false dualism because it *is* male-constructed with men's best interests at heart, the notion of a private/public split *was central* to how the feminists of the 1960s and early 1970s began to make sense of the tensions in their lives.

The dissent in the Second Stage then moved beyond its counterpart in the First Stage in that it brought with it to the academy, the fundamental insight that the "personal" could not be separated from the "political" (or the private from the public). And unlike the First Stage, it argued that the split between the private and the public was a male creation which helped perpetuate male domination. From this articulation, feminists were able to analytically examine the tensions in their own and other women's lives. In the next chapter this guiding motif is taken one step further.

Though it is clearly impossible to define the Second Stage with precision and without generalizing, it is possible, with at least some degree of certainty to say that the Second Stage of the Dissenting Feminist Academy arose and struggled amidst the activism of the 1960's and was influenced specifically by the larger women's movement. That larger women's movement, had, in turn, emerged from various radical and Left organizations protesting the alienating forces of a technocratic, corporate society. From that context feminists were able to articulate a consciousness which spoke to the alienation of *women*; to the impossibility of separate spheres for women and to the need for an autonomous, independent women's movement.

In general the period was characterized by various, sometimes divergent "senses" of collective unrest. The autonomous women's movement which developed impacted on universities underlying structures in academic theories and practice. Some of the importance of this era lie in the analyses of the contradictions between the "stillwater" of academic thinking in theory and the "storms" of educational philosophies about radical change. Centrally, it was feminist scholars who exposed the contradictions between notions of equal opportunity and what women were experiencing in practice.

In the Second Stage feminists were concerned about issues of equality in academe: equal access, equal opportunity, equal representation in the faculty ranks and so on. In large measure, equality appears to have been defined by parity, based on the reasoning that women faculty were and are entitled to the benefits and rewards equivalent to those of male faculty. From issues of equality feminist scholars provided the challenge to think beyond the boundaries of traditional sex roles, of traditional disciplines, and of established institutions. By breaking down the divisions that limited perceptions and denied women opportunities, by revising pedagogical processes as well as beginning revisions of curricula, the Second Stage laid the foundations for a unique and significant transformation of academe.

In the earliest part of this century feminist proponents of improving female education accepted cultural assumptions about women's nature and demanded a higher education appropriate to or at least compatible with women's "role". In the 1960's and 1970's, feminists began by stressing the identity of male and female intellectual capacities and called for equal *access* to positions of power in academe. With the initiation of Women's Studies, the Second Stage became more directly a strategy for institutional change. As we move to the next historical moment in feminist scholarship, we see the challenge to the male hegemony over the content of academic courses and the substance of knowledge itself. It is this recent attack on sexist scholarship and the specific uncovering of patriarchal epistemology which primarily characterizes the Third Stage.

4

THE THIRD STAGE:
THE CONTEMPORARY SETTING

We must scan the Beacons that flare along
the horizon of all culture, asking whether
any one of them is our lighthouse

Nannerl O. Keohane,
et al. 1982.

The 1970's brought with it severe economic recession and financial crises on an unprecedented scale. Education along with other social services which had enjoyed expansion in the 1960's, came under political scrutiny and, inevitably, financial scrutiny. One of the effects of the recession has been to stimulate groups and organizations to action in pursuit of changes in their situation. Within the context of the 1970's and with an eye to the legacy of the 1960's work, the Third Stage dissent once again reformulated its stance. Gone was the central focus on the institutional marginality of women as faculty. Also missing was much of the accompanying fervor, the vibrancy and buoyancy of the inimitable 60's. Instead, there appeared to be a lull, a quiet reflective period in which women re-evaluated their goals and their strategies for achieving them. Within the university setting, feminists were coping with the financial fiascos that threatened to disband programs, eliminate faculty positions, and wipe out entire departments. Feminists set the scholarship agenda into the troubling context of economic imperatives and a patriachal society, both of which the university serves all too well. Clearly the sharpening economic climate of restraint made it harder and harder to push for such things as affirmative action, day care, and a status of women's office, when many who had academic positions were in danger of losing the little security they had.

This situation in part, contributed to the shift in feminists' thinking, to the shift in their critical posture, and to feminists' attention to the knowledge which is taught and learned, produced and disseminated, in academe. In this Third and current stage, the origins and philosophic components of research theory (or of what we "know"), is described by feminists as *the* political/personal struggle for women in academe. Theory, it is argued, is an ideological practice. One of the most striking aspects of this understanding is that it moves the dissent's thinking in ways that suggest it is indeed time to abandon male modes of seeing the world, and as Keohane (1982), in the opening quotation asks, whether "any of them are our lighthouse". It is perhaps equally remarkable, that by the early 1980's the answer to that question is a resounding and an unequivocable "no". "For the functions of knowledge considered here, are precisely those that the people who construct it, are least likely to be aware of, and are usually hesitant to analyze; knowledge itself tends to conspire against those who would identify its hidden agenda. This is especially true in the university, which is the official custodian of knowledge uses and the administrative agency charged with the maintenance of theoretical hegemony."[1] The academic disciplines serve as the particular "gate keepers" of different kinds of knowledge and are the target of attack in the Third Stage.

In this chapter I will be as explicit as I dare in examining contemporary feminist criticisms of higher education. The three themes that underpinned the organization of the preceeding sections, are discussed here though I have spent more time looking at the problems of the theory, methodology and language of the disciplines simply because it has, and is, receiving so much attention from feminist scholarship. As I have stated earlier, I recognize that in this chapter I cannot possibly cover all of the groundwork that has been done in exposing gender-bias and this is not my intention. I think it more helpful to point to major trends and to attempt to make sense of where those trends are leading the dissent. Finally, I turn to the private/public ideology where I discuss the ideological practice of shaping gender through academic theory which is predicated on the assumptions of the private/public dichotomy. Though each section has its own theme and focus, the three taken together - that is, the functioning of the university as an employer, the phenotype of the disciplines and the private/public split - mirror the nature of patriarchy beyond academe and as such, reflect the problems of institutionalized education for women in all of their complexity. Which is to say that the problems with academia are not simply academic ones. The questions that are posed in this instance, and the answers which need to be answered, go well beyond the university gates and as such bring the dissent face-to-face with the contradiction of its academic survival.

The Background

Retrenchment, the dominant mode of the past two decades, replaced the social ferment of 1960's. The 1970's were characterized moreover by economic crises of unprecedented proportions since the 1930's. Recession and a depressed economy has continued well into the 1980's, and because of this, their effects have been manifold. Generally speaking, by the mid 1970's, industrial development was tentative at best; by the end of the 70's, parts of the private corporate sector had come to a complete halt. And, because education is so affected by "economic remedies" as David (1978) calls them, all levels of the education industry experienced a tightening of its belt buckles, while various groups saw the time as ripe to lobby for change in the form and content of education.

The seemingly paradoxical nature of this development is easier to understand in light of the financial problems faced by the university and imposed by the overall economic structures of the society at large. Changes in the organization of the education system for example, followed from, usually, major economic upheavals. The 1970's was no exception. It was certainly the case that regional and central governments attempted to revamp the education system. In the case of compulsory schooling, stress was put on restructuring education to make it "both more efficient and more readily serve economic ends" (David, 1978, p. 186). There was an increased emphasis on reducing the costs of the education system: teacher/student ratios became a concern; programs were slashed; pieces of school curriculum were completely removed, particularly those considered "extra-curricular" or "frills" such as French, Music, Remedial Reading in Canadian schools and Spanish, Latin, and Physical Education in some American schools. Indeed as David (1978) discovers in her study of State intervention in schooling, economy was perhaps the hallmark of the decade:

> Parents, teachers and curricula were all im-
> plicated: parents were afforded rights to
> their ... children ... teachers were to be trained
> to a graduate level, to be more professional;
> and curricula for adolescents were more
> clearly tied to the needs of industry, espe-
> cially manufacturing industry. (p. 182)

Along with these initiatives, and in response to concern expressed by academics, private enterprise and especially conservative pressure groups; governments set up advisory boards to evalu-
ate standards in schools, in particular, the teaching and learning of
the "three R's." Illiteracy was viewed as an educational invention
and an economic problem: hence the increased attention to reading
and writing ability, and a back-to-basics pragmatism. A "no-frills"
philosophy engendered official concern with the effectiveness of
the education polity. For instance, the question of the link between
schooling and the labour market was raised in a new light. The
whole question of the nature of teacher training was also raised in
connection with ameliorations in the curriculum, which would be
shaved down and made fatter with essentials. There were other
transformations made of course, but they were not divorced from
issues of educational efficiency and educational economy.

The issues of concern to higher education have evolved rapidly
in the 1970's and 1980's. In particular, changing circumstances in
the economy and in the social and political climate have brought
forward new priorities. The imperatives of government and the
public about higher education, has meant that universities, like
public schooling, have been pulled by the forces of declining public
expenditure. Priorities and perceptions, also affected by the late
1970's growing instances of rising unemployment, financial constraints and shifting economic conditions, changed with regard to
curriculum content and the orientation of research.[2] Some of these
changes reflected the opening of new fields of knowledge and the
development of new intellectual interests, while others reflected the
belief that certain types of knowledge (fields) were becoming obso-
lete and therefore, unnecessary (Symons and Page, 1984). One instance of this can be found in the tough steps governments took to

modify the system of teacher training proposing the closure of some colleges of education and the merger of others.[3]

Unlike compulsory schooling however, higher education was not and is not simply subject to governmental persuasion. "It is one of the chief examples of the peculiar theory that something can be kept outside of politics by exerting a veto on its evolution in certain directions, and by discouraging inquiry and discussion about it as much as possible" (Symons and Page, 1984, p.26). This may be an overstatement, but the point here is that higher education in the 1970's found itself caught between the Scylla of its hang-over expansion period (for e.g., in certain areas, enrollment, was continually increasing) and the Charbydis of paying the bill. In other words, "it was a time during which academic empires were built on promises to the Canadian tax payers which could not, in retrospect be fully kept" (Symons and Page, 1984, p. 26). This was the case in the period leading up to the mid 1970's. By the end of the 1970's, empires were no longer being built and those programs which had been launched in the early part of the decade were often deemed quixotic. What we see then, are programs such as Women's Studies which, having experienced the initial exhilaration of birth and growth from the late 1960's and early 1970's, faced economic hardship and the possibility of academic extinction. The expansion and growth period had left many educational initiatives frozen in the confluence of economic, social, and demographic forces.

Clearly, one cannot single out any one factor as catalyzing the evolutions we are examining. Nonetheless it is evident, that public disenchantment, and oscillations in university enrolment and participation rates, where signals that the period of growth was coming to an end.[4] At the heart of the problem lay deep-seated philosophical shifts in the public's attitudes toward the role of education. And, at the heart of those shifts lay deep-seated economic troubles. Though initially, in the early 1970's, "It was not a period for thinking much about where the money was coming from or the conditions which in later years might be imposed upon the universities in return for continued public support"; the end of the decade gave academics and academic institutions little choice but to accept the reality of the budget pinch (Leslie, 1980 as cited in Symons and Page, 1984, p. 28). Again, the forces which impinge on and help shape the paramenters of academe, are such a complex mixture of the ideological, the social and the political, that they almost defy summary analysis. This was perhaps less the case in the earlier stage, if no other reason than the fact that the university so vocally and visibly represented, what liberal democrats envisioned it should. It so palpably symbolized the meeting of confrontational minds, and it so boldly flaunted its willingness to entertain dissent, opposition and conflict. In this sense, and by comparison, the life and evolution of the university in this stage is harder to define.

To put it differently, it is difficult to separate completely the occurrences of the late 1970's - early 1980's from the preceding years. At the same time, a number of events indicate, that the university, like the feminist dissent, has not remained static and economic causes, where they do exist, have had ideological and theorectical consequences. For example, despite the 1960's critique of the left, the "new" left and of humanists, civil libertarians and various other groups; universities in the late 70's and early 1980's remained stubbornly tied to dominant group interests though less so than it had when retrenchment was not so clearly a way of academic life. I hasten to add, that the constitution of those dominant groups themselves, had taken on a new configuration, as had the focus and field of their "interests."

From a strictly philosophical perspective, financial imperatives enabled academe to once again, as it had after World War II and prior to the Progressive Era, maintain and sanction conservative thinking. This left many radicals in an extremely vulnerable position as their jobs or syllabi were used as cannon fodder in confrontation with university administrations.

Finally, the regressive stance of the university was witnessed on several accounts, more notably with regard to academic freedom and faculty citizenship.[5] It was an indication of the kind of priorities set by official policy, that despite radical groups' criticisms of the university's technological bent, there has been no significant rejection of scientific and technological association on the part of the academic community. Contrarily, the growth of science and technology proliferated, leaving what is considered the Arts and Humanities devestated by lack of support, financially, as well as philosophically.[6]

Freeman (1979) and Howe (1980) contend that this academic *gestalt* occurred partly as a result of economic cutbacks, partly as a result of labour market fluctuations, and partly as a result of overall evolutions in the cultural climate. Combined, these processes forced many radicals out of the academic community, especially as the teaching and research apparatus, which they had so ardently rejected, showed no signs of crumbling. Instead, there was every indication that academe was even more tightly integrated with larger interests, (Rich, 1976; Touraine 1974). Feminists, for instance, experienced and resolved the tensions between academe and their activism and philosophical posture, in various ways. For some it meant leaving the university along with other dissenters.[7] For others, it seemed more plausible to work within the university and to make changes where they could. Still, some women were able to "prepare for the long haul ahead", by splitting their time and their energies between the classroom and the "women's room" (Roberts, 1976).

In the midst of this crisis, (and with it, the exodus of certain groups and individuals), academic systems retained their patriarchial initiative which found expression in backlash, in attempts to impose pseudo-reform and in the transformation of institutional practices.

The notion of academic freedom as I have mentioned, and its expression, took on a different set of premises as the society which financed and to a large extent, defined its parameters, became caught in the grip of recession (Boxer, 1982). The 1970's economic state in turn, ironically appeared to be both detrimental to those seeking particular kinds of jobs, grants and educational resources, and advantageous to others. On the surface this is almost a contradiction in terms but was related to a restructuring in how and by whom universities were financed. It was also connected to the changing needs of industry, the labour market and the business sector. Business Administration for example, received impetus from these needs and from the ever-increasing role played by foundations and private corporations in financing specific types of research and policy. Scholarships, fellowships and bursaries were made highly accessible and widely available to those wishing to pursue such work (Touraine 1974; Symons and Page, 1984).

The restructuring of finance techniques within the university in the seventies reflected an expansion of, and a shift in, the sources its of pecuniary support. In juxtaposition, this reverberated the needs of a technologically-characterized labour market. One of the more remarkable trends for example, has been the proliferation of the computer market and with it, the initiation of such programmes as, Computer Science, Business Administration and Management as well as the growth of Engineering, Marketing and Environmental Design.[8]

The effect of this restructuring impacted differently on Women's Studies programmes. On one hand, we do see that Women's Studies made its way on numerous campuses, though this growth occurred mainly in the early to mid 1970's. At the height of growth however, many Women's Studies' institutes were left financially paralyzed, as they were often considered "a frill" in "back-to-basics" budgets. At the same time, feminists themselves were affected by these constraints, many were denied tenure, promotions or were simply not hired in the first place (Boxer, 1982; Canadian Association of University Teachers Bulletin, 1977; Howe, 1980; Vickers and Adams, 1977).

The constricted hiring practices with regard to women are not difficult to understand, especially in light of the fact that in times of economic constraint, women are the "last hired and first fired" (Connelly, 1978).[9] Still, the phenomenon of Women's Studies' proliferation in some areas does appear to be a curious one. We know that the dissent did survive. How then, does one make sense of the university's ambivalent context in terms of feminists' relation to it?

While Women's Studies' has faced severe threats to its survival, it it has continued to draw large numbers of students into its classrooms. Large enrollments has supported its existence. More generally, the pattern of enrollments in Canada and the United States reveals the drastic increase of female enrollment during this period. In fact, the registration of female students in both graduate and undergraduate programmes increased. In Canada, undergraduate female enrollment grew from 109,736 in 1972-73 to 165,521 in 1981-82, up by some 56,000 or more than 50 percent" (Symons and Page, 1984, p. 189).[10] Because many, if not most universities, budget departments on the basis of enrollment figures, there has been every reason to support Women's Studies at a time when enrollments in other programmes are rapidly declining. Duelli Klein (1984) suggests that two other main developments explain the peculiar situation of the dissent at this time. One involves the trend towards autonomy in terms of budget and faculty hiring procedures, the nature of course offerings, and the position of Women's Studies as a discipline of its own (often in connection with the establishment of MA and Ph.D. programmes). The second development is the movement towards the "transformation of the curriculum of the traditional disciplines (also called main-streaming) often promoted by offering so-called 'Faculty Development Seminars' that are organized by the Women's Studies Programme" (Duelli Klein, p.234).

The situation of course, has been worse in mainstream disciplines, and worse for women teaching courses from a feminist perspective in colleges and universities where no formal Women's Studies program exists. What can be stated, at the very least, is that the 1970's held both promise (in terms of the early beginnings of feminist scholarship), and later much struggle, as the financial situation of universities worsened. With less generality, though still with some measure of clarity, both optimism, and pessimism can be seen to have marked the period. This paradox, and the tensions it provoked, forced feminists to reconsider the goals they had set earlier, and to adjust their academic agenda in accordance with the circumstances which were making older strategies appear outdated or no longer useful. Out of this context, a "new form" of scholarship emerged or at least a different form. No longer was the emphasis strictly on wrestling institutional power. As Roberts (1976) saw it, the "new form" of the dissent involved coming to terms with the fact that the problem went further than gaining institutional control. Though vitally connected, it was more than a problem of economics. For Roberts, it was coming to see that sexism was a cognitive, philosophical process and an epistemological problem. And she was not alone. Feminists were feeling the angst and were describing the tensions in their work. The literature of the late 1970's describes the dissent's change in thinking, their different outlook and their call for new approaches.

The shift in form was certainly not confined to the university setting. Feminists working outside academe, were now naming the shift, depicting its impetus and forecasting its future, often in mixed tones, more frequently in definite, foreboding ones. Betty Friedan's (1981) book, *The Second Stage*, is perhaps one of the more visible, popular, chronicles of this shift in feminist thinking. In it, Friedan attempts to name the "problem with no name" arguing that the political climate over the last decade has changed and with it, the direction of feminist thought. In very personal terms she recounts an " ... uneasy sense of battles won, only to be fought over again, of battles that should have been won, according to all rules, and yet are not, of battles that suddenly one does not really want to win, and the weariness of battle altogether - how many women feel it? What does it mean?" (p. 8). Later in the book Friedan outlines what she believes the shift means:

> I believe it's over, that first stage ... How do we move on? In the first stage, our aim was full participation, power and voice in the mainstream, inside the party, the political process, the professions, the business world .. I believe that we have to break through our own *feminist* mystique now to come to terms with the new reality of our personal and political experience, and to move into the Second Stage (p. 27).

This sense of moving into what Friedan calls the "Second Stage" characterizes the move, nebulous as it may be, I am describing as the Third Stage. I believe that feminists like Betty Friedan and those directly part of the academic community, share the understanding that this stage must transcend the battle for equal power in institutions. It must somehow consider restructuring institutions and work towards transforming the nature of power itself.

Within academe, similar descriptions and prescriptions delineate the Third Stage of *The Dissenting Feminist Academy*. Broadly, people like Howe (1980), Abel and Abel (1983) and Sherman and Beck (1977), explain the stage as a "shift in thinking". In its earliest phases, this project was concerned to determine whether the processes which constitute women as institutionally subordinate, are the same processes that define women as subordinate within and beneath knowledge claims. Furthermore, having fashioned alternative forms of institutional practice (in the Second Stage), feminists now ask if it will also be necessary to devise alternative theories of knowledge. In other words, the concern is with *what* is taught as well as *how* it is taught. These questions and concerns make it apparent that it is difficult to completely untangle the two periods or to denote a dividing line between the Second and Third Stage. This is accentuated by the fact that much Second Stage continues today. And to be sure, nothing changed suddenly, just as nothing ended abruptly in the Second. In fact, and to a great extent, much of what happened and is happening now, has arisen out of the necessity feminists feel to try to resolve issues left unresolved.

The unfinished nature of the Second Stage was apparent on many accounts. The Second Stage exposure of women's *invisibility* (as faculty, administrators and as subjects and participants of research) provided a basis by which feminists had begun, in the early to mid seventies making women visible in two ways: within the academy as employees, and within the disciplines as subjects of research. The latter began occupying more and more attention as it became obvious that acquiring faculty status simply was not enough.

We also saw in the last chapter that the Second Stage was implicitly committed to the grassroots project of integrating the "personal" and the "political", at least on an individual level. And while this personal, experiential awareness was not drawn into the epistemological domain, in pointing out its practical implications for women's lives, Second Stage dissenters paved the road for the current project of analyzing the ideological character and the epistemological basis of the personal/political (or private/public) split. Feminists in the Third Stage argue that the creation of a private/public dichotomy has had negative consequences for the way women are seen and treated in the society at large, but they go further by illustrating how this dichotomy is legitimized in the very knowledge the university imparts to its students. One example of this validation of sexism occurs in science knowledge:

> The female-half of the dichotomized reality is not only excluded but is also rendered invisible — for male is defined by decree as the norm of the rational, scientific and essential human "appropriation" of the world. Thus science assumes, reproduces, authorizes, confirms and reifies the traditional dualisms of male-stream thought which have permitted men to separate, both in theory and in practice, their emotional life from their intellectual life and their personal from their public practice (Finn, 1982, p. 45).

Finn's illustration of the way in which the knowledge of science reflects and influences the male/female dualism follows in the direction of other feminists work. In a critical vein, feminists such as Finn, point out that the division between objectivity and subjectivity, like that of public and private, is problematic because it is a male construct.

The Third Stage thus affirms the necessity of making connected what was previously disconnected; of making whole what is separated and divided; and of making interdependent what traditional forms of research render strictly "dependent" or "independent". In short, feminist research in the Third Stage reveals itself as a more explicitly formulated articulation of Second Stage insights.

How are these unique developments expressed? What we begin to see by the late 1970's are feminist perspectives and analyses which continue uncovering bias (or as Harding and Hintikka (1983) call it: the "deconstructive project"), but which also recover femininity in a positive sense. These analyses move toward explanations of women's specificity. One example of this kind of analysis examines women's location in reproduction and production. Another area of inquiry explores women's unique experience in motherhood (See for example: Trebilcot, 1984). The uniqueness of women's experience has become the basis for new knowledge which validates that experience by making it central, rather than adding it to a foreign frame of reference.

In summary, a number of evolutions proceeded the actual emergence of Third Stage scholarship. First, feminist charged the academic disciplines with sexism and took the first step, by insisting that research be carried out "for", "by" and "about" women. In practice, this aspect of feminist scholarship has been largely corrective in its emphasis, because it has been concerned with filling in gaps in our basic knowledge about women (Bernard, 1973; Daniels, 1975; Sherman and Beck, 1977; Stanley, 1984). Research carried out in this strain led feminists to realize that merely adding women to existing theories was not enough and hence they began to investigate the underlying value systems of those frameworks. Feminists found that the ideological assumptions of traditional research held presuppositions about women's "proper role" and women's "nature". This is problematic not only because such notions are based on inadequate perceptions of men, women, and relationships between the sexes, but because they rely heavily on ideas about the purported biological determination of female personality and behavior. "Associated with this is the consequence that women's lives and experiences are often treated as less than fully human because different from the assumed norm of male experience" (Stanley 1984, p. 194).

It is generally agreed that the next step for scholarship is to generate original bodies of knowledge. The decision to create original knowledge signifies the dissent's departure from its previous agenda, and its full entry into the context of the Third Stage.

While such developments have obvious ramifications for the academic disciplines, the articulated need to create separate theory spills over to the understanding of, and strategies to confront, the university's institutional barriers. Simultaneously, feminists have begun to show how the private/public ideology is supported by discriminatory institutional practices and policies, and reinforced by assumptions about women's subordinance rooted in academic knowledge. In this latter moment the rejection of dualisms on the part of feminists is consonant with, and symbolic of, their rejection of all forms of false dualism. Finally, this rejection has meant, above all, that feminists have articulated how the academy both helps reinforce, and is shaped by, the private/public dualism.

This is revealed as we now examine the delineation of the barriers in this Third and current Stage.

Institutional Barriers

For the most part, the institutional barriers laid out in Chapter Three continue to exist in the same problematic forms. While more women then ever before are making their way into faculty and administrative positions (or 10 percent improvement from the 1960's), parity is far from achieved (Erkut, 1982; Horning, 1982; Perun, 1982; Speizer, 1982). In a report commissioned by the Association of Universities and Colleges of Canada (1984), authors Thomas Symons and James E. Page update Vickers and Adams (1977) findings, with data that suggests that institutional parity is far from a reality in Canadian universities.[11] One rather tell-tale indicator of this, has been a dramatic increase in female enrollments in all levels of university. Yet as Symons and Page point out, "there has not been a corresponding increase in the proportion of women in academic employment" (1984, p. 190). They add that "women represented only 15.5 percent of the full-time teaching staff at Canadian universities in 1980-81. At the same time, in 1980, women constituted over 45 percent of the undergraduate student enrollment and over 35 percent of the graduate student enrollment" (p. 191). The report also raises eyebrows at the fact that women continue to be concentrated in the lower academic ranks (e.g. 41 percent of the men and only 16 percent of women were full professors in 1980-81); continue to receive lower salaries than men (e.g. in 1980-81 and 1981-82 the median salary for women in every academic rank was lower than that for men) and; continue to be discriminated against on the basis of marital status, and age with regard to promotions and tenure.[12]

It is evident then, that prominent among the lingering issues of the last Stage are employment, promotion and pay for women (Perun, 1982). While the 1970's had brought heartening signs of gains made in terms of the social reorganization in universities; the financial difficulties in the 1980's brought "a diminution in public concern about educational opportunity and withdrawal of federal support for progressive social and educational programs that had benefited...women" (Ladd, 1982, p. 411). Consequently, women's victories have been similar to the turtles' who climb three steps and fall back two. In the following, the issues of employment, promotions and pay will be very briefly updated.

Employment, Hiring, Promotions and Pay

Ursula Franklin's (1984) editorial in Volume 5, Number 4, of *Canadian Women's Studies*, opened with the following statement:

> In the major key, so to speak, is the affirming theme that says simply: Women have made notable contributions ... Their numbers may be increasing now, but there are still major barriers to the appropriate education, the adequate employment and promotion of women ... (p. 2).

The context Franklin refers to is science and technology. However, the evidence to date suggests that discriminatory hiring practices remain ubiquitous. Women still occupy less than thirty percent of most faculties (Symons and Page, 1984). Women also continue to be clustered at the lower ranks of faculties and access to promotions and tenure remains difficult (Ferguson, 1984; Sheinin, 1984).

Finally, women "are still the lower-paid minority among the faculty ..." (Ferguson, 1984, p. 55). As Ferguson adds, it has been highly convenient that we are now in recessionary times when universities are doing little hiring. Employers can now justify not hiring women faculty on the grounds that the overall economic climate prohibits it. Ferguson dispels the myth that procedures for hiring and promotion have changed. She notes that in-house studies of the status of women appear to have had little effect on hiring, promotion, tenure and salary differentials.

Besides working toward the latter issues, feminists are still involved in activities directed at changing policies in administration that have an immediate bearing on admissions, financial assistance, health facilities, child-care programs, part-time attendance, and scheduling (Boxer, 1982). Generally speaking, feminists' efforts in combatting institutional hurdles are ongoing. Feminists are still fighting for fairer decisions on salaries, promotion, and hiring, and still fighting to increase women's participation in decision-making by seeking important administrative committee appointments. All in all, the struggle to eradicate the historical accumulation of male control persists, though feminists now have many male allies in these structural changes.

It is against this background that feminists are currently extending their analyses of institutional barriers. One feature of this extension throws a different light on the concept of "equality of opportunity". In the Second Stage much useful data was collected under this rubric: earlier work in a Canadian context, by Vickers and Adams, (1977) for instance, documented the failures of universities to achieve equality of opportunity or equality of conditions for women. In later Third Stage work, feminists "... have challenged the theoretical and methodological underpinnings of the equality debate and the educational assumptions of the liberal tradition ..." (O'Brien, 1983, p. 6). This later challenge is one more indication that strategy has been revised. On one level, there is the articulation of the importance of practicing their professions with intellectual freedom outside the structures of exclusion imposed by the still male-dominated, hierarchical structures found in most traditional academic domains. Separate autonomous support networks have been developed and independent associations exist.[13] As we saw in Chapter Three, the Second Stage argued for changes in the physical arrangements and reorganization of physical environments in institutional structures. By the end of the Second Stage, these methods were used to resist the institutional hierarchy and "professional exclusiveness that had been used to shut out women" (Boxer, 1982, p.

243). On another level then, efforts to eliminate universities' *hierarchical, authoritarian* relationships, and detached, formal *pedagogy* have attempted to present a different stance which would validate women's experience. These were the main components of a feminist methodology which was originally more concerned with institutional barriers than with disciplinary barriers.

In this instance, feminist efforts are still aimed at further development of feminist methodology, but their efforts have expanded. In other words, efforts are less directed at working within university structure *as it is*, to emphasizing and promoting *alternative*, separate feminist practices within the university. While work proceeds along earlier lines, feminists' writings reveal their rejection of adopting male modes of practice as their own. Instead, there is renewed stress on developing methods that are coherent with feminist approaches to research. In this sense, the barriers imposed by the male hierarchy, publication processes, pedagogy and the 'Old Boy's Network' (outlined in Chapter Three), have been challenged by working toward *feminist* pedagogies, devising *anti-hierarchical* practices, and by establishing separate *women's* support systems and networks. The seeds of the latter were sown in the earlier, Second Stage development of publishing companies and collectives which made women's writing their central agenda in both academic and popular publications (Boxer, 1982; O'Brien, 1984; Ruth, 1980).

These points relate to a larger issue. Third Stage feminists show how the institutional constraints of academe are connected to, and are part of, the disciplinary divisions. The divisions between academic disciplines are in reality, the university's way of *institutionally* organizing knowledge and those who produce it. This problem has led to the conscious effort by feminists to develop separate methods. Taken as a whole, the issues discussed about *meet* in the arena of the disciplines. Disciplinary divisions define the purposes of feminist method, particularly the adoption of interdisciplinary research models. The advantages of doing interdisciplinary research were discussed by Second Stage feminists and are still considered important in the current period. The growing emphasis on creating alternative structures that may be more trans-disciplinary than interdisciplinary, illustrates by example, the inclination of the dissent to less readily accept existing practices, and to consider developing completely novel practices. Without question, the issue is highly complex and characterized by widespread internal debate:

> While the relative lack of theorizing about
> women's studies may be due to a certain reluc-
> tance to engage in what is considered a tradition-
> ally male province, it may also reflect the
> widespread use of the ill-defined term "interdis-
> ciplinary" to describe a practice that has been for
> the most part multidisciplinary and interdepart-
> mental (Boxer, 1982, p. 259).

Within the debate, one strand of feminist scholarship stresses the disadvantages of interdisciplinarity—the denial of autonomy and recognition, the difficulty of transcending disciplinary think-ing. Rather than transforming established disciplines, this position articulates the potential of discovering new paradigms.

The more toward fashioning feminist methods rejects the disci-pline-based categories in which the structure of the university is grounded. Dissatisfaction with the limits imposed by the disciplines has led to speculation about *how* feminist scholarship might tran-scend traditional divisions of knowledge. According to Howe (1975), the history of the disciplines has led to a fragmented academy that stands in contradiction to feminists' holistic view. However she sees the possibilities feminist methods hold for "radi-cal reinvention" of teaching, research and learning.

The quest for original methodologies is also juxtaposed to the *deeper* discovery of dualisms not only *between* areas of knowledge, but also *within* areas of knowledge. The sexist practices and pro-cesses of academe have been made visible by feminists, as those institutional barriers enmesh with the *content* of knowledge.

One excellent review of the feminist critique of social science is Stanley and Wise's (1983) analysis which examines feminist methodology. It draws on, amongst others, Eichler's (1980) examina-tion of how sexist content, method, and purposes, affect representa-tions of women in the social sciences. Stanley and Wise agree with Eichler in her call for divergent ways of thinking about social real-ity that link, rather than separate, subject and object. The authors point to the necessary interconnection between institutional prac-tice and academic knowledge, showing that the two mutually rein-force cultural stereotypes of gender. They state that feminist thought characteristically attempts to replace dichotomies with dialectical modes of analyzing self and other, person and society, consciousness and activity, past and future, knowledge and practice. But indeed, the confusion surrounding the issue of dichotomies/dualisms has vexed feminists for some time now. It is a confusion that has never been cleared up. Stanley and Wise contribute the vital insight here, that above all, feminist research should be the "doing of feminism", using the same approaches and procedures we use in "doing" life. By exploring how we construct our everyday lives as women and researchers, we will gain insights into the mechanisms of women's oppression so that we can challenge them.

Most important of all, and more to the point of this chapter, feminists explain that institutional practices are historically grounded constructions and therefore cannot be seen in isolation from their wider social context or in isolation from the context of the university itself. The strictures of this male legacy, requires analyses which fuses oppressive facets of those practices, with an understanding of how they have come to be the way they are, and for what purposes.

We can say with some precision then, that Third Stage responses to the institutional barriers, implied and addressed, have initially followed in the same vein as Second Stage responses. These efforts are both ongoing and extremely vital for women. In this period, however, a shift occurs. The shift involves a de-emphasis on policy reform, and a concentration on forging feminist methodologies as ways of combatting institutional barriers. Perhaps the clearest index of the novelty of feminism's shift in thinking, comes in their claim that women's prescription to the "private" sphere is one and the same rationalization for their marginalization as employees, and their contortion or absence in academic research. Through feminist pedagogy, separate support networks, and collective research efforts, feminists believe they can further strengthen their autonomy. While feminist structures must exist within academic structures, the endeavor by feminists to present unique practices underscores the distinctiveness of feminist methodology. The major aim of this method, as I've mentioned, is to transcend the institutional division of knowledge into traditional disciplines. Earlier this goal was expressed through interdisciplinary work, and it still is to a large extent, but more recently the aim is expressed in a deeper rejection of the divisions/dualisms underpinning institutional knowledge itself.

The disavowal of traditional, institutional decorum, is still an important part of the agenda in the 1980's, as is the institutional problems women face. And perhaps one of the consequences of the dissent's concentration on questions of sexist knowledge, has been an unintentional neglect of those concerns which held center stage for women academics in the sixties and seventies. In fact, attention to the concerns of issues like employment, salary differentials, promotion and tenure seems to have abated to the extent that very little current research is being carried out on the status of women in Canadian and American academic life (Howe, 1984; Symons and Page 1984). Symons and Page (1984) note that as of 1984 in Canada for example, research is badly needed in this area. In-house reports prepared at universities such as: Brandon, Carleton, Dalhousie, McGill, Memorial, St. Francis Xavier, Simon Fraser, etc.; provided comprehensive overviews of the status of women at Canadian universities in the period from 1974 to 1980. Based on the literature, it is clear, argue Symons and Page, "that universities were responding to pressures to examine their structures and procedures with a view to determining the nature and extent of sex discrimination and to eliminating it" (p. 199). And yet, "..this spate of studies and recommendations appears to have had such little effect on hiring, promotion, tenure, and salary differentials". What this suggests is that superficially, women appear to have made progress. A more detailed examination however, reveals the ambiguous nature of the changes that have occurred. "Hence gains need to be defended since the continued advancement of a disadvantaged group can never be assumed" (Rendel, 1984, p. 175). Symons and Page (1984) conclude on a somber note, concurring that, "the under-utilization of the talents of educated female population, and the discrimination against women in universities, whether practiced consciously or unconsciously, is a national disgrace" (p. 210).

Disciplinary Barriers

The denial of the relevance of the study of women, and the specificity of the female case, to the central issues of a subject has important practical and intellectual consequences within the academy. One of the most fundamental of these is the production, assessment and distribution of knowledges, and the very ways we have of "knowing" which serve and reinforce dominant social values, prevailing sex-role stereotypes and cultural prescriptions of gender. "Knowing" involves the conceptual descriptions we have of social reality, the methods we employ to "know" reality and the theoretical systems we use to frame that "knowing". Within the academy, the academic disciplines were created to house these processes and in the Third Stage, these processes are the major target of attack.

Generally speaking, feminists have scrutinized "what we know", examining whose knowledge it represents; how that knowledge affects and views women; how this knowledge is produced and practiced and lastly; how knowledge connects or does not connect with women's experience. To reiterate, this particular aspect of the critique is mainly a carry-over from the preceding stage.

It is in the second phase of the project that feminists take their most concrete departure from earlier work. The emergence of *feminist* theories and *feminist* research reveals the growth of distinctively feminist paradigms.[14]

The directions of this work identifies the problems of relying on partial or distorted frameworks to understand women, and it begins to describe the kind of lived experience upon which a more human understanding of social reality can be grounded. These partial or distorted accounts *are* distorted, feminists argue, because they present partial truths as if they were the whole truth and as if they were 'objective' (in the sense that they exist independent of the knower). For example, theories attempt to provide explanations of social reality, we are told, which is held to describe how things are in some essential and 'objective' sense; when in fact they describe how things have been perceived to be by certain persons (usually males) with particular interests and goals, defined by their position in a particular social conjuncture. These partial frameworks moreover, are distorted because they presume to speak for humanity, when in fact women have been overwhelmingly left out of those frameworks. When women are included, they are frequently trivialized or incorrectly categorized (Abel and Abel, 1983; Harding and Hintikka, 1983; MacKinnon, 1982; 1983).

Consequently, feminists in the Third Stage are embracing two complementary projects: they continue to pursue the 'deconstructive project' which prefigured in the *Second Stage*; and more recently they have begun the 'reconstructive project'.

The following examination offers a glimpse at the barriers which feminists identify as urgently in need of *both* deconstructive and reconstructive work. These are: (1) The attempt by academic knowledge to model the 'hard core' sciences, (2) methodology, (3) language, and (4) theory. I will briefly examine each in turn.

Model of the "Hard Core" Sciences

"Normal Science", feminists argue, has squandered the myths that its' enterprise is both "objective" and "rational", its methods "unproblematic" and its practitioners, "detached". These myths have been attacked on many fronts.

Specifically, feminist critique of science has had two interrelated facets. First, the methods and practices of science have been investigated, with a critical view to understanding their essential features (Benston, 1982). Second, the underlying assumptions of those practices have been examined and fundamental questions have been raised about the philosophical basis of "scientific" methodology (Finn, 1982). The growth of feminist scholarship in this stage and in the previous one has meant, among other things, an examination of both these facets.

Second Stage feminists refuted (like other critics of positivism such as Kuhn, 1970; Marcuse, 1968) science's claim to objectivity and ethical neutrality, and offered evidence for the importance of subjective and ideological factors in scientific practice (Malmo, 1979; Roberts, 1976; Smith, 1975; etc.). This critique paralleled anti-positivist discourse as in the philosophy of science, though it offered further layers to the critique by referring to the gender bias of researchers. More recently in the Third Stage, feminist scholars have taken up Second Stage work and added yet another dimension that science is "also almost entirely a male enterprise" (Benston, 1982, p. 49).

The more contemporary critique by feminists *begins* with the situation of women, and "analyzes the way that women's situation has been shaped by and in turn shapes the whole social world" (Benston, 1982, p. 49). It thus *begins* in the same vein as Second Stage work, but later branches off in new directions. It is argued that because science (as social science) bears the imprint of its genderization, it is necessary to examine more fully the implications of attributing masculinity to the very nature of scientific thought

(Harding and Hintikka, 1983; Moulton, 1983).

Simply put, this ideological component in science stems from and is inherent in, the idea of objectivity which is so central to "normal science". Such a component implies that the introduction of subjective or ethical factors is incompatible with science, which is, from the point of view of scientists, the *alpha* and the *omega* of what it means to "do science".

The tenacity with which the scientific community flaunts its monopoly on "objectivity" and "objective reasoning" has much to do with its fear of biting the political and economic hand that feeds them. But it is also consonant with male norms rather than female ones (Harding, 1983; Moulton, 1983; Smith, 1980). In other words, the theory and practice of science embodies male norms — and thus exclude women almost *a prior*. Not surprisingly, a particular social identity is required to practice "normal" institutionalized science coincide with "normal" male characteristics; for example, being aggressive, strong, independent, logical etc. Women, on the other hand, are considered intuitive, emotional, dependent, respondent and passive. "The Catch 22 is, however, that at the same time as science is characterized as a male activity, it is characterized as genderless and "objective" with respect to both its methods and its concepts" (Finn, 1982, p. 45). From this vantage point, feminists explain that women are constituented as object, considered to be subjective, and yet objectivity is a male ideal.

In the first part of recent disclosures, feminists examine scientific ideology itself. This ideology separates the world into two ostensibly distinct spheres — the knower (mind) and the knowable "nature" — and prescribes the interactions which can lead to knowledge (Smith, 1975; 1980). Not only are mind and nature assigned gender, but in seeing scientific and objective thought as masculine, the very activity by which the knower can acquire the knowledge is also genderized (Benston, 1982; Malmo, 1979; Smith, 1980). The relation specified between "knower" and "known" is one of division and separation. In this process, "nature" is objectified (MacKinnon, 1983). The feminist critique rejects the subject/object split because of its impossibility for women. The subject/object disjuncture "... cannot explain experience as it is experienced by those who experience it ... This is only one way in which the object/split is fatal to the feminist enterprise" (MacKinnon, 1983, p. 638). Furthermore, the social sciences are male in that objectivity is their mode, and this construction of objectivity legitimizes itself by reflecting its view of existing society and those who comprise it, from its own stand. Because this mode inherently dismisses the possibility of women's point of view, feminists ask the next logical question: how would knowledge look from the perspective of women? While similar critiques of science and its modes of seeking knowledge have been made by scientists of the political left:

> what is potentially and ultimately revolutionary in the feminist critique is that the patriarchal structure of science, its theory and practice, will not be left intact. What is developing as a unique emphasis in feminist scholarships is the value of and the necessity for the plurality of our views ... This means the courageous and difficult task of examining and questioning all of our assumptions and the very structure of our thought processes, all clearly born and bred within a ... stratified, hierarchical, patriarchal culture. These include assumptions about dominance and subordinance, women and men, objectivity and subjectivity; about causation, truth and reality; about what is "normal" and "natural"; about control and power; about reproduction and motherhood ... (Blier, 1984, p. 206).

Blier's viewpoint, while brave in its own right, was stimulated and made possible by earlier as well as current work in this field, a trend germaine to the efforts of most feminist scholarship. Generally, feminists in the Third Stage built on the discoveries of earlier work to examine the predominance of the scientific paradigm in social science.

From feminists' perspective the adherence to the "scientific model" and the assumptions which such a practice yield and embody, leave the social sciences problematic.[15]

Wood (1977), Malmo (1979), and later Benston (1982) and Wine (1982), have argued that the modes of seeking knowledge, germaine to psychology and all sciences respectively, involve the procedure of "separating parts" — in a word, reductionism. Both Benston's (1982) and Wood's (1977) critique of this problematic feature of social science demonstrates the attempt of social science to model itself on the physical sciences.

Implicit in scientific inquiry, according to Benston (1982), is the dictum that: (a) "knowledge of the material world is gained through measurement of natural phenomena; measurement in a scientific sense consists of quantification, i.e., reduction to some form of mathematical description"; and (b) "the phenomena to be studied can be isolated out from their surroundings; the essential features of these phenomena can be described by a mathematical theory that offers some insight into the workings of physical reality" (p. 53). Earlier, Millett (1971) and Barrett (1979) had examined Benston's latter point with regard to the desire on the part of the researcher to achieve certain specific results. They argued that explanations of women's oppression (often forwarded by feminists) frequently fell into the use of biologistic or reductionist analyses. Many of these analyses were reductionist in that they subsumed socially and historically constructed phenomena under the category of biological difference, and empiricist in that they assumed that differences in social behaviour were caused by the deserved biological differences with which they correlated. Barrett's work tried to uncover masculinist distortions by demonstrating the historical association between the 'masculine' and the 'scientific', or between 'masculine' and 'objective' (Keller, 1983; MacKinnon, 1982, 1983; Moulton, 1983). From this starting point, feminists have gone on to re-examine the underlying assumptions of scientific theory and method for the presence of male bias. They have as well articulated the more fundamental question of the wider positivistic posture of science (MacKinnon, 1982).

In making central the exclusion of gender, feminists have taken the philosophy of social science one step beyond critics of post positivism. Feminists argue that society was and is created from the point of view of males, and that creation "... becomes the truth to be described" (MacKinnon, 1982, p. 537). Objectivity, "the ostensibly non-involved stance", is the male epistemological stance, which "does not comprehend its own perspectivity" (MacKinnon, p. 538). Those who create and define reality also define the conditions under which it may be viewed and verified. "Truth or its perception becomes contingent on being male" (Blier, 1984, p. 196). And, truth, reality, and objectivity are in trouble from Bliers point of view. She sees "a male-created truth and reality, a male point of view, a male-defined objectivity ... science itself, the tool for the investigation of such natural objects as women, has always been defined as *the* expression of the male mind: dispassionate, objective, impersonal, transcendent. The female mind — untamed, emotional, subjective, personal — is encompatible with science (Blier, 1984, p. 196).

Here the presumption is, that science is by its very nature, inherently masculine, and that women can apprehend it only through extreme efforts to overcome their own nature which is inherently contradictory to science (Hein, 1981). Thus, "science has not only investigated, measured, and constructed gender differences, that is, male-female dichotomies and dualisms, but has constructed itself to epitomize and represent that dualism" (Blier, 1984, p. 196).

Benston (1982) parallels Blier's line of reasoning in her thesis that the methodology of present science in widely regarded as "the" model for "rational" thought, and as such, a reexamination of the basic premises and postulates of science reveal that conceptions of scientific objectivity can be directly linked to cultural stereotypes of masculinity as "well as to the real requirements of achieving masculinity. The image of scientific method and practice...is supported by sex role processes, sanctioned by the presence of male scientists and maintained by particular interests" (p. 52). Within the context of psychology, this same juxtaposition is reflected in Wine's (1982) research, which shows how the underlying philosophy and methods of "male-stream" psychology are rigidly tied to a view of the nature of (man) that excludes women and is antithetical to "gynocentric" or "women-entered" values. To both Benston and Wine, like Hein (1981) and later Blier (1984), traditional scientific, thought *is* male thought. To promote science, " ... is to promote patriarchy, for their values are the same male-values: control, authority, and domination; and their point of departure the same condition of male alienation from the reproductive process (Finn, 1982, p. 43).

In MacKinnon's (1982) view:

> The male epistemological stance, which corresponds to the world to creates, is objectivity: The ostensibly non-involved stance, the view from a distance and from no particular perspective, apparently transparent to its reality. It does not comprehend its own perspectivity, does not recog-

nize what it sees as subject like itself, or that the way it apprehends its world is a form of this subjugation and presupposes it. The objectively knowable is object (p. 538).

Because through male eyes women are "sex objects" "women's experience of politics, of life as sex object, gives rise to its own method and theory of appropriating that reality, that experience: feminist theory and method" (p. 535). MacKinnon points out that as its own kind of social analysis, "within yet outside the male paradigm just as women's lives are, it has a distinctive theory of the relation between method and truth, the individual and her social surroundings, the presence and place of the natural and spiritual in culture and society, and social being and causality itself" (p. 536). The feminist critique of "objectivity", turns a "fact" into a "contradiction"; often features of social reality are only apprehended as contradictory from the vantage point of a radical project of transformation (Bartky, 1977, p. 26).

In identifying women and one's self as subject rather than object, the transformation is rendered both existential and theoretical. The feminist critique therefore becomes, a "life process".[16]

Finally, it is argued that because derive perspectivity from the male standpoint, the scientific model is more epistemological than metaphysical. Because it is the prevailing perspective and because anything outside of its parameters is deemed "irrational" or "nonexistent" women are forced to see reality in its' terms. In doing so, women live a "reality" which contradicts their lived experience. Underlying this perspective are the accepted practices or methodologies of science which ensure the continuation of women's "lived" contradiction.

Methodology

Method in broad terms identifies its central problem, group, and process, and creates as a consequence its distinctive conception of politics as such. Method in this sense, organizes the apprehension of truth; it determines what counts as evidence and defines what is taken as verification (MacKinnon, 1982, p. 13).

Feminists in the Third Stage by and large, agree with earlier feminist work which critiqued the methodology of the disciplines for excluding women, and by the end of the current period, feminists argue the need for entirely new forms of method based on the research conducted in the philosophy of science. Notably, the call for feminist forms of method is particularly tell-tale of the Third Stage shift. The intervening period has witnessed the appearance of several general criticisms of method which will be discussed in the following.

Thus far, it has been argued that women have not and cannot be seen in traditional, classic academic research. The theories of the disciplines lack concepts by which the reality of women's lives can be named, described and understood. This is Smith's (1979) point in her article, "A Sociology for Women" and a point frequently made by other feminists (see for example: Daly, 1973; 1978; McCalla Vickers, 1982; Miles, 1982; Benston, 1982; Wine, 1982; Finn, 1982; Spender, 1981). The omission of women in theories is one facet of the overall bias in research: the androcentric values embedded in methodologies in the other. In this section I will highlight some of the criticisms that have been made of methodology in a general way. It should be noted here, that the possibility of extending the feminist critique into the foundations of methodology has been afforded by more recent criticisms of method (and specifically scientific method) in the philosophy of science and the history of science. Feminists' challenges to particular methodologies, in other words, have in some cases, borrowed or built on the work of male critics. Because this review is only concerned with those analyses which have explicitly discussed gender, I will confine myself to feminist examinations, while acknowledging here, the contributions of those in non-feminist circles. These problems are of a general overriding nature, as are the charges that biases exist in the actual design and interpretation of theory (Gilligan, 1982; Wine, 1982), knowledge (Smith, 1980; Spender, 1981), and language or discourse (Spender, 1980). Finally, the assumptions of "objectivity" and "rationality" underlying the methodological enterprise in Education, have been questioned and challenged (Malmo, 1983; Smith, 1975; Wine, 1982).

Feminist have shown how the ideological dimensions of the methods used in research, can be revealed in the fact that what is hidden in the methods, is the reality that science is produced by actual living individuals as an actual, concrete activity (Smith, 1980). The ideological dimensions are equally made visible when one sees that, women "are outside the frame. They are largely silent in the discourse that develops the conceptual apparatus, the relevances, and themes" (Smith 1980, p. 149). Smith (1980) in her work, actually shows how methodological practice "constructs the female" and includes in her discussion, how the very language that is used in scientific methodology reifies women. Benston's (1982) analysis of the scientific methods supports Smith's (1980) proposal. She says that not only are conceptions of scientific objectivity linked to cultural stereotypes of masculinity, but are connected as well, to the achievements of masculinity. For example, the linkage between different types of method and male and female stereotypes and their differing valuations was made by Millman and Kanter (1975). Further, the use of empiricist research, and to some extent empirical methods, has, like the ideology of objectivity which lies embedded in them, been found to be associated with masculinity itself (Roberts, 1976). Roberts (1976) attributed the "objective", controlled approach in establishing neutral facts to a masculine approach and pointed out that the valuing of empirical methods and hard data as superior to the softer types, parallels society's valuing of the masculine (Malmo, 1983).

In this vein, Walker describes the way in which the male has been made the "prototype/standard" (pp. 112-113); how male subjects have been studied more frequently in research; how "male is normal — female is abnormal" (p. 114); "how male psychologists have magnified sex differences and ignored sex similarities and; how the use of "psychological testing" has contributed toward the perpetuation of sex-role stereotypes" (p. 117). This latter problem was also demonstrated by Vaughter (1976) who argued that the failure of male psychologists to understand female dynamics is compounded by their search for inner traits which agree with stereotypes and their failures to examine the social context. Wood (1977), in her essay "Bias in Psychology", covered a wide range of problematic areas such as the restriction of the framework for study, the lack of cross-cultural, cross-disciplinary perspectives and the historical propensity of psychology to be apolitical and ahistorical. Her main concern however, is with the lack of attention paid to the social context of personal experience. Overcoming such implanted predilections may require the use of interdisciplinary or even transdisciplinary methodologies. The use of interdisciplinary methods however is not without its drawbacks as we have seen. Walker (1981) points out that "we perpetuate a methodology which accentuates differences and militates against an emphasis on similarities. We develop tests which serve to maintain the status quo ..." (p. 121). Some feminists argue that the widespread use of the ill-defined term "interdisciplinary" to describe a practice that has been for the most part multidisciplinary and interdepartmental, has been detrimental to feminist work. Stressing the disadvantages of interdisciplinarity — the denial of autonomy and recognition, the problems of transcending disciplinary thinking — feminists such as Boxer (1982) warn of the energy-draining and still unsuccessful efforts at transforming the disciplines. Furthermore, some feminists have rejected disciplinarity *itself* as a fragmentation of social experience, a male mode of analysis that cannot describe the whole of women's experience. There are questions which are unanswerable by disciplinary thinking (Howe, 1980).

A somewhat different twist to the feminist critique has come in Malmo's (1983) study on how women are treated as the "other" in social science research. The author does a superlative job in my estimation, of unearthing the ways in which social science knowledge has conceptualized and theoretically constructed women as "other", that is, as "object" not "subject". Research methodology has done this, Malmo explains, by studying "woman" rather than women; by singling out one or two aspects of women's experience and proceeding to generalize on the basis of these; by ignoring the psychological aspects of women's experience and focussing purely on the social structural facets of women's lives; by imposing on women, models of behaviour derived from male experience (or from abstractions of women's experiences; by consciously ignoring androcentric bias which perceives behaviour to be exclusively rational and ignoring the significance of emotions and finally; by presenting simplistic interpretations which assume women to be passive victims. Malmo concludes by arguing that as feminists, we must treat our subjects with respect, and involve them as true subjects in the research process. We must share with them the research process and the results, so that they can learn and grow as a result of the experience. In these ways feminist methods can go beyond the "other".

The fundamental problem with methodology, argue feminists,

is its absolute objectification of gender in the research process. This male understanding distorts our models of inquiry and inevitably disconnects unique aspects of women's social reality from the methodological tools we employ. The male-as-normative domination of method moreover penetrates to the means by which information is gathered, the kind of information gathered and the interpretations of what is gathered.

In response to these concerns, feminists have attempted to *recontextualize* women's experiences and have rejected the separation of knower and known in much of their research. Recontextualization has forced us to acknowledge that objectivity and subjectivity are modes of knowing, analysis, interpretation, understanding. They are not independent of each other, should not be and inevitably cannot be. Du Bois (1983) has made the point succinctly and concisely when she stated:

> "As women, we inhabit our world with a double consciousness. We are in and of our society but in important ways also not 'of' it. We see and think in terms of our culture; we have been trained in these terms, shaped to them; they have determined not only the ways in which we have been able to perceive and understand large events, but even the ways in which we have been able to perceive structure and understand our most intimate experiencing. Yet we have always another consciousness .. We are aware ... of the reality of own perceptions and experience; we are aware that this reality has often been both only unnamed but unnameable; we understand that our invisibility and silence hold the germs of both madness and power, of both dissolution and creation (1983: 112).

Most feminists agree that *new* methods must be found to study women. In fields such as the "New Sociology of Education", feminists have found ethnography, ethnomethodology and phenomenology useful, alternative methods, to the more widely used statistical, quantitative methods. Recent work in this field has also yielded exciting approaches with the help of symbolic interactionism

(Smith, 1977).

In sociology, the use of these alternatives to empiricist practices has provided research tools by which feminists have made visible women's subjective and intersubjective lives; how women make sense of their social locations and finally how their lives are organized. As Smith (1979) has said: "... in opposing women's oppression we have had to resort to women's experience as yet unformulated and unformed; lacking means of expression; lacking symbolic forms, images, concepts, conceptual frameworks, methods of analyses; more straight-forwardly, lacking self-information and self-knowledge (p. 144). As such, we have a long way to go before we can actually say that the methods we use in our research are purely feminist.

"Resorting to women's experience" takes us back to the changes that are occurring in feminist methodology — changes resulting from an awareness of the problems in traditional approaches.

In psychology, as in sociology, feminists researchers have considered traditional methodologies, inappropriate for the study of women's behaviour and experience. Instead, "they prefer qualitative methods, such as informal interviews, case studies and participant observation, which allow them to "take the role of the other", to see the world through the eyes of the people being studied." (Mackie, 1983, p. 19).

Feminists research then has shifted from using the kinds of research methods employed in many studies delineated in Chapter Three. It appears that the major impetus has been a need to examine women's lives in a way that makes women *subjects* of that experience. Feminist research, research "for" women, stands inside and is part of the subject it studies. Perhaps the most compelling and profoundly innovative proposal has emerged from MacKinnon's (1982; 1983) thesis. In it for example, she explores the reasons for the incompatibility of marxism and feminism and claims that this incompatibility is a function of the methods that define class and sex as each system's governing categories:

> The marxist criticism that feminism focuses upon feelings and attitudes is also based on something real: the centrality of consciousness raising. Consciousness raising is the major technique of analysis, structure of organization, method of prac-

> tice, and theory of social change of the women's movement. Because marxists tend to conceive of powerlessness, first and last, as concrete and extremally imposed, they believe that it must be concretely and externally undone to be changed. Women's powerlessness has been found through consciousness raising to be both internalized and externally imposed ... (p. 520).

The basic feminist concept, 'the personal is political', implies that the politics of gender can be discovered through women's collective analysis of their experience of sexual objectification. This politic is necessarily different from the politic of class and the difference emerges at the level of method. Like Haraway (1983), Keller (1983) and Blier (1984), MacKinnon perceives a feminist perspective as a critique of the claim to objectivity. Unlike these authors, MacKinnon sees feminism as a method in itself. Consciousness raising, in MacKinnon's view, is the glue which holds method and theory together. Like the separation of ideology and practice, theory and method cannot be disjunctured. "Consciousness raising is the major technique of analysis, structure of organization, method of practice, and theory of social change of the woman's movement" (p. 5). Feminism is unique to consciousness raising as consciousness raising is unique to feminism.

The response to the problems of method, has been a crucial part of the dissent's work. In history for instance, feminists have fashioned alternative methods to uncover the unique historical experiences of women. Among them are dialectical approaches to women's history, that acknowledge *both* the strengths and constraints in women's roles, and assert the long oppression of women and women's long tradition of struggle (Cott and Pleck, 1979). "Opposing the notion that women's history was one of undifferentiated oppression, .. authors ask for deeper and more inclusive investigations of *ordinary* women's lives ..." (Cott and Pleck, 1979, p. 15) (emphasis mine). Feminist history methods also dispute "the conventional division of history into eras or periods. All such demarcations are arbitrary, in the last analysis, since historical change is constantly taking place" (p. 15). Cott and Pleck (1979) also add that new methods in feminist history deny traditional periods or eras because history has made man as its subject and measure, hence, "its periodization has little to do with changes in women's lives". Within the History of Education specifically, Pierson and Prentice (1982) believe that feminist methods should avoid studying "women worthies". "We must recognize the flawed nature of analyses which assign importance to women only insofar as they have contributed to or supplemented the work or achievements of men" (1982, p. 110). The authors caution against the use of traditional periodization, as do Cott and Pleck (1979), and add that feminist research on women creates new schemes of periodization. "Among these are women's domestic work and domestic arts, childbirth and child-rearing, female networks and female sexuality, as well as women's health and reproductive lives, including menstruation and menapause" (1982, p. 111). Finally, Pierson and Prentice outline some of the information sources feminists are exploiting to get at the actual experience of women in the past. They explain that "Historians of women ... recognize the necessity to go beyond the prescription of and debate over roles where ever possible, in order to examine women's actual behaviour and their lives through whatever sources are available. New approaches have been discovered: official statistics and their categories have been challenged, different questions have been asked and put to old sources and new sources have been found" (1982, p. 111).

In educational psychology, feminist have abandoned to a large extent, the use of empiricist models. Rather, they have begun to examine women's experience in its social context and to listen to women's experience as they experience them (Gilligan, 1982).

Feminists on the whole, argue that new, alternative methods are necessary in all fields of academe. In Malmo's (1983) work it means "going beyond the other"; in Smith's (1980) formulation it is "doing a Sociology for women"; in Robert's (1982) anthology it is "doing feminist research"; in Wine's (1982) opinion it is moving "toward a gynocentric psychology". Like the critique of theory which accompanies it, feminists' actual call for new methods stands at the very front of the feminist agenda in academe now.

Language

Language is our means of classifying and ordering the world: our means of manipulating reality. In its structure and in its use we bring our world

> into realization, and if it is inherently inaccurate, then we are misled. If the rules which underlie our language system, our symbolic order, are invalid, then we are daily deceived (Spender, 1980, pp. 2-3).

The issue of language is one which has occupied feminists' attention since the 1960's. However the focus on language as a barrier to academic work appears more visibly in the late 1970's as reflected in the literature mentioned in this section.

Feminists assert that the problems with language occur on two general fronts. The first one concerns the *linguistic* and *conceptual* difficulties of using language which by its nature precludes the experience of women (Kramer, 1974; Lakoff, 1975; Strainchamps, 1971). The second has more to do with its *philosophical* basis (Daly, 1975; 1984). Currently, there is activity on both fronts, though quite recent work reveals that feminists have begun to transform the English language "so that it is more amenable to encodings of women's increased strength" (Spender, 1984, p. 2).

Second Stage feminist scholarship exposed sexism in language use and language structure (Hole and Levine, 1971; Kramer, 1975; Lakoff, 1975; Martyna, 1975; Strainchamps, 1971). This work revealed speech patterns, linguistic practices and general modes of communication as intrinsically patriarchal. Feminists showed as well that the problem of language was not specific to academic contexts, but arose as a barrier within and outside of academe. For example, Miller and Swift (1977) explored the extent to which the sexist content and structure of language defines, ignores or deprecates women. Other similar studies examined language usage in teaching materials, children's books, dictionaries, advertisements, and legal documents, and uncovered explicit bias in favor of a masculine perspective (Kramer, Thorne and Henley, 1978; Spender, 1978).

Researchers such as Martyna (1980) deciphered the differing speech patterns of women and men, and examined the stereotypes and social functions of women's and men's speech, and Fishman (1977) concluded from her study that women do the interactional work, while men retain the control of topics and turns of talk. Thus the control men retain over language structure is reinforced in language usage. Recent developments reflect further connections between language structure and its use in a social context. Feminists engaged in discourse analysis have also considered the way in which the interruptions and reinforcements of particular linguistic styles reveal and support the existing social structure (Zimmerman and West, 1975).

In the late 1970's, an enormous amount of research was conducted on social interaction from the point of view of gender — differentiated communication (Chodorow, 1972; Kramer and Henley, 1978).

The way gender identification affects communicative behaviour, is one particular area of interest to feminists in psychology for instance (Bem, 1974). As a result of this, assertiveness training for women emerged as a strategy for helping women express themselves openly and clearly. Similarly, feminist ethnographers have outlined the cultural parameters salient in the study of gender and language (Hymes, 1972; Philipsen, 1975). They argued that we need to know much more about how people actually use speaking as a cultural resource, in order to have a firm foundation for communication theory in general.

Perhaps the most publicly recognized research has focused on the "he/man" approach to language. This approach to language involves the use of male terms to refer both specifically to males and generically to human beings (Grim, 1977; Martyna, 1980; Miller and Swift, 1977; Moulton, 1977; Spender, 1980; Valian, 1977). The "he/man" approach has received most attention in current debates of sexist language, not only because of its omnipresence but also because of its status as one of the least subtle sexist forms (Martyna, 1980).

Similarly, in articulating the question, "Who is Man?" Miller and Swift (1977) discovered the use of the male to represent the norm. "The use of man to include both women and men may be grammatically "correct", but it is constantly in conflict with the more common use of man as distinguished from woman" (p. 18). Moreover, "A word means what it means not because of what dictionaries say about it, but because most speakers of the language use it with a certain meaning in mind and expect others to use it with the same meaning" (p. 21).

Hence, implicit in the language is the insistence that males take precedence; males come 'first' in the natural order (Spender, 1980). A patriarchal society claims "... not just the superiority of males but that this superiority should be reflected in the structure of language" (Spender, 1980, p. 147). This "superiority complex" is historically contingent and institutionally administered.

These earlier documentations opened up areas which recent work has subsequently investigated. One broad research strand has expanded the study of the generic "he" to explore the impact of the generic "he" on women's and men's thought processes, as will as the misnomers patriarchal reconstructions of language origin and change entail (Martyna, 1980; Spender, 1980).

For example, feminists who have made connections between the general employment of the "he/man" approach and the ideology of the academy, argue that this relation occurs on the level of the politics of knowledge.

Smith (1978) explains the significance of women's absence from the production of knowledge and therefore from academic discourse in the following: "Insofar as women's work and experience has entered into it, it has been on terms decided by men. This is why women have had no written history until very recently, no share in making religious thoughts, no political philosophy, no representation of society from their point of view, no poetic tradition, no tradition in art" (pp. 281-282).

The use of male-biased language and androcentric concepts has been shown to structure conceptualizations about reality as those concepts are used in academic disciplines. When particular words or concepts are used, they automatically carry with them the "... entire complex of meanings and assumptions stereotypically associated with humans" (Blier, 1984, p. 34). Thus the employment of disciplinary-premised jargon is especially problematic with regard to its *a priori* ideological treatment of women. (Blier, 1984; Lips, 1981; Roberts, 1976; Smith, 1977; Spender, 1981; Stimpson, 1979; Wood, 1977).

Many of the concepts we employ are biased not only in their use, but more problematically, in their construction. Schepner-Hughes (1983) attends to a significant aspect of the language critique: the use of specific words whose connotations and contexts of theoretical examination imply an underlying patriarchal persuasion. In psychology, for example the use of concepts like "success", "achievement", "power", "ambition" and "moral development" etc. have been re-evaluated and found to contain explicit notions that leave women '"deviant" at best or non existent (see Gilligan, 1982;

Lips, 1981; MacKinnon, 1982, 1983; Vaughter, 1976; Wine, 1982). Vaughter (1976) has questioned the validity of the constructs "fear of success" and "motive to avoid success". She concurs with the suggestion that patterns of negative consequences, which typically follow women's achievement, must be changed. "But until such changes have occurred, the recommendation that success be defined as the avoidance of disapproval from men and that success is avoiding punishment in a sexist society is unacceptable to me" (p. 138).

Contemporary feminist scholarship has dramatically displayed how this underlying patriarchal persuasion extends to the deeper, philosophical, and conceptual problems inherent in language. At the forefront of this work are Daly's (1978; 1984) groundbreaking explications of the interconnection of patriarchy as a mode of existential being and language as an existential description of that being. Daly's highly complex statement goes to the very heart of language, and reveals it as the matrix by which words, naming, meaning and logic are ontologically, metaphysically and verbally connected by a patriarchal web. She writes that "deceptive perceptions were/are implanted through language — the all-pervasive language of myth, conveyed overtly and subliminally through religion, great art, literature, the dogmas of professionalism, the media, grammar" (1978, p. 3) She believes that our liberation from patriarchy will come in part through our studies of male control over language and through our "wrenching back some word power" (p. 3).

In her earlier book *Beyond God the Father: Toward a Philosophy of Women's Liberation* (1973) Daly places the language issue at the center of her philosophical inquiry. She argues that language makes woman "a stranger ... an outsider, ... an alienated person not as a daughter who belongs or who is appointed to a marvelous destiny" (p. 20). Women's revolution as a structural, social, psychological and existential event, can eliminate sexist symbol systems and sexist conceptual apparatuses, by going beyond them, because a new language must come from women's new consciousness: To exist humanly is to name the self, the world, and God. The "method" of the evolving spiritual consciousness of women is nothing less than this beginning to speak humanly — a reclaiming of the right to name. The liberation of language is rooted in the liberation of ourselves" (p. 8).

The significance of Daly's writings appears most vividly in the interconnections she draws between method, theory, ontology, and language. Her work which was written in the mid 1970's was seminal to both her own, later work, and to the work of other Third Stage feminists who like Daly, view the process of feminist consciousness as the rejection of patriarchal forms of methodology, and language. The emergence of feminist consciousness in turn, potentially involves the coalescence of method, theory, thought and action: "the method of liberation, then, involves a castrating of language and images that reflect and perpetuate the structure of a sexist world. It castrates precisely in the sense of cutting away the phallocentric value system imposed by patriarchy ... that value system ... has amounted to a kind of gang rape of minds as well as bodies" (Daly, 1975, p. 9).

This method signifies women hearing and speaking our own words, and simultaneously, "the development of this hearing faculty and power of speech involves the dislodging of images that reflect and reinforce the prevailing social arrangements" (p. 10). The main point, Daly insists, is that women are not merely "rethinking" language, and philosophy, "but are participating in a new creation" (Daly, 1975, p. 9).

The November, 1984 edition of *Resources for Feminist Research*, is dedicated to the issue of women and language, and to recording the feminist work which is beginning to carve out this "new creation". The various articles, reviews, comments and analyses found in it, confirm Daly's belief that feminists are beginning to deconstruct patriarchal language (as theory and method), and reconstruct women's language. The reconstructive phase is the most difficult because so few words exist which women can claim as their own. The reconstructive phase is as well, the most fundamental project because in devising a new language which symbolizes a new conceptual scheme, feminists will be less constrained to create new theory, new method and new ways of imagining and being (Godard, 1984; Rooney, 1984).

The language barrier then, underpins the entire feminist project of transforming scholarship. The question of how one writes about one's oppression; how one verbally articulates the oppression; how research is constructed and disseminated; and how one thinks about that research confronts the ubiquitous issue of language (Lundberg, 1984).

The "problem of naming" becomes acute from a feminist perspective and hence it is clear that the task ahead involves a thor-

ough reexamination of language definitions and assumptions in order to determine the extent to which we assume a male bias, value
the masculine stereotype, and remain unconscious of the source of
our own attitudes and values. Failing to do this, we will be treating
all women, ourselves included, as "other" (Malmo, 1983). In reading
through this bias, feminists argue, the potential exists to revolution-
ize knowledge about women and ultimately about all of hu-
mankind.

Such a project remains arduous, yet works by feminists suggest
that the project is well underway.

Theory

> "The dependence of women on theories whose
> primary aim is other than the liberation of
> women has limited women's ability to seek an end
> to their own oppression. The time has come for a
> theory which is unique to women's experience.."
> (Hughes, 1979, p. 16).

As we have seen, the most fundamental and as some suggest,
perhaps the most powerful criticism made of traditional scholarship, is that it omits the experience of women in this conceptualization and therefore in its research. We have also seen that the "ideology of gender" within academic paradigms leads to research that
construes social reality in sexually dichotomous and patriarchal
forms. In other words, women have been defined as "not-a-man".
Consequently, the androcentric perspective in disciplines has rendered women not only unknown, but virtually unknowable. Feminists since the mid to late 1970's, have emphasized that this has to
do with both the substance of particular theories and with the processes of research. In short, it has involved what is seen as worthy
of study, and what is not, with how it is studied and how it is
known.

A purusal of some of the dominant theoretical frameworks in
various disciplines indicates that women have not be seen as worthy
of study. As Weisstein (1971) said of psychology in her classic article, 'Psychology Constructs the Female: or The Fantasy life of the
Male Psychologist', psychology has little to tell us about women are
like, because quite simply, psychology does not know. Analogously,

our history, philosophy, biology, literature, sociology, political science, etc., has had little to say about women because until recently, they did not know and did not care to know. Here I will go one step further, as did Weisstein, and say that what the disciplines have known, has largely been ideological in nature.

As such, we have no history, philosophy, sociology, psychology of women, or at least no coherent theory about women in these fields. Through feminist scholarship nevertheless, we are beginning to learn and understand women's relationship to the disciplines and the practice of those disciplines.

In the 1980's, and through feminist scholarship, we have demonstrated and learned that the theoretical paradigms which make up our intellectual milieu marginalize women: their presence is minimal if they are not totally absent (Arnot, 1980; Howe, 1985; Spender, 1981). The exclusion in theories has been bo less pernicious than the exclusion in subject matter and when women are studied, the same modes of study have remained sexist (Du Bois, 1983). The male perspective, once again, is axiomatic, unquestioned. The point to be developed here is that "women have not been part of, and may even (contradict), predominant theoretical accounts of human life" (Keohane et al, 1982, p. vii).

This distortion has created theoretical problems that are inseparable from practical, empirical questions, as well as from the need to conceptualize in a different way, both women's oppression and exclusion in the larger society, and that same treatment in the academy. This problem marks the inescapable requisite once again to create a new knowledge of ourselves and other women.

In this section we examine both facets of the theory issue: the critical exploration of problems in theory, and the various challenges feminist have posed to those barriers. It is here that we reach the *core* question facing the Dissenting Feminist Academy: the relation between feminist scholarship and the need for a solid, unique theoretical framework.

Let us first revisit the Second Stage. Feminist scholars argued that the failure of academic theory to incorporate women's experience and/or perspectives resulted in the predominance of male theories of social behaviour.

First, feminists argued that much of the theory in academic disciplines was inaccurate or involved because of lack of evidence for its claims (Huber, 1973; Maccoby and Jacklin, 1964; Sherman,

1971; Weisstein, 1971). Second, in uncovering the blatant bias in some theories, feminists found that even when credible evidence was determined, the values of the theorist "himself" led to conclusions that "proved" women's inferiority or women's subordinate status (Acker,1973; Bardwick, 1972; Bernard, 1973; Miller, 1974; Wood, 1977). Third, it became clear that previous theoretical formulations were objectionable: "Since they are rooted in male perception an experience and omit the feminine perspective, it is hypothesized that these partial views of reality have limited explanatory power (Mackie, 1983, p. 17). Further, Mackie says, "some theory is criticized on the grounds that scholarly arguments are used to justify a sexist status quo" (p. 17). For example, Acker (1973) noted how wives' status-creating resources (their education and occupations), are ignored in studies of social stratification, as if these had no effect on the family's status. Millman (1975) questions theories of female deviance that explain women's behaviours in sexually stereotyped terms, e.g., seeing prostitution as a sexual act rather than as an occupation. Bernard (1973) wrote that the (then) "present cohort of women critics of sociology has been largely normal science in nature, modifying, correcting, sharpening, or refining the classic paradigms and analyses of traditional sociology, often with the effects of exposing their male bias" (p. 16).

Huber's (1976) review of sociology ended with a conclusion not unlike Bernard's. Bernard saw the feminist critique of theory as "remedial, a patching up, merely a first installment of the potential contribution women can make" (p. 18). Huber reiterated that, "What is needed is a theory of sex stratification to explain women's apparently subordinate position in every era and in all societies. Such a theory will be slow in coming because the data are scattered in several disciplines and across many cultures" (p. 696).

Huber believes that the emergence of a "new" critique of sociological theory can only occur from a "new" sociology, as does Smith (1977).

From a critique of the male-centeredness of traditional theory, then, feminist scholars in the 1970's, responded (in their respective disciplines) by trying to modify paradigms to account for women's oppression. As part of this response, feminist scholars selected particular theoretical systems which appeared to offer the most promise in explicating women's position.

The significance of this trend in psychology is most clearly revealed in the work of feminist psychologists who have seen the possibilities of psychoanalytic theories' reconstruction, but also believe in the challenge of recovering Freud, who they see as offering explanations of how women's subjective understanding can be shaped by the objective structures of the society (Chodorow, 1978; 1979; Miller, 1976; Mitchell, 1974).

Feminists in psychology have as well, embraced social learning and behaviourist theoretical models to attend to the society's "external processes" of inculcating socially defined sex roles, and the effect this has on women (Fenemma, 1976; Frazier and Sadker, 1973; Greenglass, 1983; Maccoby and Jacklin, 1974; Medrick and Tangri, 1973).

A third theoretical system in psychology used by feminist scholars is what Mackie (1983) coins the "interactive" or "cognitive-development" model. One important transformation of this model occurs in Gilligan's (1982) demonstration that women's divergence from the standard model of Kohlberg's theory of moral development has been seen as a problem in theory. She argues that traditional psychology has, on one level, omitted the female from this account of moral development and on another level, distorted the female experience it includes.

Similar patterns are observable in sociology. The possibilities of explaining women's relation to the family, work and school have been envisioned in the used of reproduction theory and political economy theory (Arnot, 1978, 1979, 1980; David, 1978; Deem, 1978; Gaskell, 1979; Smith, 1974, 1979; Wolpe, 1978). Correspondingly, the employment of Marxism as an explication of ideology and ideological practices, has also proved useful in analyzing how our subjective lives are contoured by the work and practices of the institutions in the society. (Benston, 1978; Eisenstein, 1979; Hartmann, 1976; Held, 1976; Kuhn and Wolpe, 1978; Rowbotham, 1973; Smith, 1977, 1978; Weinbaum, 1978; Zaretsky, 1974).

Going beyond accounts which earlier accepted wholesale Marxism, some feminists have argued that an adequate understanding of patriarchy requires a theory of the struggle for sexual recognition that can account for the repressive form that this struggle has assumed throughout history. It requires an approach that treats the formation of sexual identity as problematic, and therefore worthy of independent theoretical attention. It is in Freudian theory that this attention is both most original and sustained. Thus Marxists who are also feminists, have turned as well to Freud for an illumination of the problem of patriarchy that Marx does not provide.

The 1970's then, witnessed feminists' efforts at placing "women's experience at the center of inquiry" and efforts in challenging "basic theoretical frameworks in most academic disciplines" (Abel and Abel, 1983, p. 2). This feminist project "sensed the tantalizing possibilities of reconstruction here: ideas devised in male-centered systems nonetheless offer promise of a new centering in women's lives" (Keohane, et al., 1982, p. viii). However, once women's experience was taken into account, those theories/systems changed.

It was clear in the latter part of the 1970's that feminists were still contributing to the "deconstructive" project. The March, 1979 (Volume VIII, No. 1) issue of *Resources of Feminist Research*, opened its edition on Political Theory with the following.

> The contours, values, procedures and presumptions of all existing scholarly disciplines are thrown into question as soon as women begin to try to add information about women to existing knowledge. Since established *partial* theories are structured as if they were *whole*, their truths are distorted as well as incomplete: research in neglected areas therefore points up theoretical inadequacies in addition to providing corrective data. *Qualitative rather than simply quantitative change in existing scholarship is required to correct these distortions* (Miles and O'Brien, 1979, p. 15).

Moreover there were hints or signs that the publication saw as fundamental, the task of identifying "distinctive aspects of women's experience which can provide resources for the construction of more representatively human understanding" (Harding and Hintikka, 1983, p. x). Hints were also given that the reconstructive project was needed. "Most of the contributions are, at this stage, primarily concerned to identify new problems and sketch new questions which both express and promote the emergence of a new, specifically women's perspective within political science" (Miles and O'Brien, 1979, p. 15).

While the actual reconstruction work had not as yet been fully launched, the literature revealed authors' feelings that the dissent had reached a stalemate. The widely held view was, and is to some extent, that creating new theoretical systems is the only way forward (Blier, 1984; Clark, 1983; Clark and Lange, 1979; Comer, 1978; Daly, 1984; Huber, 1976; Hughes, 1981; Keller, 1982; Lowe and Hubbard, 1984; MacKinnon, 1982, 1983; Malmo, 1983; Oakley, 1981; Okin, 1979; Roberts, 1981; Smith, 1978, 1979, 1981; Spender, 1981).

Within various academic disciplines, statements could be heard about the *need* for reconstruction. Quite a bit earlier, Lopata (1976) concluded in her paper: "We all catch ourselves falling back on traditional vestiges, and even whole frameworks, of theories about the family. "Consciousness raising" in a scientific discipline may mean reexamination of the whole paradigm and the store of knowledge which form the foundation for our construction, of reality" (p. 176). Hughes (1979), who had previously seen the importance and centrality of political economy theory for explicating women's oppression, was now calling for entirely unique paradigms. And, in sociology, feminists such as Smith (1979), Roberts (1976) and Roberts (1981a) were planting seeds of dissent. Psychology was witnessing a similar phenomenon. Walker (1981) argued that while feminism had provided psychology with "extra problems to look at and ... additional ways to analyze data" (p. 111), fundamental changes were still needed. Vaughter (1976), described the ways in which feminist psychologists had begun developing a non-sexist psychology. She concluded first, by delineating the changes that have occurred as a result of feminism, and second, by suggesting: "..., when one examines the science (psychology) from a feminist perspective, with an awareness of sexism or racism, foundations shake. The response called for is the methods, subjects, apparatus, materials, procedures, discussions, and references" (p. 143).

It was repeatedly argued that it is time a new psychology was built, whose underlying philosophy and reference is not male defined, and until such a paradigm was developed it was apparent we would stay at a "stalemate" in our work.

Schepner-Hughes (1983) felt the stalemate and explained that from the beginning, feminist critiques of anthropology were "troubled by internal contradictions and inconsistencies" (p. 116). She feels that the question of importance now is: "... if anthropology is androcentric, how can feminist anthropologists be certain they are raising questions that are not overdetermined at the outset, questions and concerns reflective of male theoretical frameworks?" (p. 112).

The sociology of education as well, experienced analogous changes within a feminist context. Finally, philosophy, history and the natural sciences were scrutinized, and currently have feminists working within them engaged in critical examination of their "western" androcentric and ethnocentric assumptions. Recent publications in these areas, are Marian Lowe and Ruth Hubbard's (1984), *Women's Nature: Rationalizations of Equality* and Ruth Blier's (1984), *Science and Gender: A Critique of Biology and its Theories on Women*. Blier (1984) says in her introduction that "In the 1970's and 1980's, theories that attempt to explain human behaviors and potentialities by reducing analysis to the level of the gene have emerged once again as dominant cultural influences" (p. viii). The response called, for, she believes is a "feminist science", which "proceeds instead with an understanding of the constant change, complexity, contextuality, and interaction that characterize natural and social phenomena and our lives. Fee (1984) agrees with Blier, but is more overt about what the next step in feminist work should be.

It is the reality then, of the most current feminist thinking, to separate from the earlier project of integrating women's experience into male theoretical systems. This of course, is not a wholly exclusive occurrence, but the tendency is clear from the writings reviewed. That the seeds of this theoretical direction were planted and growing was also made clear in the fall of 1983, with the publication of *The Signs Reader: Women, Gender and Scholarship* and Sandra Harding and Merill Hintikka's *Discovery Reality: Feminist Perceptives on Epistemology, Metaphysics, Methodology, and Philosophy of Science*. As the titles suggest, the authors fundamentally reject positing a dogmatic line, or a single way forward, though it is visibly apparent new forms of knowledge underline the agenda. It is feminists' *proof* of the problematic nature of male epistemology which leads towards the direction of finding *our* reality. The Spring 1982 issue of *Signs: Journal of Women in Culture and Society*, was dedicated to the question of the future of feminist theory:

> A crucial task for feminist scholars emerges, then, not only as documenting pervasive sexism as a social fact, or showing how we can hope to change, or have in the past been able to survive it. Instead, it seems that we are challenged to provide new ways of linking the particulars of women's lives, activities, and goals to inequalities whereever they exist (Rosaldo (in memoriam), 1982, p. 514).

1982 saw the publication of *Feminist Theory: A Critique of Ideology*. This collection of works raised the question, "How far can we use these theories, these languages? Are they irrecoverably centered in male experience, so that we must somehow begin from the beginning and devise our won languages, our own discourse?" (Keohane, et al., 1982, p. viii). Perhaps even more to the point:

> As feminist theorists, we must come to terms with the ideological constructs that form our milieu, and with the theorists who first produced those constructs as living thought — Marx, Confucious, Freud, Saint Paul. We must scan the beacons that flare along the horizon of all culture asking whether any one of them is our lighthouse (pp. vii-viii).

Charlotte Bunch in her introductory comments to *Building Feminist Theory: Essays From Quest* (1981) quite movingly gave hindsight and future to the new feminist direction:

> As we enter another decade of feminist activism, the articles collected here grow in importance. They contribute to analyzing our past and passing on what we have learned so that each individual or group does not have to reinvent the wheel of feminist thought and experience ... Some of the authors fear their essays are dated because particulars have changed, and each of us has changed in her own thinking ... (p. xi).

Clearly then there is evidence that feminists are "changing their own thinking". The perspective is indicated in the continued commitment to pursue personal, cultural, political and theoretical redefinition, which feminists earlier identified as the central task and contribution of feminism.

Private/Public Barriers

Feminists in the Third Stage have exposed and attacked the dualistic structure of knowledge as an intrinsic problem for the development of feminist scholarship. In the process of writing this book, it has become evident that one of the distinguishing elements of this critique has been the *concomitant* challenge to the analytic and concrete separation of the private/public spheres, and the exposure of the split as an ideological devise.

The critique of the private/public barriers is a highly complex one, characterized by debate and tangled with confusion. Without attempting to make a definitive statement, and in the interests of untangling some of the arguments, this section examines some of the more general points raised by Third Stage work about the concept of separate spheres.

It seems useful to point out at the start, that the analyses of the private/public barriers have two broad elements, one more recent than the other. First, feminists earlier (mid to late 1970's) explained the way women's lives are organized in terms of the private/public split, and with this explanation asked how women experience the split. Second, feminists in the current period analyze the concept of a private/public split as ideology. By ideology, feminists mean that the private/public principle is a representation of reality at the level of ideas and practice which systematically conceals that reality first by mystifying it and second by reifying it (Finn, 1982). There are important links between ideological aspects of the split and women's concrete experience of it, particularly from the perspective of feminist work which shows how the ideology of the split is reflected in the assumptions of knowledge and the practices of universities. However, it is important to bear in mind the analytical distinction between these two aspects of the critique in order to grasp the contradiction within the logic of the ideology which distinguishes and defines them. Finally, examining the issue in this way makes somewhat clearer how Third Stage research connects the problems of the private/public barriers to other barriers.

The private/public conceptualization was first considered deleterious because of the way it organized women's lives, and made women's relation to men unequal. At the base of this argument was an explanation of how women have always been associated with the "domestic": the social sphere of bringing up children and kinship relations, a cultural consequence of their biological ability to bear children. Men, on the other hand, are always oriented to the "public", the outside world, the sphere of authority and power (Oakley, 1974; Rosaldo and Lamphere, 1974). This division is so universal that Rosaldo (1974) concluded that, "the opposition between domestic and public orientations provides the necessary framework for an examination of males and females in any society" (p. 24). According to Rosaldo, and to some degree Ortner (1974), it is evident that the association of women with the domestic sphere results from sexist chains of association which begin with notions of female "nature". Other critics like Rosaldo and Ortner, used "domestic" and "public" to make women active subjects within their own reality or in other words, to examine how women experience their lives within the framework of these realms (See for example, Smith, 1977; Zaretsky, 1973). They refused to accept the limitations of women's lives imposed by the parameters of the private/public at the same time that the domestic and public framework made it possible to investigate the unacknowledged exercise of power by women in the domestic sphere (Rosaldo, 1980; Zaretsky, 1973).

The key element is this early Third Stage exposition is the insight that since the nineteenth century anyways, women have been defined mainly by their place in the domestic sphere as wives, mothers and "homemakers". Women are developed as social beings according to the model of femininity which fluctuates a great deal according to the time *period*, the social context, and the social class *vis a vis* "feminine nature". Beneath these variations, feminists argue that the societal definition of femininity refers to those qualities, dispositions and skills, inculcated through sex-role socialization, which are associated with the performance of tasks and the exercise of women's domestic functions (Hartmann, 1980; Sargent, 1980). Women's participation in the non-domestic labor force is not irreconcilable with femininity because institutions like the family and education system have assumed an organization on the basis of sex differentiation, making those institutions a pretext for forms of discrimination and segregation (Smith, 1977; 1980).

The fundamental problems with women's definitional relegation to one side of the private/public split, is that even though women have access to the "public", their participation there is organized so as to maintain the "privatization" of women (Smith, 1975). Seen as an extention of the domestic functions of wife and mother, women's participation in non-domestic work is limited to the free time that procreation and housework allow. For women, moreover, this organization represents a real lived dilemma. Women experience this juggle of responsibilities on an immediate and concrete level. In the case of the university, for example, the association between models of femininity and particular kinds of "domestic" or "para-domestic" studies is evident (i.e., Child Care, Nursing, Home Economics). By this association, these "public" areas become "female" and their specific qualities and activities are "feminized" (Armstrong and Armstrong, 1979). At the same time, then, that women's public activities enable them to reduce their domestic subordination, these activities paradoxically make possible women's direct subordination to the central and principle agents of social control. In practical terms, by its very association with a female populace, certain types of activities have been conferred a low-status.

From this standpoint, the private/public dichotomy is real to the extent that the tensions women experience within it are real and to the extent that the institutions of society employ real, concrete practices to perpetuate the split. So, for example, the experience of women in academe is different from that of men: women are paid less, given tenure less frequently, excluded from male hierarchies, and generally treated in a way which remains consistent with the notion they "belong rightfully" in the home. In short, the historical construction of gender within the framework of separate spheres, fragments women's experience, making that experience lived structurally and psychologically different than men's. In this sense, the "career-versus-family" dilemma, is actively promoted by particular institutions, and directly felt by women.

This earlier groundwork enabled feminist analyses of the private/public barriers, which are currently underway. These analyses propose that the domestic/public is an historical framework with division at its center (O'Brien, 1979). The point here is that we should first look for the connections between the two rather than divisions. Second, as O'Brien's (1983) article suggests, we lack a dynamic, historical element between the domestic and the public. Patriarchal power has many dimensions and is produced in many relationships; in labour, sexuality, motherhood, children and ideology. The myth of the domestic/public division as all-encompassing reduces the relation between the sexes to one dimension and does not for example, explain the history of the division or delineate how the dividing line has shifted over time. More importantly, the fact that women's participation in the "public" is organized in a way which extends their definition in "domestic" organization, suggests that the division between the so-called two realms, is in reality ideological. It is ideological to the extent that the pull women feel between the demands of their role as wife, mother and housekeeper, and the roles of their professional, social commitments, is imposed by the ideology which constitutes them as women *(vis a vis* the model of femininity) in both the "private" and "public" spheres. In both so-called realms, femininity is the source of feelings of alienation. In both so-called spheres women are subordinated: "... we must bring to light the actual interconnected processes by which, in a particular place in a particular period of industrialization, patriarchal relations were being reformulated in both the home and the workplace" (Lown, 1983, p. 43).

The interconnected nature of the private and the public, and the concomitant exposure of the split as ideological, is central to current feminists' critique of how the barrier works in an academic context, particularly in terms of the way this specific interconnection is generally tied to the institutional and disciplinary barriers in universities. This critique begins with the insight that the main feature of the split is division, the split itself, a dualism. This dualism is also characteristic of knowledge. Both the private/public framework and knowledge are "patriarchal creations which serve patriarchal interests" (O'Brien, 1984, p. 49). O'Brien (1984) elaborates this point in the following:

> There simply is no single clear way to the trans-
> formations of institutions, pedagogy or practice.
> It is not simply a choice of reform or revolution,
> education or politics. The mode of dealing with
> reality by separation and categorization is the
> very heart of patriarchal culture, with its furi-

ous, futile terrorisms of the either/or. Divide and
rule has been the practice by which patriarchal
canonists and conquerors have ruled the natu-
ral/historical world, including the separation of
that world itself into nature and history (p. 6).

Feminists argue that the traditional dualisms of "male-stream"
thought, assumed and reverberated in academic knowledge, are
epitomized by the private/public dichotomy (Harding, 1983; Keller,
1983). The interrelation between "male-stream" thought and the pri-
vate/public split is sharply apparent in terms of the way both view
women. Hence women are equated with one side of dualisms found
in knowledge such as; subject/object, inner/outer, emotion/cogni-
tion, soft/hard, irrational/rational. In turn the "subject", the "inner", the "soft" and the "emotion" are stereotypical attributes of
femininity which have ideologically defined the "private" as feminine. Academic knowledge, then, ideologically locates women on
one end of the split, justifying and maintaining the split's ideological survival. In this sense, we can see the vital linkage between
these two sets of barriers.

Benston (1982) also illustrates that the private/public framework is merely one feature of a post-industrial society in which all
aspects of life are fragmented and compartmentalized into: na-
ture/culture, inner/outer, objective/subjective, rational/irrational.
She stresses that at the core of this organization is man/women,
public/private or dominator/dominated. Benston notes that such a
scheme is necessarily oppressive to women insofar as it implies antithesis, rather than complementarity, and to the extent that it supports women's oppression both in knowledge claims, and in the institutional practices which treat women as different from, though
ultimately subordinate to, men.

Benston's latter point introduces another component of the
Third Stage account of the private/public barriers. So far we have
seen that the split between the "private", and the "public" does not
actually depict the way women experience their lives as women.
The academic disciplines, through their knowledge, ideologically
reinforce the split's perpetuation. However Third Stage work also
shows how the barriers erected through the university's institutional actions, further reinforces the split's perpetuation. Here, the
three sets of barriers form a matrix, though it is asserted that the

private/public barriers acts as an undrergirding to both the practices of academe and the ideas of academic theory (Harding, 1983; Keller, 1983; MacKinnon, 1983; Moulton, 1983).

How do we make sense of this matrix in terms of its reformulation of patriarchal ideology? On one level, the ideology of the private/public split is manifested in the material policies and practices of the university which define feminists' experience as employees. Mechanisms of hiring, promotion, and tenure, (elaborated in Chapter Three and updated in this Chapter) have built-in assumptions about women as waged workers which are a part of the private/public split. These mechanisms operate ideologically (through their underlying rationalizations and their concrete work) in accordance with the split to reinforce the notion of women as "secondary" labour participants, and "primary" domestic workers. These notions are also reflected in the scant provision of day care facilities.

The ideology of the private/public dichotomy is embedded as well, in the theoretical justification of women's subordination *vis a vis* academic knowledge. That justification as we've seen, operates through the language, and the methods of science; it lies beneath and within the actual theory we use to explain social reality, and it predicates the very posture of "objectivity". Taken as a whole, these elements of the disciplinary connection to the private/public, can be understood as working with (albeit not necessarily in harmony) elements of the institutional barriers, in the interests of keeping the private/public ideology operational. Each set of barriers supports the other (Allat, 1983; Lown, 1983).

Finally, at the crux of this issue is the fact that the division itself, between two realms, is ideological. At the same time, a significant part of the Third Stage "reconstructive" project is beginning to subvert this system, by attempting to break down the imaginary line which constitutes the two spheres as the only two facets of existence. One of the ways this is being done is through feminists' assertion of the need for a holistic feminist "metatheory" which reflects women's complete and complex experience. This need has been spurred by the awareness that women's oppression is perpetuated in the dualistic structuring of knowledge and maintained by the private/public division. It has also been brought about by the realization that women experience the split interconnectedly. What is specifically subversive about the development of feminist theory, is precisely its concern to understand women's lives as they experience it, and its lack of cooperation in dividing that experience into polarities. In other words, feminists currently emphasize the historical manifestation of the private/public ideology as one form of patriarchal organization. In feminists' rejection of the split's separation, is the simultaneous project of collapsing the division between "private" and the "public". In another, similar vein, much of that same work has begun to collapse the boundaries between other offshoots of this dualism: subject/object, nature/culture etc. (see for example: Allat, 1983; Gamarnikow, 1983; MacKinnon, 1982; 1983; Miles, 1982; O'Brien, 1979; 1983; Pollert, 1983).

In summary, recent literature suggests that *The Dissenting Feminist Academy* is moving in the direction of viewing the private/public split as a prime constituent of a patriarchal conceptualization. This private/public conceptualization is first considered problematic because women's lived experience contradicts its truncation. Women's lives attest to the interdependence of private/public realms (O' Brien, 1983). Second, it is considered problematic to the extent that its ideological construction necessitates its ideological practice. So while women experience the split as oppressive on both private and public levels, the patriarchal organization of academe (as elsewhere) materially and theoretically ensures that the dichotomy in fact, remains ideologically viable.

The major point here is that the significance of Third Stage thinking stems from the uncovering of the patriarchal underpinnings in knowledge itself, which have necessarily led to the exposure of the private/public dichotomy as an ideological tool and an epistemological problem.

In the final analysis, we can say with some degree of certainty that the emergence of the Third Stage cannot be pinpointed by one or a number of specific concrete events, although it consciously expressed itself as an academic arm of the larger women's movement. For the most part, the Third Stage has been and is an extension of the Second. Its defining characteristic however, arises in feminists' gradual movement toward developing feminist theory. This development in turn has been triggered by the uncovering, and later the rejection of, the male hegemony over knowledge. Feminists in academic contexts believe that the time has come in Keohane's words, to "build our own lighthouse". This vision in a general sense, defines and shapes the Third Stage agenda which moves from "squeezing into a suit that did not fit", to "designing and making our own clothes".

The literature testifies moreover, that unlike the Second Stage, feminists in the contemporary setting laud femininity as a more fully human principle. This stems from the rejection of equality on male terms, but equally from the commitment to fashion alternative systems of thought, language and practice which reflect alternative value systems.

The Third Stage rejection of all false dualisms, is perhaps the most radical insight. This rejection arose out of the complicated and tangled debates about what a "new" feminist or would epistemology should look like. It is argued, that because the whole of the male scientific approach to the world is characterized by dichotomies, (things are either rational or irrational; thesis or antithesis; objective or subjective; us or them; pure or impure; and even male or female) a feminist epistemology must insist on integrating what these dualisms tear apart.

In the Third Stage, the main emphasis is given to understanding the pervasiveness of bias in academic disciplines, though the central shift to separation has had ramifications for each of the barriers and, most notably, has led the dissent to view the barriers as interdependent.

The articulation of feminists' separation from mainstream theory and practice, first appears in the institutional barriers where they are moving away from the established practices of academe, to create new forms of structure sustained by feminist principles. Here the importance of feminist method has underlined the need to see how historically-rooted institutional processes are tied to the academic knowledge which informs them.

Within academic disciplines, feminists have also revealed bias in the posture of science, the discourse of language, the consequences of methodology and the construction of the first level of the feminist response. The second involves creating feminist alternatives which resist dichotomizing categories like rational/emotional, hard/soft, and objective/subjective. Feminist methods and theories seek explanatory systems which unite polarities, and which show the connectedness of women's experience in all aspects of life. Such a commitment has brought the feminist dissent into abrupt confrontation with the private/public barriers which is the epitomizing dichotomy. In the Third Stage, the private/public split is drawn into the epistemological domain. Feminists argue that the split inself is a creation which is tied to knowledge. Both are characterized by dualism which contradicts women's experience, and both serve patriarchal interests within and across both public and private spheres. Hence, the feminist project of constructing new paradigms (which undo dualisms) potentially promises the destruction of the private/public notion, or at least the eradication of the imaginary blurring line between the so-called two realms.

5

CONCLUSION

It is no longer a sight merely a photograph, or
fresco scrawled upon the walls of time, at which
we can look with merely an aesthetic apprecia-
tion. For there ... we go ourselves and that makes
a difference. The questions we have to ask and
answer .. during this moment of transition .. may
well change the lives of all men and women forever..

Virginia Woolf.

I would imagine that at this very moment, I feel somewhat like
Mary Putnam Jacobi did in 1892 when she was about to disseminate
her research.[1] She too, had written a work which attempted to chart
male bias in research and as a feminist, she too was concerned that
her research and its dissemination, would mean moving one step
closer to the path of equity in higher education. Here, my shared
experiences with Mary Putnam Jacobi must part ways, for to pursue
the analogy would be to deny Jacobi's experience its historical
specificity and its individual uniqueness.

It is also now almost fifty years ago since Virginia Woolf so
iconoclastically denounced higher education not only as a male bastion, but as a hostile and impossible environment for women.[2] She
did not perceive women's *access* to academe as a worthwhile goal
for women because for Woolf, the institution of education was rampant with misogyny. Basing the well-spring of her ideas on her
exclusion from Oxford University, she pointed out the extent to
which the university represents male values, perspectives and beliefs. Finally, all of this led Woolf to the conclusion, that women

might do better to pursue intellectual work independently, trusting they have a "room of one's own" and "three guineas."[3] Clearly Woolf was one dissenter who believed that in numerous ways, institution-alized education is a major threat to women's learning and she was not alone. Unlike Jacobi however, Woolf did not necessarily believe women *should* work inside the academy. In fact, the conflicting relation between women and academe led her to argue consistently for an education over which women have control, instead of an education controlled - as it is still today - by men.

My reason for looking back in time, to the feminist ideas of Woolf and Jacobi, is to demonstrate that male dominance in academe is no less today than it was in the time of Virginia Woolf or, for example Elsie Clews Parsons.[4] This would be a depressing revelation if it were not for the fact that the dissent of feminism is, perhaps, stronger now than ever before.

Yet the first point to be made here is that *The Dissenting Feminist Academy* has a history. What I have tried to say here, in this book, has, in different forms and in different times, been thought about, grappled with, and said before. And it is perhaps a measure of how far we have *not* come that we are still fighting the same battles; still speaking to a largely hostile audience and still struggling to be heard - inside the academy and outside. On the other side of the coin, feminists today have the benefit of knowing Jacobi and Woolf's words. We have the advantage of a history that feminists themselves have retrieved and made real, in literary terms. The countless ways earlier dissenters unsettled the university "Fathers", has made our work less arduous than it would be otherwise. I can take this for granted until I realize just how much that earlier work made this volume academically possible now, when century ago my energies might be spent fighting to gain entrance, still struggling for the right to go to university in the first place.

Though similar patterns exist among the earlier dissenters and their contemporary counterparts, the history of *The Dissenting Feminist Academy* has not been marked by a steady path of "progress", so much as it has been a continuous search for *educational*, and therefore personal, identity. Dale Spender (1982), is one of many who rejects this notion of "progress" or of the construction of history as a steady march of uninterrupted human improvement. Speaking about the history of feminist ideas, she describes the history as "more like the repetition of the same pattern, than 'progress', the pattern of interruption and silence which denies women's consciousness so that men's creations can be justified ... the pattern which constitutes, women's culture ... where women's intellectual ... resources are taken away by repeated interruptions partly through the role men have imposed on them." (p. 732-33). The three stages of feminist scholarship have shared these patterns, but have as well, shared the pattern of dissent and of vocal rejection which reflects women's consciousness, so that men's creations can be rejected. They share the pattern which attempts to recognize that women and their culture, exist intellectually in their own right. Finally, the stages share the pattern where women's intellectual resources are kept, through repeated confrontations with that system which has denied they exist. In a general broad sense then, this history has been a history of conflict and ultimately, one of contradiction. The theme of contradiction is the one I would most stress in this final analysis. Though others will be discussed, they too are underscored by the larger characteristic of contradiction: the theme of separation versus integration; the theme of identity versus structure and; the theme of marginality versus innovation. Following this core theme, I have attempted specifically to show how feminist scholarship has *both* flourished in, and been thwarted by, the university. I have tried to demonstrate through listening to feminist voices, that as feminists and as academics, women have found themselves entangled within a *web* of contradictions. Finally, I have tried to argue that the nucleus of the problem is women's need to define themselves in a site that has always made it difficult for them to do so.

In the following I wish to examine briefly, the nature of this relationship between feminism and academe in each of the three stages. It seems important as well, to make some general comments on the stalemate feminists are presently identifying in their work, and about how the patterns of the history forewarn the future of feminist scholarship. Finally, certain themes emerge, not from any one single stage in this book, but from a reading of them all. These will also be discussed within the context of the dissent's future prospects.

A. The Stages Revisited

In Chapter two, I showed how the nineteenth century dissent

developed as women were gradually seen as needing higher education and yet were also seen to be moral guardians of the family and of family life. The dissent sought to empower women by gaining access to higher education and public life in general. Winning women's physical presence in the university *was* an important watershed for women's education, as feminist historians suggest, particularly in view of the social restrictions women faced in this period.

Beyond the importance of gaining access, however, was the persistence of the idea by educators, reformers, philanthropists, and the church - all of whom had supported women's higher education - that women are to be wives and mothers first, but "that they may require special training to adequately pursue these tasks" (David, 1978, p. 239). This double-edged concession was, however, a product of a variety of social evolutions. In the mid nineteenth century, as argued in Chapter two, ideologies of femininity expressed themselves through religious/social concepts; through economic shifts in the shape of the family unit; through theological doctrines of moral piety and the "feminine ideal" and later; through reform, philanthropy and the "scientific" ethos of Darwinism. Granting women access to academe was not only seen as a "progressive" measure, but a means by which a society in turmoil could ensure compliance with a particular socio-economic system - a system that could no longer rely on antiquated methods of social control and social philistinism.

Through education, the State was able to create and sustain notions of women's "proper sphere", by making the university an arena of feminine negotiation. Hence, higher education for women was established along gender divisions. If we are to grasp therefore, the efforts of the first stage feminists, it is crucial to recognize that these women were responding to the "benevolent" motives of a state, and not just to the university community around them.

The dissent was largely comprised of women who felt that the domestic propensities of women were not incompatible with the paternalistic world of academic study. They may have differed from women who attended single-sex institutions insofar as they saw women's access to male-dominated enclaves as vital to achieving equality; but they nonetheless championed women's right to equal educational opportunity on grounds that were not entirely irreconcible with cultural definitions of femininity. The acceptance of these terms was evident in feminists' conceptions of their role, and in conceptions of the roles they felt women had to fill. As the educational provision they received reinforced in feminists' minds what was ideologically sanctioned in the society; it also provided a forum for challenges and alternatives from women, who were still able to carve out a distinctive feminist scholarship tradition.

As the themes of social science, social unity, labor reform, moral education and progressive spiritualism resonated throughout the larger society and echoed in the academy, feminists struggled to forge a new, rational union between the sexes, a union that demanded that both sexes have equal symmetrical development. They expanded the concept of symmetry to include the social system. They contended that both sexes needed equal access to scientific knowledge, and therefore championed *equal* educational and economic opportunities for both sexes in the public realm. Coming from an adherence to liberalism, and a strict belief in the liberation of human potential, feminists saw the "political problem" of women's subjugation as having been resolved by the new forces of authority, except for the lingering tasks of attaining legal equality, suffrage, protection of private property and interests. Certainly this did not hold true for all feminists, who came from a multifarious network of associations. But it is safe to say without overgeneralizing, that organized, nineteenth century feminism was largely made up of middle-class women whose alliance with reform and reform movements, and whose commitment to an egalitarian ideology, contoured their educational demands.

This much said, it is clear that the theme of reform during the Progressive Era, informed the ways in which women's educational provision was perceived. It also had a vital influence on the ways in which women themselves saw their evolving roles. Finally, and perhaps most importantly, reform work allowed women to expand their "proper sphere" without altering the pattern of sex roles that prescribed that sphere. In this sense, reformers were not so much rejecting Victorian concepts of femininity, as they were re-defining it (Dyhouse, 1984).

Against this backdrop, it is understandable how dissenters must have experienced this tension. "They were torn between on the one hand mollifying public opinion and proving their respectability by scrupulous adherence to the standards of 'proper' or 'decent' 'ladylike' behaviour, on the other by the need to assert themselves as intellectually confident and well able to mount an offensive on the bastions of the male academic establishment" (Dyhouse, 1984, p. 55). Rosenberg (1982), writes that notions of women's propensity for "domesticity", "purity" and "piety", were not easily reconcilable with the male-world of academe. Indeed, but of the various reasons for granting women access to higher education, the institutional re-establishment of gender divisions was the main one. Education in this regard, became an effective instrument, to both measure and enforce social control. This is *not* to say that the new colleges and schools functioned solely or primarily to reinforce conventional notions of women's role. The issue at hand, is far more complex, particularly when one examines the single-sex or "separate" academy, alongside the social experiences of women in coeducation institutes. It *is* to say that universities and colleges played a vital role in maintaining sexual divisions.

In the single-sex colleges, women carved out a different dissent than those in coeducation colleges, a dissent that was reflective of the single-sex experience. But the differences notwithstanding, some themes are echoed in both. In both forms of provision, women were presented with images of male authority; were expected to exemplify in their own lives the quintessentially "feminine" virtues; were almost always unmarried and; were considered to need preparation for marriage, family life and domesticity. "Learning was *not* to be seen as a form of self-development, let alone a route to personal liberation, it was an act of discipline or a form of service" (Dyhouse, 1984, p. 58). How it was seen by *women* was a different question.

The coeducational dissent has been both lauded and castigated by historians. It has been the focus of attention, specifically because during this period, most feminists took the coeducationist, not the separate education position. Within this setting, the dissent managed, within the parameters of the forces we have been discussing, to engender reconsiderations of the scientific bedrock of sex-role perpetuation. In a rather curious twist, and combining "Hegelian" idealism with "Spencerian" positivism, psychology with physiology, feminists took up the question of women rights, while never losing hold of their belief in women's "moral superiority". More important, they tried to create a "new" ideology that would propound a society organized along cooperative, humanitarian principles. Feminists saw women's "moral distinctiveness" as a guide to developing such principles, and they believed that a community predicated on cooperation and equality would eliminate the divisions between the sexes. These claims were reflected in their rally for coeducational provision, where it was felt, men and women could work together, in harmony and as equals. In the same vein, the larger plea for scientific knowledge and the promotion of equal physical development, like the hope perceived in coeducation, echoed the themes of progressive reformism: physiological and institutional symmetry, human improvement, equality, benevolence, biological purity and cooperation. "Because morality itself, they believed, depended on health, vigorous development was imperative for both sexes" (Leach 1980, p. 65). Because the sexes had to work and live equally and, because the theme of health was expressed in coeducation institutions; coeducation was considered the best possible situation in which to establish the physical health of both sexes. In such environments, men and women could be prepared for more "congenial relationships, more cooperative friendships and marriages" (Leach, p. 65). The importance of cooperation, while coached in pseudo-scientific rationalizations for preserving separate spheres, made those qualities feminists felt were innately or uniquely women's, the *initial* basis for new educational arrangements.

Some might argue that these activities, in and of themselves, did not challenge the sexual status quo and therefore, would not consider the women, dissenters, so much as they helped reinforce prevailing attitudes about women and actually helped maintain ideologies of separate spheres. Others may argue, that consideration must be given mainly, to the "truimphs", to the achievements accumulated, and to the "citadels" feminists "stormed" in the name of sexual equality. Finally, and still others may stress that the new developments in women's education were brought about largely by the "pressure-group tactics" and reform-spirited tenacity of feminists bent upon eliminating the barriers around women's education and employment (Dyhouse, 1984). There are problems with all three approaches. The first would seem to favor traditional histories: it incorrectly assumes women were "passive victims" and it loses sight of the veritable interaction of nineteenth century feminism with the society in which it flourished and was constrained. The second argument underplays the ambiguities, the complexities and the contradictions, which women's educational experience entailed. Their struggle for, and their daily experience in education, were processes that existed within the larger historical processes of mid century North America. Having fallen into the trap of the third assumption, earlier in the process of this research, the difficulties of exerting a critical eye toward women's work in the past is one with which I am only too familiar.

What I believe we can say, with some clarity and precision, is that the First Stage dissent emerged from its social setting with the interests of women in mind. Taking on the social restrictions of the Victorian-age "hangover", the feminists in the mid to late nineteenth century embraced what they needed from the theoretical doctrines of progressivism, liberalism, social science, and moral reform, to make their signature on the social science tradition. With the security of women's "unique" qualities, and with the sanction of benevolent movements; they were better able to exert their opinions and to participate in the public world of academe, without risking alienation, hostility or ostracization. Frequently taking on the terms in which their "roles" were socially defined, may have helped reinforce attitudes of "proper" femininity; but it enabled them to break through monopolies which had previously excluded women, and to some degree, it made the espousal of women's rights more palatable, if not accepted.

Higher education *did* secure a valuable environment in which women could study and research, but it *did* maintain gender divisions. Within that paradox, women dissented in their research, as well as in their beliefs. Arguing from a "woman as a group" position, they emphasized the similarities between the sexes in their rejection of theory which purported women were different and therefore inferior. In sociological terms, they "negotiated" their gender identities to make sense of both their roles, as women and as academics. The ambivalence of their provision, like the contradictions of their dissent, was part and parcel of the changing educational system in North America. Having managed to find a place in that system, the dissent built an academic foundation that women could later use. Finally, while the re-organization of higher education actually instituted a new sexual division of labor, its reverberation of the ideas that spurred the dissent, made it more easily penetrable.

In terms of the barriers which were laid out in Chapter two; the feminists who worked in the social science-dominant universities, did not and clearly could not, focus on the institutional barriers. This would be a later concern, precluded by the more immediate goal of gaining access and, later, the task of accommodating to the academic community.

In the latter years, of between 1880 - 1920, the university as we know it today had been firmly established. The agenda having been concretized, overtly displayed the "hidden curriculum" with male domination of the governing structure of the colleges and the construction of "privatized" and differentiated curricula (e.g., the domestic studies such as Child-Care Studies, Social Work, Home Economics and later, Education).

How though, did the university maintain its control prior to the early twentieth century? Again, the growing sanctions of scholarly acceptance were not entirely successful in their attempt to reorder the sexual division of labor. Their sorting abilities however, soon proved pernicious to the survival of the dissent. The gradual establishment of the university's hierarchy and with it, the development of standardized academic procedures, both reinforced the notion of the university as a *male* bastion. Generalizations here are risky, but within these barriers, we do know that some women managed to acquire the necessary qualifications and, many forged brilliant careers with graduate degrees. Lucy Maud Montgomery for example, (a Canadian writer from Prince Edward Island and author of the world-renowned *Anne of Green Gables*) was one such women, and describing Dalhousie University in 1896, she noted that women had distinguished themselves in Mathematics, Physics, English, Philosophy, and Medicine (Fingard, 1985). Similar patterns existed at McGill University and in American institutions, particularly Cornell, and Bryn Mawr (Fingard, 1985; Gillett, 1982). These "exceptions" were frequently a large group.

The crystallization of the social sciences, the growth of specialization and, the rise of a professional ethos in the academic world, were, as Rosenberg (1982) demonstrates, three further forms of exclusion that posed hurdles to women. First, the breakdown of social science into individually-defined disciplines, led to the disavowal of its reform commitments. Second, specialization meant identifying with narrowly-defined research, that no longer validated reform-related community involvement, but instead, legitimated scientific, "laboratory-produced" scholarship. In conjunction with the demands of professionalization, women were forced to increasingly "trust the tools of their trade" and pushed to identify more fully with their scientific commitments than with their feminist, reformist commitments. Many were pushed out of academe.

The demands of the disciplines and of specialization, further enforced limits on women. Feminists pursuing research in psychology and sociology, for example, embraced the theoretical paradigms levied by their male mentors and used them to ask questions about women. This occurred concomitantly with a new determinism for scientific rigor and measurable "objectivity". These processes left women on the fringes of academe, forcing many out, and thwarting the reform-spirited radicalism of those who remained. Detrimentally, women were cut off from their colleagues who were dispersed in different fields, and were forced to sever their affiliations with support groups outside university. Because women believed, with good reason, that activist work would compromise the objectivity of science and women's tentative place within it, they lost the important networks which had been such a source of strength.

As noted in Chapter two, the private/public barriers did not occupy a central place in feminists' *documented critiques* of academe. Academic, American feminists like Helen Woolley Thompson and Leta Hollingsworth hoped to reduce the limitations on women within their own sphere and; maintain the virtues of the female sphere while eliminating discrimination against women in public domains (Rosenberg, 1982). The university's growing preoccupation with professionalism forced feminists to adopt an integrative stance both professionally and politically. Such a stance was necessary in order to survive and be accepted as academics, but it also meant integration and assimilation on male terms, at the same time denying the significant and vital female culture which had largely given impetus to women's fight for access to education in the first place.

It is in, mid nineteenth century feminism's conception of the private/public ideology and women's negotiation of it, that we find the very *crux* of the dissent's contradictory juxtaposition to academic thought in the Progressive era. Rejecting the restrictions of each "sphere", feminists relied on science and organization in their effort to construct a new social ideology. As Leach (1980) suggests, they hoped to create new places and roles for both sexes in their larger attempt to, "reconstruct the private and public life of the educated bourgeoisie while at the same time securing for it a solid position within institutional and professional structures" (Leach 1980, p. 12). But in largely accepting the terms in which the ideology was defined, and in relying on the discourse of "individualism", their cooperative, humanitarian vision receded, leaving them caught in the grips of the public/private divisions that their philosophy rejected. The academic system tightened these divisions through the institutionalization of the same theories feminists embraced. In a cruel paradoxical twist, feminists were caught within the barriers of this ideology that in some respects, they had supported.

Some historians have argued that feminists' lack of a separate support network within the university and isolation from their ties outside, may indeed have contributed to the decline of the dissent after 1920 (See for example: Antler, 1980; Freedman, 1979). Stranded without support systems and/or a separate feminist political base, women were alone and vulnerable in the face of extreme male resistance and conservative backlash in the 1920's (Freedman, 1979).

Other external factors notwithstanding, a few feminist scholars after 1920 carried on the research of earlier feminists. But for the most part, as Rosenberg (1982) asserts, the fervor of the previous iconoclastic work was gone. A full understanding of the dissent's hiatus awaits further research, though a number of social, economic, and intellectual forces, contributed to its decline. Against the wider background of the Depression, the overall repression of radicalism, post-war propaganda, coupled with new views of women, motherhood and the family unit, added to the suppression of organized feminism. Later the feminine mystique of the '50s, and the establishment of the university as a fully operating social mechanism, limited and circumscribed the previously expanding opportunities for women.

These larger considerations aside, two specific factors had a direct impact on feminism in academe. The first condition, intensified by economic and political events, involved drastic financial cutbacks in university hiring, research funding and reduced subject area expansion as a by-product of the Depression and economic crisis. The second condition, a product of the first, manifested in conservative backlash to all forms of radicalism, particularly feminism. In the fact of severe economic depression (in the 1930's), the kinds of research carried on by earlier feminist dissenters seemed frivolous at best and the question of sex differences receded into the background (Rosenberg, 1982; Rossiter, 1980).

We can conjecture that the effects of conservative backlash, economic recession and right wing "morality" were at least contributing factors to the *Dissenting Feminist Academy*'s hiatus after 1920. These are also familiar conditions facing feminists in 1986; the parallels serve as sharp reminders of the lessons to be learned by the First Stage response to its social context.

In Chapter three we saw that the response of the dissent has shifted. With the advantage of *access*, feminists in the '60s and early '70s, aimed both to overcome the barriers which prevented women from equal participation in the society and, to confront the male dominance of the university.

Unlike the larger feminist movement in the nineteenth century, feminists in the late sixties and early seventies viewed the family or the private sphere as the social/psychological foundation for the perpetuation of the patriarchal system. The family, in other words, was seen as a unit of social control: the model of marriage, motherhood, conjugal and parental relationships within the nuclear family unit entail the reinforcement of male dominance. This political understanding of personal life was one of the crucial insights brought with feminists to the university.

Like many other public institutions, the university in the meantime had benefitted from outpourings of federal funding for research. In addition, the mood was right for expansion in the mid 1960's: students unrest and antiwar activity increased the possibilities for the participation of radical groups in academia. Within this state of flux and institutional imbalance, feminists found an opening to voice their concerns in an academic context. Compared to the conservatism of the '40s and '50s, the '60s were marked by rapid social change - the proliferation of protest movements, the rapid growth of federal domestic programs, the reform of higher education. "Access" and "equal opportunity" were key themes of the liberal-based philosophy that enveloped the university community and were resonated throughout the sectors of the feminist community that largely comprised the academic dissent.

As in the First Stage, the co-junction of prevailing reform-oriented persuasions with the expansionist, "free-thinking" attitude of universities, shaped the reform agenda of the dissent. Within the pulls and tugs of these forces, feminists wrought revisions in the university's hierarchical structure and in the content of the curriculum. The gains they made, and the losses they suffered, were partly a result of the limitations to the ideologies defining their politics. Again, there is a contradictory clash between the informing threads of liberalism and the male-orientation of liberal reform. And again, we see in this period, the paradoxical promise of liberation offered to women by doctrines of equality and, the strengthening of gender reproduction through the class/sex bias of progressivism. An emphasis was placed on presenting women as equal, and as requiring "equal space" - within the curriculum within the faculty ranks and within the upper echelons of the academy's administration. These were the areas women focussed on and in turn, the successes the dissent experienced, were determined by the politics they adopted, the response of the system and, the extent to which their efforts engendered transformation.

It was argued in Chapter three that women's invisibility as faculty members catalyzed concern with institutional policies which perpetuate women's devalued status as employees through hiring, promotion and remuneration procedures. The strategy of basing organization on lived experience did not at that time, extend so far as to justify an independent mode of political action oriented to the *unique* needs of women. Both the form and the program of the Second Stage did reflect however, its analysis of how women were subordinated in academe and of what would be initially necessary to initially overcome it. According to the Howe (1984), three ensuing actions sprung from that analysis. First, feminists focused attention on the problems that were of specific relevance to women as faculty. Second, they argued that engagement in academic struggle requires a changed sense of the way the *disciplines* portray or do not portray women. In response, they expanded the curriculum through Women's Studies, which were explicitly designed to make women a *central* part of the academic agenda. Finally, feminists followed-up such moves with concrete challenges to the sexism and the masculinist hierarchy of the university, (*vis a vis* feminist pedagogy) and the masculinist distortions of academic knowledge (*vis a vis* interdisciplinary epistemology).

By the late 1970's, academic disciplines were exposed as male-dominated particularly in terms of their subject matter, method, theory and language. The differentiation of roles and power between students and professor was rejected in the relationships between feminists and students and students were encouraged to utilize their subjective experience when learning new material. The lectern model was considered passe. Instead, small group discussions were modelled after forms of interaction found in women's consciousness-raising groups. In short, feminists contributed to the development of a new paradigm of pedagogy and a new curriculum. The novel character of both contributions, pioneered women's unique establishment in the academy in a way it had not been before and propitiously, these initiatives paved the way for further separatist feminist work carried out in the Third Stage.

The response of the Second Stage to the university's barriers was as I have said, part of the historical conditions which strengthened women's interests, but which limited their choices. The reasons for this are complex, but in using political strategies without a full consciousness of the way those political forms of struggle themselves are part of the socio-economic system that perpetuates sexual inequality, it is clear that inroads were made without forcing substantial alteration in the actual underpinning structure of the university. Albeit this preliminary struggle was a necessary prelude to more far reaching institutional transformations, the incorporation of traditional types of political strategy limited the extent to which the dissent could make visible how the university supports women's *specific* oppression. Our analysis enables us to offer an additional interpretation. The use of mainstream institutional channels to fight for women's equality, contradicted the dissent's claim, that women's struggle derived from their lived experiences *as* women. This contradiction was reflected in analyses of the private/public split for example, in which feminists denounced women's relegation to the private sphere but frequently issued their uncritical acceptance of the split's categorical separation. The contradiction is shown as well in the "add women and stir" method of altering knowledge in the disciplines. The "add women and stir" method holds the underlying assumption that the frameworks to which women have been attached are, in themselves, unproblematic and because of this, it has not recognized the depth of the antagonism between women's experience and the way that experience is contorted in academic theories. Similarly, those who stressed the need to transform women's *attitudes* about sex roles failed to see the deeper dimensions by which both women's attitudes and roles are circumscribed and defined in patriarchal cultures. The emphasis on "attitudes" moreover, precluded understanding how psychological models which abstractly define achievement motivation are in themselves used to legitimize women's subordination and, cultural standards of femininity.

The problems which feminists in the 1960's confronted were ones of pragmatic immediacy to women in universities. Their responses to those problems, were reflective of how they perceived and experienced them in their own lives. They use of available strategies may have fallen short of their purposes to act as correctives, but in measure at least, most of the correctives succeeded in terms of the fact that they made issues of relevance to women, and indeed women themselves, an important part of the academic setting, concomitantly transforming that setting through these actions. The dissent's challenge threatened, at least in the short run, to upset the structure and practice of sexism in higher education. In retrospect, it was strong enough to allow contemporary feminism, to argue that women must now transcend the same contradictions which beset feminists in the Second Stage.

The political climate over the past decade has changed and educational production has followed; where protest embraced the possibilities of academia in the '60s the current mood of universities is somewhat narrower and their ideologies less tolerant. The curriculum, with its strict adherence to "bread and butter" knowledge and technological specialization, to the economy of job obsolescence and fashionable corporate *elitism* is a political chronicle for these more conservative times. Finally, feminist studies, in having achieved scholastic acceptance, now fails to pass as a trend. During the last decade, and enriched by the advantages accorded by its social circumstances, feminist scholarship has grown in scope and complexity. In this latest period and within the structures of a depressed university economy, the dissent has taken on a new form that reflects this growth and which acknowledges its' benefactors.

Feminists in the Third Stage have had at their disposal a mammoth corpus of documented knowledge about women and their experiences, which has afford their scholarship the opportunity to forge sophisticated and complex analyses of gender inequality based on that knowledge. The same knowledge which has prompted and facilitated general critiques of women's subordinate status in the wider society, has yielded deeper explanations of the university's various roles in reproducing that subordination: the male hegemony over knowledge (academic/"legitimated"), language, methodology, and the ideological functions of separate spheres.

Access to archives, the use of records which have been preserved, and available distribution of historical documents has enabled feminists to make it clear that the underlying conflict between academe and feminism is itself an expression rooted at least, in the nineteenth century conception of two separate spheres. It is this historical conception, that Third Stage feminist scholarship is at the point of dismantling — not by dismissing oppositional dichotomies, but by explicating and insisting on the systematic connections between them and by explaining how the ideology itself, forms the underbelly of our institutional treatment as women.

The shift which this volume has laid the groundwork to examine is the Third Stage shift in position toward developing and carving a distinctly feminist epistemology/methodology while working inside academic systems. Feminists presently find, the same pushes and pulls of a conservative milieu, though the gains are deeper because of the Second Stage legacy. Their advocacy of *separate* struggle (in terms of rejecting traditional theories and philosophies) develops from an analysis of the particular nature of patriarchial ideologies and their hold on the university.

The seeds of the movement towards academic self-definition were planted in the Second Stage when feminists argued that separate organizations are necessary for consciousness-raising and when curricular transformations supplanted "adding and stirring". Explicitly within the larger feminist movement, and implicitly in feminist critiques of institutional, and disciplinary practice, was the argument that without separate "female institution building", (as Freedman (1979) coins it) women's transformed consciousness may take on the terms in which it is appropriated. The feminist scholarship in the late 1970's - early 1980's illustrates the extent to which those earlier concerns have been echoed in contemporary debates. It reveals the same determination to provide an academic context and knowledge which address the specific needs of women. In the current situation, the changed consciousness on the part of women has been sustained within the context of scholarship and practice, established by and for women, which addresses these concerns.

We also see in the Third Stage radical departures from previous work which are related to their commitment to build independent theories/methods, and involves in a broad sense, feminists' perceived need to structure an autonomous feminist community *within* the larger social context of the university. The existence of this community is evidenced on several counts. Feminists have encouraged the re-emergence of feminist networks across disciplines both informally and formally in channels such as faculty organizations, and associations, health collectives, status of women groups etc. In many universities women's centers, libraries and ad hoc committees have been formed among women faculty, as well as women students. The development of feminist institutional practices and feminist theories also suggest that energies lie in the direction of tightening a characteristically, feminist, organization through the introduction of counter forms of scholarship and pedagogy. In this manner, the work of feminists in the academic setting today is not so much a program of *reform* as it is a *revolutionary* process. Informed by the historical retrieval of women's encounters with educational institutions in the past, the dissent no longer sees the potentials of a reform-oriented strategy, based on male notions of "progress", "equality", and "amelioration". The hope offered by liberalism, pseudo-radicalism, civil libertarianism and other types of classic humanitarianism have been seen as a circumscribed politics or as a politic that offers women a proferred place in a patriarchal society. In short, feminist scholarship has reached that point where the angst is most acute: it now considers whether or not feminist scholarship can begin the process of rebuilding theories of social reality and if so, if that kind of process will survive within academic jurisdictions.

Finally, in their analyses of the private/public barriers, feminists have made connections between the ideology of the private/public split and women's subordination in all aspects of the university and, indeed, the society.

Feminists argue first that the physical, spatial separation of the two spheres, has been used ideologically to perpetuate women's oppression. A second aspect of the private/public split's critique has been to show that while the two spheres are considered distinct, women's experience of both reveals how the split is determined by patriarchal definitions of women's "proper" roles. In feminist work, attention has been given to the interconnections between the "private" and the "public", and the delineation of the interconnected process (in the university specifically) by which patriarchal ideology is worked in both the home and the workplace.

While internal disagreement continues to characterize contemporary debates about the use and role of the private/public dichotomy, within feminist scholarship there is growing agreement that it is an oppositional dualism which has been manipulated to ensure women's subordination in the home *and* in waged labor. Because women's experience has been circumscribed in both spaces, and because women's treatment in both has been a product of the ideology that holds them to the "private"; feminists challenge the analytical and structural distinction by insisting that the systematic connections between them not be obscured. I would add here that feminists do not reject all dualisms and in fact view some as helpful and necessary. Rather, the use of false dualisms or those constructed from a male perspective and which serve patriarchal interests are opposed by feminist epistomology; one such dualism has been the private/public split.

What can be observed nevertheless in the 1980's, are both encouraging and discouraging signs as one considers the status of academic women specifically and the position of women generally. The social parameters of the current period holds potential promise and potential problems. We must be wary then, when we suggest that the work of the present dissent has become more radical relative to its developments in theory. If we have learned from our history, we must understand that increased radicalism as a measure of historical change and as a benefactor of previous struggles in feminist scholarship. The gains and losses moreover, imply that the struggle which is so integral to feminists' interaction with academe, has not ended in the Third Stage. Rather, the struggle has merely shifted with its historical circumstance, and one of the distinguishable elements of that struggle has been the firm establishment of women's voices in academia. The in-roads which feminist research has made are far-reaching: in knowledge, by recreating it; in methodology by reworking it; in pedagogy by redefining it; in traditional institutional structure by rejecting it; in women's historical process by documenting and recapturing it.

These and other transformations wrought by *The Dissenting Feminist Academy*, take on added significance in light of the glaring obstacles which have hampered feminist work at every phase of its development. These obstacles have come from within the university as well as from outside.

Historically, the academy's resistance to feminism, like its resistance to feminist scholarship has been an inevitable consequence of the tensions between academic sites which work patriarchy and women's work in those sites which reject patriarchy. And historically, these tensions have been deliterious. Contemporary conditions make these same tensions no less real and no less inconsequential. The present project, which has seen the problems with and the incongruencies of, our political-philosophic inheritances, now faces the task of devising bodies of knowledge unencumbered by patriarchal persuasion and, at the same time, faces the decision of modelling an academic strategy after these independent theoretical creations. Knowing the work of higher education in keeping alive cultural notions of "womanhood", makes the task all the more frightening and the position of the dissent, all the more vulnerable. The task is an enormous one for which no other models exist. On one level, the struggle against the university's resistance to feminism has involved feminists in searching for a new knowledge bedeviled by the fact that they must live in a patriarchal society and work in patriarchal institutions like the university. The task of creating that knowledge becomes even more formidable in view of the fact that historically women have not been able to produce what has "counted" as knowledge (see Chapter two); they have been kept outside publishing processes (see Chapter three); and until recently, have not had their history documented or recorded (see Chapter four). Women's writings of their own and other women's oppression have been hidden in "his story". As a result, we have been unable to build on, and identity with, the experiences of women who lived before us. Feminists have been left to initiate the process of investigation and documentation without a sense of women's collective history as a source of identification.

Another, interrelated way in which the university's resistance has expressed itself, has been through the legitimization mechanisms which characterize and delineate the university as an academic institution, and through the sinecure procedures its members must adopt, in order to be "accepted" in the academic community. The ambivalence created through these practices and seen throughout the dissent's history, is reflected, for example, in feminist critiques of academic disciplines and their internal components.

Feminists have had to become knowledgeable about the university's discourse to challenge it. Perhaps the most ubiquitous paradox is the *language* we use to expose sexist ideology in knowledge practice and ultimately *language* itself. Language involves not only verbal communication, but, as Daly (1978; 1984) powerfully argues, encompasses our very way of conceptualizing reality and our very way of being. The language we *de-mystify*, must be conceptualized in ways which perpetuate its mystification. In order for that realization to be communicated, we have had to stand inside the processes by which discourse is made, to show just how and why those processes are wrong to women. In this sense, the dissent has suffered an existential angst, living inside and outside of what passes for, or is defined as, reality.

Similarly, much of the knowledge we produce "about", "for", and "by" women has been preframed, and, in our need for survival and legitimacy within the academy, that knowledge may be more "academic" in its form, content and structure than we would have it otherwise. But to the extent that the beginning and end points reveal and reflect women's *lived experience*, the academic legitimation allows for other women to see it, relate to it, and gain strength from it.

Beyond resistance inside academic structures, reaction to feminism from the larger society continues to grow. This backlash recently comes in the guise of the "New Right" moral majority. The "New Right" has seized the initiative at a time when crises in personal life have become a widespread central concern for numerous women. Economic openings for women, raised consciousness of their social and political possibilities and of course, the dramatic evolutions spurred specifically by feminists and through feminist work, have led to some extent to increased backlash, opposition, hostility and in its extreme form, violence.

It is not simply that feminists have scrutinized the nuclear family, the sexual division of labor and standards of "normative decency". The breakdown of marriages, the corresponding increase in the divorce rate and the high incidences of depression, drug and alchol addition and suicide have also given this backlash its opening. Much work remains to be done by the dissent to bring about changes in the legal, political, health and financial establishments. And much is left to do to work through the personal tensions of women's everyday lives. This point speaks to the question of how much energy should be spent, working out the barriers to women in an academic context. It also subtly points to the need to ask if too much time is not being spent *away* from securing ties with the larger grass roots feminist movement.

It seems safe to speculate that part of the dissent's energies must also lie in working to create the structural changes which will make the possibilities of its scholarship accessible to and real for all women taking into account the social class, racial, religious, and age considerations which draw boundaries around women's lives. Again, however, confronting the pervasiveness and tenacity of male dominance as it is embodied in the university, is much more difficult than the consciousness-raising and value change which must precede it. Both jobs are nevertheless, vital in the face of opposition and both are difficult. Broadly, reaction has ranged from petty remarks to outright hostility and violence. The attack on feminism from the "New Right" is not only strong, it is omnipresent: anti-abortion, anti-gay movements, as well as the deluge of articles, books, media propaganda espoucing misogyny, and "pro-family" religious movements represent a complex, well-financed effort to stop feminist work and destroy feminism. Within such a climate, it becomes imperative that feminists look to their history, which has served in more ways than one as a cautionary tale.

At this point in time, it is important that *The Dissenting Feminist Academy* look inward to the patterns it can discern from the historical moments its life. From the experiences of the First Stage, it appears fundamental that in addition to forging independent theories, feminists must also affirm the centrality of their own culture by refusing individual integration of the kind that undermined the dissent at the end of the First Stage. Separate support networks and female interest groups within universities *and* outside of universities are vitally needed and endemic to its active movement into the Fourth Stage. The history of feminist scholarship shows that the loss of ties with an active, solid, feminist community dislocates the feminist dissent, fragments its members and splinters its efforts. While some fragmentation is inevitable, larger splits have posed serious difficulties for feminism historically. Such an important lesson cannot be overlooked as the dissent moves toward the 1990's.

Theoretical gains for women in intellectual forums, have not necessarily meant practical gains for women in their everyday lives. The majority of poor are still women; their numbers are increasing. Awareness of the astonishingly high numbers of female children and women who experience incest and sexual violence does not in itself lead to decreases in the numbers, which in fact appear to be increasing. Women are battered; their health engineered by the male establishment. The compulsory clitoridectomy still in effect in some African provinces, manifests in North America in the mass mutilation of women's bodies - all in the name of institutionalized professional medicine. It is further apparent that feminists are increasingly acting on these issues, as the recognition grows that it is time to *act* on the political consciousness that feminist analyses have instilled through the study of interacting systems of oppression. Work on pornography, abortion, reproduction, contraception, sexuality and motherhood is in progress, though it is clear that greater cohesion is still needed between the work of feminists who are devoted mainly to activism and those whose work lies within the parameters of educational institutions.

Despite backlash, feminist scholarship continues to grow, but so too does the urgency of systematically working through the ideas embodied in its scholarship in order to survive financial cutbacks, and in order to work toward transforming academic structures. Again, history has shown that a simple increase in number of women in academic positions will not answer the problem; such of an increase must be accompanied by a willingness academic communities to self-examine its' values and its' structures.

With the strength of its historical legacy, current developments in feminist theory and feminist practice in academic systems are consistent with and a part of, the embellishment of feminist culture in those systems. The separatist project of reconstruction moreover, and the gradual movement towards it, suggests that feminists sense the need for an autonomous female sphere within an exclusionary male sphere. Developments in this direction suggest that the strength of feminists' vision lies less in the access to and incorporation of male-defined domains, and more in the concrete creation of alternative feminist institutions within those domains. The promise of equality through strict assimilation no longer holds the same promise, as we have seen the tentative nature of integrating on terms that women have not defined as their own.

B. Visions

This brief history of feminist ideas does make it clear that women's marginality in relation to the university, is a process with roots that lie deep inside the structure of higher education, itself historically influenced by norms and values of the wider society. It will clearly then, be a monumental task to change that structure.

But what of the university? The university has been an arena in which the dimensions of our culture have been measured, an environment for validating an elite at one period and for accommodating the emergence of a different class at another. It has been one of the places where we have been told who we are or who we are not. In this sense, it has been an important province.

But thinking about the university historically presents problems, particularly from a feminist perspective, and requires a willingness to accept ambiguity, and a certain unavoidable messiness. The discovery that we as women have been told who we are and are not, and that *what* we have been told is wrong, though touted as "the truth" is a difficult one, and a challenge to anyone who would view higher education with clarity. The pain of discovery goes further. Certainly the university cannot be understood without acknowledging all the elements that give it life - curricula, knowledge, teachers, students, courses, programs and its' mandate (sic). Also, the university is both structure and content. In exploring both, the stuff of which learning and becoming educated is made, we bump into questions of: what is learned?; what does it mean to become educated?; for whom do universities work? and; why does provision work as it does? Answering these questions requires some notion of what the university is expected to do, which has frequently not been the same for all people. And it is clear that the elements which give it life, - its structure and content, and the agenda of learning and becoming educated - have all been outside of women. The university has ignored, and ideologically construed respectively, that majority which it would call the "second sex", and it has done this with the gracious appeal of a psychiatrist who tells his deserted mother of seven, that a lobotomy is for "her own good".

The first point, to be noted then , is that the issue of women's relation to academe is not merely an educational one - a matter of curricula, texts, courses or classrooms. It is, rather, a profoundly moral one - at least from the ideological perspective of educators - and it has always been tied to questions of "the betterment of" or "the right to". The issue has involved, what administrators and earlier, philanthropists and reformers have made of educating women and how they have constituted, in women's educational provision, questions of family life, society's "morals", the sexual division of labor and motherhood. These points have always been considered in light of women's "access" and likewise, women's scholastic participation has always been an ineluctable question, coached in terms of how the family is affected, and ultimately settled in favor of the State. Benevolent motives to have women educated have spurred the question at intervals. But more frequently it has not. The universities have "hosted" women, and at times been more genuinely generous in what they have offered, while never losing sight of their more prestigious guest. This double-edgedness has made the university all the harder to prosecute and its work of education, all that much harder to indict. Education for women or higher education for women has not just been "granted" or "won", but has required a confrontation between the morals of false ideology and the resistance of constrained experiences. Women know this tension best, not because their experience has been the only one which has been denied by education, but because that education has so thoroughly appropriated, through its' denial and its' simultaneous perjury of their identities and self-definition. Their "otherness", their "social construction", their marginalization, pinges on their connection with the morality of the family, the moral fabric of the next generation, and the moral fibre of the young now. Quite a responsibility for one woman. It is more than the fact that the academy prescribes women's individual identities; through its knowledge, it disallows women having identities as *individuals* and worse, it effectively instills the kind of psychological guilt that squashes the pursuit of individual needs, when a few women have bravely broken the picket line.

I see the dissent I have described, as a pyscho-political response to that appropriations, and specifically, a response to the institutionalization of that appropriation. But the university has not just organized women and their identities in particular ways. It has needed and gotten the help of a discourse which sustains the sense of education's ameliorative posture, while establishing the "male" as the generic and it has done this in the name of "progress". The university after all, is an institution that has always taken great pride in the fact that it reflects the conscience of democratic liberalism. It's nineteenth century benevolent stance was perhaps more blatant, both in its intentions and its ideology, but the message it wants to give its public is the same. And indeed it must. But the liberal democracy it purports to represent and, the message it gives, have both been in the interests of the male gender. Even the roles it has laid out for men have been more comfortable, more powerful and more flexible. Moreover, they have been individual - for men. Finally, the message the university gives us has been mythical. Academe is imbued with "myth-addicts" and its platform tends therefore to be drawn up by "moral myth-makers" who saddle those under its jurisdiction with half-truths and falsehoods, destined to outlive their occasion and to have their cover blown. These myths are in their way "facts", but the central fact about them is that they are myths are must be treated as such. More than anything, *The Dissenting Feminist Academy* is an articulation and rejection of these myths. More than anything, it has historically-exposed the myth that "education is power" or at least the notion that exposure to knowledge is the panacea of oppression. It is a myth because it has not told women that the knowledge they have struggled to "know", is in itself oppressive, or that to be educated as women, is to be educated in a certain way. More than anything, this has been *The Dissenting Feminist Academy's* message.

The debate concerning feminists' separation from the university is one which will undoubtedly continue to tug at the dissent for some time to come, but will continue, undoubtedly, to force revitalization and inevitably renewal. In the meantime, and for those who work in universities, it is a reality that academe can be transformed, partially because of the tenacity of the dissent, and partially because of the nature of the university.

Stripped so far as possible of myth, universities are immensely complex living organisms, at intervals strikingly successful, at others, dull and inert, or tangled in tension and conflict. Tiresome and frustrating for those who experience it from within, and bafflingly incomprehensible to those who regard it from outside, academe remains full of promise, with flashes of brilliant fulfillment and longer stretches of tedious eclipse. Diverse in it human resources, (of which the dissent is a vital part) continuously throwing up new ideas which collide with deeply embedded beliefs, feelings and habits, academia has for decades been troubled by the difficulty of ensuring education for all, and maintaining "equality" for its lively dissenters, who create such incessant discomfort and stress for the settled status quo. The point that such boasted and mythical opportunities are not enough, and that the insights of uncomfortable women are among the academy's most precious, but wasted resources, is still a shockingly unbelievable concept to the complacent public, who feel they have been "damn liberal" to women and that for them to expect even more is unreasonable. The economic morality and reasonableness of women defining their own education, in terms they have set out is an integral component of the muddled, controversy about the future of higher education which is raging in North America today.

One of the objects of this book has been to show that the university's polity forms a larger and more essential part of women's history and life than is commonly supposed, and that to give more attention to it would be useful, while to go on neglecting it will cost us dear.

The modern university now seems more understandable, if only because its financial embarrassment has forced it to "hang its laundry" in public. Being more understandable, it carries with it potentially liberating influences. By contrast, the now obsolescent educational forms have been rigid and ardent. The need now is to look at what women require and want from education, to see it as a place to begin in all its human diversity, and to match it with a basically integrated but generously diversified and responsive new academy, not a *feminist* academy necessarily, though its philosophy would reflect the abolition of gender as an oppressive reality, but a more fully "human" academy.

Hard as it is to reflect that centuries ago, women were saying what we are saying now, what they are saying is not meant to speak of utopia, but to something which could happen here and soon. That is, the creation of a different type of academy which will be less constricted by the appeal of sexual selection. It would of course, be ludicrous to suggest that the transformations which need to be wrought, can occur without concomitant shifts in the posture of all institutions. But the changes have already begun and they are felt throughout the society.

In Chapter four, I described the range of issues affecting higher education in the 1970's and now. The litany of problems are familiar ones: inflation, fiscal constraints and budget deficits, a decline of the traditional applicant pool, reduced funding from all sources, loss of public confidence, rampant vocationalism, and the moribund state of the liberal arts. Relief from these interrelated pressures is obtainable by continuing to attract students and dollars and by stretching revenues as far as possible. This is, by and large, the prescription for survival for the majority of universities and colleges. And clearly, these difficulties will affect the different kind of academy I am talking about. But I believe such an academy can be created *within* these constraints and possibly, *because* of them. It could happen, not as a new prescription artificially imposed from outside, though the need will be to utilize the community around higher education, but as something which feminists see as possible and which a few educators have had it vaguely in mind to do some day.

But what of the barriers that have stubbornly persisted despite the social context of academe? In some respects the barriers in women's way have either been removed or reduced to more manageable proportions. Yet as some difficulties have lessened, others have worsened. Having our consciousness-raised and our research agenda replenished by feminism, has not always led to tension-free identities or to more fully integrated personal lives. Many women have lapsed into a muddle about who they are, what they want to do and how it might be done. The mainspring of this tension is the dialectical relation between women and institutions such as universities. Women have found a kind of self-conscious liberation and newly-found identity in the university, mainly through feminist scholarship, but its growth and good health have been jeopordized by the academic environment that gave it life. Because we cannot separate out, one form the other, the proportions which a different educational system takes on are astronomical. How does one or *can* one then, even begin to work through the spider web that is woven around the university? Surely piecemeal efforts at changing structure from inside will be just that - piecemeal. How can one begin to unlock academe from the fetters of its history? Surely such a task is impossible.

But it isn't though and the remainder of the book will be devoted to explaining why I believe it isn't. The first point to be made is that the academy *can be* transformed because it *must* be. At this point in time, it must respond to the growing discomfort people as a whole are feeling or risk extinction. A dependable preparation for life is not to be found in the knowledge we are given. As Woolf declared in her banishment of the "ivy league mentality", and as we have seen in this decade, education cannot be counted on, to make us as women, whole. At best, the mainstream curriculum will seem to instruct. What I am suggesting is that the curriculum is not simply misleading women about gender. It is not simply a failure on the part of academics to teach, or a mechanism by which educational systems perpetuate a sexual divide and, differentiate on the basis of cultural stereotypes. The university shares this quality with most of the institutions in our society. However, with the university, the level of conflict between what women feel are their identities, and what they are told are their identities, seems especially high. This is partly due to the espoused "equality" goal of academe. Its eccentricity, its hospitality to iconoclasm, and its sometimes four-star accommodations for radicalism have all contributed to the myth that it is just *the* place to "find oneself". Up until now, it has not been that kind of place for women. And as the opportunities we assumed were "ours" for the picking, wane under the crunch of economic forces, so too, does the belief by men *and* women, that higher education is worthwhile. Simply put, men and women are ready for new roles, some of which have been imposed by sheer necessity, and the university must be willing to respond to those needs. I think Betty Friedan (1981) is correct in saying that the consciousness evoked by the feminist movement, and the social changes which have resulted from that evolved consciousness, have left our society with a general overall awareness that grows daily. But the resultant confusion in women *and* men's minds about "what do we now" is still to be worked through. The reality of changed consciousness can no longer be ignored. It is an economic, political and social reality and the institutions which we live and work in, have little choice but to respond. Above all, education must respond. I think that feminist scholarship has offered a guide to that response not only because it has articulated the existence of women and the existence of gender construction in all facets of life, but also because it so centrally deals with those questions that are affecting all of our lives now.

The university can and must change because it has been exposed, and because it can no longer rely on myth. The reality of the grave problems it is now facing have dispelled our illusions of its grandeur. It's "fall from grace" could be its greatest "godsend". Feminism has engaged in this debunking and now is offering alternatives. It has done this by identifying the university's functions and by recognizing its workings. This identification in itself has come as a shock to many, but it has been a healthy one. Such bold movements in education deserve our attention. But in doing so, we must contend that universities have been a troubling phenomena for some time. And certainly it is the case that the initial shock of exposure has given way to intense re-evaluation. To many, including educators themselves, education systems have not been working: they have not helped to prepare people for employment; they have not guaranteed a quality life; they have not promoted equal opportunity despite the rhetoric and in short; they have done their job, but the job is no longer required or wanted. Seen in this light, the issue at hand, is not the validity of transformation, but the necessity of changing course and direction.

Another reason that the state of higher education must change, is that the increasing worries of the State that sanctions it are spilling over onto the rest of society. Crippling unemployment rates, and chronic financial crises have broken down the hope for education. Where once there was opportunity through gaining a university degree; today, there are no promises, guarantees or certainty that higher education will provide for the future. Women feel this, but so too do men who are experiencing the disjuncture between academic myth and personal reality. In light of these imperatives, it is doubtful that any university or college can reasonably afford to retain a laissez-faire approach.

There are come of the many problems, complexities and ambiguities which surround *The Dissenting Feminist Academy* and which sculpt the nature of the dissent. In light of these thickly tangled complexities, one could be tempted to forecast a pessimistic epilogue on the future of feminist scholarship and the future of women's higher education in general. With full acknowledgement of the pressure of convention to end on an optimistic note; I cannot help but conclude, that within the contradictions and within the barriers, *The Dissenting Feminist Academy* holds the best possible promise for women in academe today.

Whenever feminists precisely entered the Third Stage, they now see things they cannot "un-see". "Seeing" has led to explication. While intellectual and political analyses do not in themselves solve the contradiction between feminism and the university, feminist theories, for example, are a means by which feminists can bridge gaps left by disciplines. Feminist theories are also tools with which one can avoid the pitfalls of false analysis. On this level, feminist theory may prove vital in struggling our way into the future.

Feminists can either give up in disgust on the frustrations of working in the academy or live with the sacrifices and compromises necessary to survive there. If feminists segregate politically and intellectually, they run the risk of losing the momentum that has taken a century to develop. The other alternative, of never being completely comfortable in an institution which considers women's "proper" place in the home is equally painful, tiring, and frustrating. Both alternatives run far from representing ideal solutions, but for those who believe that gradual changes in policy will cumulatively being larger transformation, the reality of academic survival, involves confronting the paradox of that survival, head on, within the university.

Practically speaking, institutional struggle means working to wrest some control from those in power so that feminists can stay alive and retain a feminist vision of social change. It also means supporting other women inside. In the long run, it means fighting in the university as *part* of the struggle to change society. Women are in all major institutions and are deeply affected by them, but women in turn, have re-defined aspects of those institutions as part of their larger struggle for social transformation. As it stands now, we cannot propose rupturing women's lives from existing structures because in doing so we assume that women do no (even in their subordination) constitute parts of those structures and most certainly they do.

Our evidence suggests that the university is very much enmeshed in the larger processes through which patriarchy is maintained, but as that structure is not isolated from the feminist dissent; it is not purely conspiratorial or successful in its attempts at domination. The contradiction is acutely focussed at the point where just as the university has needed the consent (to some degree) of the dissent to sustain its stability, the dissent has needed the academy to legitimate its critique within academic boundaries. Feminists have shown us that the major obstacles to women, imposed by the university, are different manifestations of the same disease. The three particular barriers I have concentrated on do not *always* work in harmony, but they do work in concert to produce a "reality" of femininity that is in fact mythical. But the analyses of this interconnection have only been made possible by feminists' direct and immediate experience of those barriers — first hand. Concurrently, the emergence of feminist inside academe structures within an academic context suggests that while tied to larger social processes, the university is also a social institution with its own inherent contradictions — its ideological underpinnings fluctuate and can be contested and resisted. In fact, the university's continual work at maintaining barriers to women, and feminists' continual work at breaking them down, makes it evident that while feminism and the academy are contradictions in terms, feminism can survive and thrive there enough to bring about profound dramatic changes. Whether it be the progressive, social evolutionary reformism of the nineteenth century, or the liberal pseudo-radicalism of the 60's; the fact remains that such discursive inheritances have *never* been women's; *never* made it clear why women are oppressed; *never* purported to speak to issues of sexual inequality and; never offered the kinds of answers women have always asked. It is a reality as well, that our agenda, and the theoretical character that has shaped it, has always been contoured by the academic setting in which we work. This in itself has been, perhaps, the ultimate contradiction, but the point is that the development of novel, intellectual paradigms have already begun and there is no turning back.

The present dissent is at a critical juncture. In its move forward, it has two vital resources. First, the stalemate feminists' felt they had reached in their work in the late 70's and early 80's, has given impetus to the re-examination of the very frameworks upon which all knowledge rests. The possibilities are just beginning to be visible, because the thrust of all research until recently, has been done from within the paradigms that are finally being called into question on a scale never before imagined.

Feminist issues have never before reached such large groups of people and even the backlash against feminism is a reflection of its power, a reminder of its implications. Feminist scholarship is not merely rethinking the academic world; it is also illustrating the wrongness of the academy's lack of perspective through a confident and solid argument for the necessity of women's perspective. I think that from the perspective of those feminists in the Fourth Stage, it will be clear that feminism produced the major paradigm shift of the twentieth century.

The second resource exists in the commitment of the dissent to embellish its autonomous feminist culture *vis a vis* feminist theory. True to its interpretation of women's experiential specificity, the current dissent's advocacy of separate struggle stems from more than a commitment to direct action. It develops from an historical analysis of the *particular* nature of women's experience, on women's *own terms*.

Arguably at least, these resources challenge male dominance, empower women rather than patriarchies, and hold the potential of moving toward (they do not get there) a new academy, and necessarily, a new relation between life and scholarship. These resources also give feminists themselves reason to be optimistic about the dissent's future in the face of opposition and hostility. While the precise extent of the transformation is clearly impossible to "measure", it is clear that the dissent of feminist scholarship will be the twentieth century's most important dissent.

In the meantime, feminist work continues to contribute to modelling that future transformed academy, whose one redeeming feature will be, a structure and organization that will make feminist dissent unnecessary.

NOTES

Chapter 1   Introduction

1. The private/public dichotomy has been used by feminists, as a conceptual device to explain how women and men's lives are shaped by the social institutions of a particular society. As a culturally-specific organizing principle, feminist research shows that the modern division between the public and the private spheres "is seen as serving to reinforce patriarchy by circumscribing women within the domestic realm, or, insofar as they are drawn into the public domain, relegating them to menial and low status positions" (Pierson and Prentice, 1982, p. 106).

2. Of the bibliographic compilations I have seen on the historical participation of women in academe, Rosalind Rosenberg (1982) provides an extremely comprehensive, cross-disciplinary reference section in her book, *Beyond Separate Spheres: The Intellectual Roots of Modern Feminism*. New Haven: Yale University. For a more general, Canadian guide to documented sources of women's historical experience see Jeanne L'Esperance's *The Widening sphere: women in Canada, 1870-1940*. Light and Strong-Boag's (1980) bibliography of Canadian women's history is also excellent.

3. There are various assertions about the ideas, actions and "beginnings" of contemporary feminism. Many of these assertions have taken on the air of received "truths". In the attempt to distinguish the three time periods, I have used the term "First Stage" to denote what I have perceived as a first major influx of feminists in North American universities. It should not therefore be confused with previous usages. Similarly, the second time period has been coined the Second Stage and, the third period the Third Stage. These also should not be equated with previous usages, regarding the emergence of feminist thought. Finally, I do not mean to imply (in the use of "First Stage") that these periods represent the only or first emergence of feminist ideas. As Spender (1982) makes clear, feminists' ideas have existed in the thinking of women from Aphra Behn (1670) on. .sp 11n

Chapter 2   The First Stage

1. The term "social moralism", is not to be found in the litera-ture of this period, nor to my knowledge, is it used in contemporary historical works. I use it advisedly here, to refer to the inclination on the part of reform movements, to equate the necessity of improv-ing social conditions, with the need to improve the moral spirits of the sexes through hygiene, preventative medicine and sexual absti-nence. Such social appeals to repress all forms of licentiousness, had deep roots in the religious doctrines of Protestantism.

2. Arnot (1893) in her article *A Cloud Over Co-Education*, (in S. Walker and L. Barton (eds.) *Gender Class and Education*, Falmer Press, 1983, pp. 69-93) argues that the class interests of higher edu-cation have always shaped the form that gender has taken. "The history of class reproduction, of class relations and bourgeois priv-elege includes, not as a marginal but as an integral feature, family forms (of the norms of heterosexuality, female virginity, and mar-riage) as well as particular concepts of masculinity and femininity which held together the gender division of labour within paid em-ployment and family life." (p. 88).

3. The origins of the nineteenth century women's movement were similar to those of the mid twentieth century women's move-ment (Actor, 1974). Like its twentieth-century successor, the nine-teenth-century women's movement was born inside other social movements. Just as the activism of women within the civil rights and anti-war movements prompted them to challenge accepted no-tions of gender relationships in the 1960's, so female participation in the anti-slavery and evangelical movements of the early nine-teenth century caused women to oppose the gender restrictions that limited the extent of their social activism. Participation in each of these movements carried women beyond the parameters of their *own class* and into a consideration of their rights and responsibili-ties as *women* and as *human beings*.

4. These themes echo throughout nineteenth century femi-nism. As Strong-Boag (1980) argues, most feminists during this time sought to create within themselves a "more perfect womanhood". "This effort at human improvement is an essential ingredient in the feminism of this time" (p. viii). Such perfection would mean that women could participate in the public sphere of politics and em-ployment as well as in the private sphere of the home and family. It did not necessitate the challenge that such divisions were in

themselves a problem. Nor did it undermine the notion that women were by *nature* meant to stay in the private sphere. Very often this was the case because women on the whole accepted the doctrine that perpetuated separate spheres and women themselves frequently contributed to entrenching the ideology.

5. For example, within changes of curricula, the new universities came to delineate social reform and pedagogy as the "special" domains of women and later the rise of Home Economics and Child Development further attested to what was considered appropriate study for women.

6. Again, we must keep in mind that the university itself was in the midst of highly complex construction, and because of this, was not as yet, in the "business" of *social maintenance*. According to Touraine (1974), the university could not aid in the perpetuation of an established order (like previous academies had) because the society was in a state of flux as was the new research academy itself.

7. This aim, as we have seen, was in keeping with the overall reformist character of the academy. The economic imperatives of making the universities financially viable also prompted the "concern" to open its doors to people of different backgrounds, particularly at a time when tuition resources were badly needed.

8. The German word meaning "apprentice" or "pupil".

9. Many feminists, especially those who conducted research in the social sciences, argued that women and men were essentially equal and similar. One group who opposed this vehemently were feminists who worked outside the university. For them, to challenge the belief that women were innately unique was to undermine the premises and ideological underpinnings of the suffrage movement and protective legislation for women (Berkin and Norton, 1979; Klein, 1979). This is not to suggest that clean-cut divisions can be made without mention of the complex overlapping of the goals of feminists. In the case of law provisions, industry coverage, and protective legislation, Kessler-Harris (1982) suggests in another vein, that evidences of the split come from the fact that women who worked in factories gave alternate support and rejection to these issues. She also shows that organized efforts to legislate boundaries on working conditions became gender-linked only after the courts struck down a series of hard-won laws. Other groups found that protective legislation served their needs as well. Middle class fe-

male reformers (according to Kessler-Harris), acting out the imperatives of the "cult of true womanhood", denounced especially the physical and moral conditions and consequences of women's participation in non-domestic production through work at home and in the factory. To relieve the female worker's problems of hygiene, health and morality became the objective of these women, while the model of bourgeois conjugal and domestic life, was the solution proposed. It also represented the reverse side of laws and policies which limited and regulated the paid labour of women and children.

Chapter 3   The Second Stage

1. My purpose here is not to describe a specific sector of intellectual and scientific activity in North America; it is, rather, to understand the changing place of the university at a time when a type of production is developing in which science and technology play a central role.

2. For a fuller examination of the tensions that universities' experienced in the 1960's, see Chapter five in Touraine (1974).

3. This development is discussed specifically in the context of feminist politics in the late 1960's in Miles (1982).

4. In section two of Bunch and Pollack's (1983) *Learning Our Way*, the authors cover the pitfalls and "highs", of feminist efforts to create autonomous environments for education. Some of the problems that such institutions face are: "decisions must be made at the very outset about how much, or whether, to pay teachers, how much to charge students, and where to get money to start. Another difficult question for alternatives is who the students will be: where will they be recruited, who will be interested in what issues, who will be able to afford what costs)and what kinds of class and race biases does that assume), what will the incentives be to attend if there is no degree involved, and so on. Perhaps the most difficult problem that alternatives face is the issue of money and how to survive without relinquishing their political goals" (p. xiv).

5. The equation of women with deviation and men as the norm has been discovered in virtually every discipline. See for example: Acker (1973), Barrett (1979), Benston (1982), Bernard (1973a), Blier (1984), Wood Sherif (1977), Clark (1979), Clark and Lange (1979), Cohen (1982), Cott and Pleck (1979), Spender (1981a).

6. Wood Sherif (1977) points out that Mary Calkins, Helen

Thompson Woolley and Leta S. Hollingworth vocally expounded on the problem of bias in psychological research. Thompson Woolley "had critically exposed the bias in sex-difference research, dismissing much of it as drivel, in 1903 and 1910" (p. 95). As I have discussed in Chapter two, she and other women like her were keenly aware of the actualities of sex bias, and in answer to Wood Sherif's question: "If the possibility and the existence of sexual bias was recognized by the turn of the century why and how could academic...psychology continue to perpetuate its myths up to the present?"; I would suggest that the reasons lie within the historical role and function of psychology in supporting sexual divisions.

7. In some ways Parlee actually appears to be fishing for "the" way forward in feminist research. Her own uneasiness about psychology of/for women is reflected here: "... but the underlying conceptual framework, as reflected in the formulation of problems and operationalization of terms, remains fundamentally unchallenged. ... The question of what we may actually know (in the scientific sense) about women's behaviour and experience seems less important at this stage than knowing what investigators have tried to find out, what questions they have not asked, and how their methods and procedures have helped or hindered the development of a psychology that is relevant to women" (1975, p. 121).

8. The phrase "themes of relevance" was used by Smith (1977) in her brilliant article, "A Sociology for Women". For an elaboration of this also see her article, "The Ideological Practice of Sociology" in *Catalyst*, 8, 1974b.

9. Worsley (1970) depicts sociology as that study, primarily concerned with the analysis of social structure. Social structure has in turn been defined as encompassing certain "core" organizations such as work, economics, politics and education etc. Feminist sociologists have recognized that beyond the restrictions of these topics, there is the tendency of male sociologist to, "focus their attention on social institutions and settings in which males predominate, such as the occupational, political and legal systems. Where women were noticed at all, it was their connection to men that counted" (Mackie, 1983, p. 13).

10. In his brilliant study, Willinsky (1984) is careful to explicate how the significance of Standard English is formulated in social class *and* in gender terms. The significance of gender distinctions, he argues, belies the work of schools in formulating female

and male language differences.

Chapter 4   The Third Stage

1. Friedenberg (1984) has fashioned this notion of the school's custodial function. His classic work, (1970) *The Vanishing Adolescent* explores the dimensions of this concept as it has been used by the school to construct the experience of adolescence.

2. See Symons and Page's (1984) study, *Some Questions of Balance: Human Resources, Higher Education and Canadian Studies.*

3. In Nova Scotia for example, such a plan was initiated in 1980 by the Department of Education, to consolidate the various Education faculties across seventeen universities and colleges in this province. The impetus for the merger came from the financial breakdown of those faculties and declining enrollments.

4. See Chapter one in Symons and Page (1984).

5. See Chapter four in Touraine (1974).

6. See Symons and Page (1984).

7. Rich was one of those who decided that academic life was irreconcilable with her feminism and other radical commitments (Rich, 1976). Freeman (1979) says that the backlash which manifested in financial cutbacks resulted in many feminists leaving the university. The "decision" to leave was not always a decision but rather a move with no alternative.

8. The growth of these specialties is not a ubiquitous evolution. This point is referring to the Canadian context specifically.

9. This theme is examined in more detail in Connelly's (1978) book, *Last Hired, First Fired.*

10. See Chapter nine in Symons and Page (1984).

11. As a further illustration of these processes, Vickers and Adams' (1977) monograph also reveals the profound effect that academic women's role has had and is having on society and government in general, and on the status of women in particular. The data they present suggests that the current low rate of participation among women in higher education is an important factor contributing to the overall inability of Canadian women to gain a status and condition equal to that of men. The authors try to demonstrate that the academic profession is little different from other professions insofar as the university has played a vital role in supporting the existing socio-economic and political arrangements in the society.

However, "we can expect the members of the academic profession to take some action to put their own house in order. Because academics are dependent on government and, to a lesser degree, benefactors and student fees, as a group, they are the most susceptible to outside pressure and intervention with regard to the status of women" (p. 141). While the university alone cannot be blamed for the plight of women, the authors clearly indicate those areas in which the universities can, and must be held accountable. One area reflects deliberate discrimination on the part of the Faculty. Other areas are accessability, the sexual division of labor, and management practices.

12. See Symons and Page (1984). Also, CAUT has a Standing Committee on the Status of Women and reports regularly in the *Bulletin*. The Association of Universities and Colleges of Canada (AUCC) set up a committee in 1971 to examine the *Report of the Royal Commission on the Status of Women* and one of the outcomes of this was a basic statistical survey by Jane Adams (Psychology, University of Calgary) entitled, "A Profile of Women in Canadian Universities" (p. 69). These are all Canada-wide bodies that have produced national reports which, dismally, show a consistent subordinate position for women on Canadian campuses.

13. For example, in Canada: The Canadian Women's Studies Association; The Canadian Research Institute for the Advancement of Women. For example, in the United States: The National Women's Studies Association; The National Organization of Women. In terms of separate forms of communication the growth of this research has become widely available in books and articles in Canada, the United States and Britain. In Canada, see for example: *Atlantis*; *Fireweed*; *Our Generation*; *Canadian Women's Studies*; Resources for Feminist Research; *The Journal of Educational Thought*. In the United States, see for example: *Signs: A Journal of Women in Culture and Society*; *Feminist Studies, International Women's Studies Quarterly*; *Women's Studies*; *International Journal of Women's Studies*; *Feminist Teacher*; *Frontiers*. In Britain, see for example: *Feminist Review*; *Women and Education*; *British Journal of Sociology of Education*.

14. See Keohane, Rosaldo and Gelpi's (1982) *Feminist Theory*.

15. The feminist critique of knowledge as "neutral" and "objective" is not confined to the social sciences. The critique extends to the natural sciences as discussed in the work of Benston (1982)

and more recently, in the work of Blier (1984) and Hubbard (1984). Further, the problems found in social science offer a direct and necessary parallel with the discrepancies and contradictions in the natural sciences. The blueprint of social science has been taken from the natural sciences and thus evidences the biases in both.

16. See Bartky's (1977) article "Toward a Phenomenology of Feminist Consciousness" in M. Vetterling-Braggin et al. (eds.) *Feminism and Philosophy*, New Jersey: Littlefield, Adams, 1977, pp. 22-35.

Chapter 5   Conclusion

1. See Wood Sherif's (1979) article "Bias in Psychology" for a discussion of Mary Putnam Jacobi's work.

2. See Virginia Woolf's (1938) *Three Guineas*, Hogarth Press, London: and *A Room of One's Own*, London: Hogarth Press, 1928. Also, Dale Spender (1983), in her book *Women of Ideas* examines Woolf's ideas about women's educational (See specifically pp. 672-681).

3. See Woolf (1928; 1938).

4. For a review of Elsie Clews Parsons contribution to *The Dissenting Feminist Academy*, see Rosenberg (1975; 1979; 1982).

REFERENCES

Abel, Elizabeth and Abel, Emily (eds.). *The Signs Reader: Women, Gender and Scholarship.* Chicago: University of Chicago Press, 1983.

Acker, Joan. "Women and Social Stratification: A Case of Intellectual Sexism." *American Journal of Sociology,* 78, 4 (1973), 936-945.

Acker, S. and Warren Piper, D. (eds.). *Is Higher Education Fair to Women?* Great Britain: SRHE and NFER-Nelson, 1984.

Acton, Janice, et al. (eds.). *Women at Work, Ontario, 1850-1930.* Toronto: Canadian Women's Educational Press, 1974.

Adam, June. "A Profile of Women in Canadian Universities." A Statistical Survey Commissioned by the Association of Universities and Colleges of Canada, University of Calgary, 1971.

Ahlum, Carol and Howe, Florence. *The New Guide to Female Studies No. 1.* Pittsburgh: KNOW, Inc., 1971.

Allen, S. et al. (eds.). *Conditions of Illusion.* Leeds: Feminist Books, 1974.

Allen, Christine Garside. "Conceptual History as a Methodology for Women's Studies." *McGill Journal of Education,* 10, (1975), 49-58.

Antler, Joyce. "Feminism as a Life-Process: The Life and Career of Lucy Sprague Mitchell." *Feminist Studies,* 7, 1 (1981), 78-86.

Apple, Michael. *Ideology and Curriculum.* Boston: Routledge and Kegan Paul, 1979.

Ardener, Shirley. *Perceiving Women.* London: Malaby Press, 1975.

Armstrong, Pat and Armstrong, Hugh. *The Double Ghetto: Canadian Women and Their Segregated Work.* Toronto: McClelland and Stewart, 1978.

Arnot, Madeleine. "Culture and Political Economy: Dual Perspectives in the Sociology of Women's Education" *Educational Analysis.* 3, 1 (1981), 97-116.

Arnot, M. "A Cloud Over Co-Education: An Analysis of the Forms of Transmission of Class and Gender Relations." In S. Walker and L. Barton (eds.), *Gender, Class and Education.* New York: Falmer Press, 1983, pp. 69-91.

Association of Universities and Colleges of Canada. *Report of the Royal Commission on the Status of Women, 1971.* Ottawa: 1971.

Association of Universities and Colleges of Canada. *The Status of Women in Canadian Universities, 1975.* Ottawa: 1975.

Association of Universities and Colleges of Canada. *Rank and Salary Differentials in the 1970's: A Comparison of Male and Female Full-time Teachers in Canadian Universities and Colleges.* Ottawa, 1979.

Astin, Helen et al. (eds). *Women: A Bibliography of Their Education and Careers.* Washington, D.C.: Human Service Press, 1971.

Astin, Helen. *The Woman Doctorate in America: Origins, Career, and Family.* New York: Russell Sage Foundation, 1977.

Astin, H.S. and Bayer, A.E. "Sex Discrimination in Academe." In A. Rossi and A. Calderwood (eds.), *Academic Women on the Move.* New York: Russell Sage Foundation, 1973, pp. 333-356.

Astin, H.S. and Hirsch, W. *The Higher Education of Women: Essays in Honor of Rosemary Parks.* New York: Praeger Press, 1978.

Atwood, Margaret. *Women on Women.* Toronto: York University Press, 1978.

Banks, O. *The Sociology of Education.* London: Batsford, 1976.

Bardwick, Judith (ed.). *Readings on the Psychology of Women.* New York: Harper and Row, 1972.

Bardwick, Judith and Douvan, E. "Ambivalence: The Socialization of Women." In V. Gornick and B.K. Moran (eds.), *Woman in Sexist Society.* New York: Basic Books, 1971, pp. 147-159.

Barrett, Michele. *Women's Oppression Today: Problems in Marxist Theory.* London: Verso Editions, 1979.

Bartky, Sandra Lee. "Toward a Phenomenology of Feminist Consciousness." M. Braggin-Vetterling et al. (eds), *Feminism and Philosophy.* Totowa: Littlefield Adams & Co., 1977, pp. 22-37.

Barton, L. et al. (eds). *Schooling, Ideology and the Curriculum.* Barcombe: Falmer Press, 1981.

Baxter, Annette. "Women Studies and American Studies: The Uses of Interdisciplinarity." *American Quarterly,* 26, 4, (1974), 433-439.

Beard, Mary. *Women as a Force in History.* New York: MacMillan, 1946.

Benston, Margaret. "The Political Economy of Women's Liberation." In N. Glazer and H.Y. Waehrer (eds.), *Woman in a Man-Made World.* Chicago: Rand McNally, 1977, pp. 216-225.

Benston, Margaret. "Feminism and the Critique of Scientific Method." In A. Miles and G. Finn (eds.), *Feminism in Canada: From Pressure to Politics*. Montreal: Black Rose Books, 1982, pp. 47-66.

Berkin, C. and Norton, M.B. (eds.). *A History of Women in America*. Boston: Houghton Mifflin, 1979.

Bernard, Jessie. *Academic Women*. New York: New American Library, 1964.

Bernard, Jessie. "My Forth Revolution." In J. Huber (ed.), *Changing Women in a Changing Society*. Chicago: University of Chicago Press, 1973a, pp. 11-29.

Bernard, Jessie. *The Future of Marriage*. New York: Bantam Books, 1973b.

Bernard, Jessie. *The Future of Motherhood*. New York: Penguin Books, 1974.

Bernard, Jessie. "Afterword." In J. Sherman and E. Torton Beck (eds.), *The Prism of Sex: Essays in the Sociology of Knowledge*. Madison: University of Wisconsin Press, 1979, pp. 267-275.

Bernard, Jessie. "Foreword: A Quiet Revolution." In E.C. Snyder (ed.), *The Study of Women: Enlarging Perspectives of Social Reality*. New York: Harper and Row, 1979.

Bernard, Jessie. "Women." S. Ruth (ed.), *Issues in Feminism: A First Course in Women's Studies*. Boston: Houghton Mifflin, 1980, pp. 26-40.

Bernstein, Basil. *Class, Codes and Control: Towards a Theory of Educational Transmission*. London: Routledge and Kegan Paul, 1977.

Berry, Margaret C. *Women in Educational Administration: A Book of Readings*. Washington, D.C.: National Association for Women Deans, Administrators and Counsellors, 1979.

Bienen, L., Ostriker, A. and Ostriker, J. "Sex Discrimination in the Universities." In N. Glazer and H.Y. Waehrer (eds.), *Woman in a Man-Made World*. Chicago: Rand McNally, 1977, pp. 370-377.

Bird, Caroline. *Born Female*. New York: David McKay, 1968.

Bishop, S. and Weinzweig, M. (eds.). *Philosophy and Women*. California: Wadsworth Publishing, 1979.

Blier, Ruth. *Science and Gender: A Critique of Biology and Its Theories on Women*. New York: Pergamon Press, 1984.

Bloch, R.H. "Untangling the Roots of Modern Sex Roles: A Survey of Four Centuries of Change." *Signs*, 4, 2 (1978), 237-252.

Bowles, S. and Gintis, H. *Schooling in Capitalist America.* New York: Basic Books, 1976.

Bowles, G. and Duelli-Klein, R. (eds.). *Theories of Women's Studies.* Berkeley: Women's Studies, University of California, Berkeley, 1980.

Boxer, J. Marilyn. "For and About Women: The Theory and Practice of Women's Studies in the United States." In N.O. Keohane, et al. (eds.), *Feminist Theory: A Critique of Ideology.* Chicago: University of Chicago Press, 1982, pp. 237-271.

Braverman, Harry. *Labour and Monopoly Capital: The Degradation of Work in the Twentieth Century.* New York: Monthly Review Press, 1974.

Bridenthatl, R. and Koonz, C. (eds.). *Becoming Visible: Women in European History.* Boston: Houghton Mifflin, 1977.

Brodie, Janice. "Book Review: Women, Power and Politics." *Atlantis.* 7, 2 (1982), 153-154.

Braverman, I.K. et al. "Sex-Role Stereotypes and Clinical Judgements of Mental Health." *Journal of Consulting and Clinical Psychology*, 34, (1970), 1-7

Brubacher, J. and Rudy, W. *Higher Education in Transition: An American History, 1636-1956.* New York: Harper and Row, 1958.

Bryant, M. and Briggs, A. *The Unexpected Revolution: A Study in the History of the Education of Women and Girls in the Nineteenth Century.* London: University of London Institute of Education, 1979.

Bunch, Charlotte. "Not for Lesbians Only." *Quest: A Feminist Quarterly*, 3, 2 (1975).

Bunch, Charlotte. "Beyond Either/Or: Feminist Options." *Quest: A Feminist Quarterly, 3, 1 (1977), 2-17.*

Burnstyn, Joan. "Educators' response to scientific and medical studies of women in England 1860 - 1900." In S. Acker and D. Warren Piper (eds.), *Is Higher Education Fair to Women?* Great Britain: SRHE & NFER Nelson, 1984, pp. 65-81.

CAUT Bulletin. *Women and Pensions.* ACPU. December, 1978.

Canadian Association of University Teachers. *Tabulations of Data and Partial Comment on 1979 Status of Women Survey.* Ottawa, 1979.

Carlson, Rae. "Where is the Person in Personality Research?" *Psy-*

chological Bulletin, 75, (1971), 203-219.

Carlson, Rae. "Understanding Women: Implications for Personality Theory and Research." *Journal of Social Issues*, 28, 2 (1972), 17-32.

Carlson, E.R. and Carlson, R. "Male and Female Subjects in Personality Research." *Journal of Abnormal and Social Psychology*, 61, (1960), 482-483.

Carroll, B.A. (ed.). *Liberating Women's History: Theoretical and Critical Essays*. Urbana, Illinois: University of Illinois Press, 1976.

Centra, J.A. *Women, Men, and the Doctorate*. Princeton, N.J.: Educational Testing Service, 1974.

Chapman, J.R. and Gates, M. (eds.). *The Victimization of Women*. Beverley Hills: Sage Publications, 1978.

Chesler, Phyllis. *Women and Madness*. Garden City, New York: Doubleday, 1972.

Chetwynd, J. and Harnett, C. *The Sex Role System*. London: Routledge and Kegan Paul, 1978.

Chicago, Judy. *Through the Flower: My Struggles as a Woman Artist*. Garden City, New York: Doubleday, 1975.

Chisholm, Lynn and Woodward, Dianna. "The Experience of Women Graduates in the Labour Market." In R. Deem (eds.), *Schooling for Women's Work*. London: Routledge and Kegan Paul, 1980, pp. 162-177.

Chodorow, Nancy. *The Reproduction of Mothering: Psychoanalysis and the Sociology of Gender*. California: University of Berkeley Press, 1978.

Chodorow, Nancy. "Feminism and Difference: Gender Relations and Difference in Psychoanalytic Perspective." *Socialist Review*, 9, 4 (1979), 51-70.

Chomsky, Noam. "The Responsibility of Intellectuals." In T. Roszak (ed.), *The Dissenting Academy*. New York: Pantheon, 1967, pp. 254-298.

Clark, Lorenne. "Women and Locke: Who Owns the Apples in the Garden of Eden?" In L. Clark and L. Lange (eds.), *The Sexism of Social and Political Theory*. Toronto: University of Toronto Press, 1979, pp. 16-40.

Clark, L.M. and Lange, L. (eds.). *The Sexism of Social and Political Theory: Women and Reproduction from Plato to Nietzsche*. Toronto: University of Toronto Press, 1979.

Cohen, Marjorie. "The Problem of Studying Economic Man." In A. Miles and B. Finn (eds.), *Feminism in Canada: From Pressure to Politics.* Montreal: Black Rose Books, 1982, pp. 89-101.

Cole, J. *Women's Place in the Scientific Community.* New York: John Wiley, 1977.

Collier, J.F. and Rosaldo, Z.M. "Politics and Gender in Simple Societies." In S.B. Ortner and H. Whitehead (eds.), *Sexual Meanings: The Cultural Construction of Gender and Sexuality.* Cambridge: Cambridge University Press, 1981, pp. 275-329.

Collins, Jean. "The Feminist Press." Editors of *Change* Magazine, *Women on Campus.* New York: Change Magazine, 1975, pp. 102-109.

Comer, Lee. "Women and Class: The Question of Women and Class." *Women's Studies International Quarterly*, 1, 3 (1978), 165-174.

Connelly, Pat. *Last Hired, First Fired.* Toronto: The Women's Press, 1978.

Cooper, T. and Cooper, F. *The Roots of American Feminist Thought.* New York: Random House, 1973.

Cott, Nancy. *The Bonds of Womanhood.* New Haven: Yale University Press, 1977.

Cott, Nancy and Pleck, Elizabeth, H. (eds.). *A Heritage of Her Own.* New York: Simon and Schuster, 1979.

Culley, M. and Portuges, C. *Gendered Subjects: The Dynamics of Feminist Teaching.* London: Routledge and Kegan Paul, 1985.

Curti, M. (ed.). *American Scholarship in the Twentieth Century.* New York: Russell and Russell, 1967.

Daly, Mary. *The Church and the Second Sex.* New York: Harper and Row, 1968.

Daly, Mary. *Beyond God the Father: Toward a Philosophy of Women's Liberation.* Boston: Beacon Press, 1973.

Daly, Mary. *The Church and the Second Sex: With a New Feminist Postchristian Introduction by the Author.* New York: Harper Colophon, 1975.

Daly, Mary. *Gyn/Ecology: The Metaethics of Radical Feminism.* Boston: Beacon Press, 1978.

Daly, Mary. *Pure Lust: Elemental Feminist Philosophy.* Boston: Beacon Press, 1984.

Daniels, A.K. "Feminist perspective in sociological research." In M. Millman and R.M. Kanter (eds.), *Another Voice: Feminist Perspectives on Social Life and Social Science.* New York: Anchor Press/Doubleday, 1975, pp. 340-380.

Daniels, A.K. "A Survey of Research Concerns on Women's Issues." A Project on the Status and Education of Women, Washington, D.C.: Association of American Colleges, 1972.

Darwin, Charles. *On the Origin of Species by Means of Natural Selection, or Preservation of Favoured Races in the Struggle for Life.* London: Murray, 1859.

David, Miriam. *The State, the Family and Education.* London: Routledge and Kegan Paul, 1978.

Davis, A.B. *Bibliography on Women.* New York: Science History Publications, 1974.

Davis, E.G. *The First Sex.* Baltimore, Maryland: Penguin Books, 1971.

Davin, Anna. "Imperialism and Motherhood." *History Workshop*, 5, (1978), 9-65.

Deaux, K. *The Behaviour of Women and Men.* Monterey, California: Brooks/Cole, 1976.

deBeauvoir, Simone. *The Second Sex.* Trans. by H.M. Parshley. New York: Alfred, A. Knops, 1953.

Deem, Rosemary. *Women and Schooling.* London: Routledge and Kegan Paul, 1978.

Deem, Rosemary. (ed.). *Schooling for Women's Work.* London: Routledge and Kegan Paul, 1980.

Deem, Rosemary. "Gender, Patriarchy and Class in the Popular Education of Women." In S. Walker and L. Barton (eds.), *Gender Class and Education.* New York: Falmer Press, 1983, pp. 107-123.

Department of Education Division of School Services. *Statistical Report for the Minister's Committee on Women's Issues in Education.* University of Alberta, 1980.

Dinnerstein, Dorothy. *The Mermaid and the Minotaur: Sexual Arrangements and Human Malaise.* New York: Harper and Row, 1976.

Dixon, Marlene. "Why Women's Liberation?" *Ramparts*, (1969), 57-63.

Douglas, Ann. *The Feminization of American Culture.* New York: Random House, 1977.

DuBois, Ellen. "The Radicalism of the Woman Suffrage Movement: Notes Toward the Reconstruction of Nineteenth-Century Feminism." *Feminist Studies*, 3, 1/2 (1975), 63-71.

Duelli Klein, Renate. "The Intellectual Necessity for Women's Studies." In S. Acker and D. Warren Piper (eds.), *Is Higher Education Fair to Women?* Great Britain: SRHE and NFER-Nelson, 1984, pp. 220-242.

Dye, Nancy Schrom. "Feminism or Unionism? The New York Women's Trade Union League and the Labor Movement." *Feminist Studies*, 3, 1/2 (1975), 111-126.

Dye, Nancy Schrom. "Clio's American Daughters: Male History, Female Reality." In J. Sherman and E. Beck (eds.), *The Prism of Sex: Essays in the Sociology of Knowledge.* Madison: University of Wisconsin Press, 1977, pp. 9-31.

Dyhouse, Carol. "Storming the Citadel or Storm in a tea cup? The Entry of Women into Higher Education 1860-1920." In S. Acker and D. Warren Piper (eds.), *Is Higher Education Fair to Women?* Great Britain: SRHE & NFER Nelson, 1984, pp. 51-65.

Eichler, Margrit. "Discussion Forum: the Future Direction of Women's Studies." *Canadian Newsletter of Research on Women,* 5, 3 (1976), 10-12.

Eichler, Margrit. "Review Essay: Sociology of Feminist Research in Canada." *Signs,* 3, 2 (1977), 409-422.

Eichler, Margrit. "The Origin of Sex Inequality: A Comparison and Critique of Different Theories and Their Implications for Social Policy." *Women's Studies International Quarterly,* 2, 3 (1979), 329-346.

Eichler, Margrit. *The Double Standard.* London: Croom Helm, 1980.

Eichler, Margrit. "Sexism in Research and Policy Implications." Unpublished paper presented to the Conference of the Canadian Research Institute for the Advancement of Women, Ottawa November 1982.

Eisenstein, Zillah (ed.). *Capitalist Patriarchy and the Case for Socialist Feminism.* New York: Monthly Review Press, 1978.

Eliot, C.W. *Stanford University: The First Twenty-Five Years.* Stanford: Stanford University Press. 1937.

Epstein, C.F. "Encountering the Male Establishment: Sex-Status Limits on Women's Careers in the Professions." *American Journal of Sociology,* 75, 6 (1970), 965-982.

Epstein, C.F. *Woman's Place.* California: University of Berkeley Press, 1971.

Erikson, Erik. *Childhood in Society.* Chicago: University of Chicago Press, 1963.

Erkut, Samru. "Issues of Educational Equity in the 1980's: Multiple Perspectives." In P.J. Perun (ed.), *The Undergraduate Woman: Issues in Educational Equity.* Mass.: Lexington Books, 1982, pp. 399-419.

Fee, Elizabeth. "The Sexual Politics of Victorian Anthropology." In M. Hartman and L. Banner (eds.), *Clio's Consciousness Raised: New Perspectives on the History of Women.* New York: Harper and Row, 1974, pp. 86-103.

Fee, Elizabeth. "Science and the Woman Problem: Historical Perspective." In M. Teitelbaum, (ed.), *Sex Differences: Social and Biological Perspectives.* New York: Anchor Press, 1976, pp. 6-28.

Fee, Elizabeth. "A Feminist Critique of Scientific Objectivity." *Science for the People*, 14, 5-8 (1982), 30-33.

Feldman, S. *The Rights of Women.* Rochelle Park, N.J.: Hayden, 1974.

Fenemma, Elizabeth. "Women and Girls in the Public Schools: Defeat or Liberation?" In J. Roberts (ed.), *Beyond Intellectual Sexism: A New Woman, A New Reality.* New York: David MacKay, 1976, pp. 343-352.

Ferguson, K.E. *Self, Society and Womanhood.* Westport, Connecticut: Greenwood Press, 1980.

Ferguson, Janice. "The Equation Doesn't Balance." *Canadian Women's Studies*, 5, 4 (1984), 24-26.

Fingard, Judith. "They had a tough row to hoe." *Dalhousie Alumni Magazine.* 1, 2 (1985), 27-30.

Finn, Geraldine. "On the Oppression of Women in Philosophy — Or, Whatever Happened to Objectivity?" In A. Miles and G. Finn (eds.), *Feminism in Canada: From Pressure to Politics.* Montreal: Black Rose Books, 1982, pp. 145-173.

Finn, Geraldine. "Why Althusser Killed His Wife." *Canadian Forum.* (1981), 28-29.

Firestone, Shulamith. *The Dialectic of Sex: The Case for Feminist Revolution.* New York: William Morrow, 1970.

Fishman, P. "Interaction: The Work Women Do." *Journal of Social Problems.* 26, (1978), 63-86.

Flax, Jane. "Do Feminists Need Marxism?" *Quest: A Feminist Quarterly*, 3,1 (1976), 114-130.

Flax, Jane. "Political Philosophy and the Patriarchal Unconsciousness: A Psychoanalytic Perspective on Epistemology and Metaphysic." In S. Harding and M. Hintikka (eds.), *Discovering Reality: Feminist Perspectives on Epistemology, Metaphysics, Methodology, and Philosophy of Science*. Boston: D. Reidel Publishing, 1983, pp. 245-281.

Frazier, N. and Sadker, M. *Sexism in School and Society*. New York: Harper and Row, 1973.

Franklin, Ursula. "Editorial." *Canadian Women's Studies*, 5, 4 (1984), 2.

Freedman, Estelle. "Separatism as Strategy: Female Institution Building and American Feminism, 1870-1930." *Feminist Studies*, 5, 3 (1979), 109-120.

Freeman, J. "Women's Liberation and Its Impact on the Campus." *Liberal Education*, 57, 4 (1971), 468-478.

Freeman, J. "Women on the Move: Roots of Revolt." In A. Rossi and A. Calderwood (eds.), *Academic Women on the Move*. New York: Russell Sage Foundation, 1973, pp. 1-32.

Freeman, J. *The Politics of Women's Liberation*. New York: David McKay, 1975.

Freeman, J. (ed.). *Women: A Feminist Perspective*. Palo Alto, California: Mayfield Publishers, 1979.

Freeman, J. "The Women's Liberation Movement: Its Origins, Organizations, Activities, and Ideas." In J. Freeman (ed.), *Women: A Feminist Perspective*. Palo Alto, California: Mayfield Pub. Co., 1979, pp. 448-460.

Freize, I.H., Parsons, J.E., Johnson, P.B., Buble, D. and Zellman, G.L. (eds.). *Women and Sex Roles*. New York: W.W. Norton and Co., 1978.

Friedan, Betty. *The Feminine Mystique*. New York: Dell Books, 1963.

Friedan, Betty. *The Second Stage*. New York: Summit Books, 1981.

Friedenberg, Edgar. *The Vanishing Adolescent*. New York: Dell Pub., 2nd Edition, 1970.

Friedenberg, Edgar. *Coming of Age in America*. New York: Vintage Books, 1963.

Friedenberg, Edgar. *The Dignity of Youth and other Ativisms*. Boston: Beacon Press, 1965.

Furner, Mary O. *Advocacy and Objectivity: A Crisis in the Professionalization of American Social Science, 1865-1905*. Lexington: The University Press of Kentucky, 1975.

Furniss, W.T. and Graham Alberg P. (eds.). *Women in Higher*

Education. Washington, D.C.: American Council on Education, 1974.

Gagnon, Madeleine. "My Body in Writing." In A. Miles and G. Finn (eds.), *Feminism in Canada: From Pressure to Politics*. Montreal: Black Rose Books, 1982, pp. 269-282.

Gamarnikow, E. et al. (eds.). *Gender, Class and Work*. London: Heinemann, 1983.

Gamarnikow, Eva, and Morgan, D., and Purvis, J. and Taylorson, D. *The Public and the Private*. London: Heinemann, 1983.

Gardiner, Jean. "Women's Domestic Labor." *New Left Review*, 89, (1975), 47-58.

Garfinkel, Harold. *Studies in Ethnomethodology*. Englewood Cliffs, N.J.: Prentice Hall, 1967.

Garskoff, M. (ed.). *Roles Women Play: Readings Towards Women's Liberation*. Belmont Cal.: Brooks/Cole, 1971.

Gaskell, Jane. "Equal Educational Opportunity for Women." In J.D. Wilson (ed.), *Canadian Education in the 1980's*. Calgary: Detselig Enterprises, 1981, pp. 173-193.

Gaskell, Jane. "Reproduction of Family Life: Perspectives of Male and Female Adolescents." Paper presented at the Annual Meetings of the Canadian Sociology and Anthropology Association, Ottawa, June 1982.

Gillett, Margaret. "Sexism and Higher Education." *Atlantis*, 1, 1 (1975), 68-81.

Gillett, Margaret. *We Walked Very Warily: A History of Women at McGill*. Montreal: Eden Press Women's Publication, 1982.

Gilligan, Carol. *In a Different Voice: Psychological Theory and Women's Development*. Cambridge, Mass.: Harvard University Press, 1982.

Glazer, Nona and Waehrer, Helen Youngelson. (eds.). *Women in a Man-Made World*. Chicago: Rand McNally, 1977.

Godard, Barbara. "Translating and Sexual Difference." *Resources for Feminist Research*, 13, 3, (1984), 26.

Gorden, A.D., Buble, M.J. and Dye, N.S. "The Problem of Women's History." In B.A. Carroll (ed.), *Liberating Women's History: Theoretical and Critical Essays*. Urbana, Illinois: University of Illinois Press, 1976, pp. 75-92.

Gordon, M. et al. (eds.). *The American Family in Social-Historical Perspective*. New York: St. Martin's Press, 1971.

Gordon, Linda. *Women's Body, Women's Right*. Baltimore: Penguin

Books, 1976.

Gornick, Vivian. "Women as Outsider." In V. Gornick and B. Moran (eds.), *Women in Sexist Society: Studies in Power and Powerlessness.* New York: New American Library, 1971, pp. 70-84.

Gornick, V. And Moran, B. (eds.). *Women in Sexist Society: Studies in Power and Powerlessness.* New York: New American Library, 1971.

Gould, Carol and Wartofsky, Marx. (eds.). *Women and Philosophy: Toward a Theory of Liberation.* New York: Capricorn Books, 1976.

Graham, Patricia Albjerg. "Women in Academe." In C. Safilios-Rothschild (ed.), *Toward a Sociology of Women.* Lexington, Mass.: Xerox College Pub., 1972, pp. 261-276.

Graham, Patricia Albjerg. "Expansion and Exclusion: A History of Women In Higher Education." *Signs*, 3, (1978), 759-773.

Greenglass, Esther. *A World of Difference: Gender Roles in Perspective.* Toronto: John Wiley, 1982.

Griffin, S. "The Way of All Ideology." *Signs*, 7, 3 (1982), 641-660.

Grim, Patricia. "Sexism and Semantics." In M. Vetterling-Braggin, F. Elliston and J. English (eds.), *Feminism and Philosophy.* Totowa, New Jersey: Littlefield, Adams and Co., 1977, pp. 109-116.

Groake, L. "Beyond Affirmative Action." *Atlantis*, 9, 1 (1983), 13-24.

Group for Equal Rights at MacMaster. *The Status of Women at McMaster University.* Ontario: McMaster University, 1971.

Gruchow, Nancy. "Discrimination: Women Charge Universities, Colleges With Bias." *Science*, 168, 3931 (1970), 559-561.

Halliwell, J.E. *Career Profiles of University Research Fellows.* Natural Sciences and Engineering Research Council. Ottawa, Ontario and Report to the Alberta Conference on Women in Science, Engineering, and Technology, Panel on Grantsmanship. Edmonton. May 12, 1984.

Hanlin, O. and Hanlin, M. *The American College and American Culture: Socialization as a Function of Higher Education.* New York: McGraw Hill, 1970.

Haraway, Donna. "Animal Sociology and a Natural Economy of the Body Politic." *Signs*, 4, 2 (1978), 21-60.

Haraway, Donna. "The Biological Enterprise: Sex, Mind and Profit From Human Engineering to Sociobiology." *Radical History*

Review, 20, 1979, 206-237.

Harding, Sandra. "Why Has the Sex/Gender System Become Visible Only Now?" In S. Harding and M. Hintikka (eds.), *Discovering Reality*. Boston: D. Reidel Publishing, 1983, pp. 311-324.

Harding, S. and Hintikka, M. (eds.). *Discovering Reality: Feminist Perspectives on Epistemology, Metaphysics, Methodology, and Philosophy of Science*. Boston: D. Reidel Publishing, 1983.

Harris, A.S. "The Second Sex in Academe." *American Association of University Professors Bulletin*, 56, 1970, 283-295.

Harris, A.S. "The Second Sex in Academe." J. Stacey et al. (eds.), *And Jill Came Tumbling After: Sexism in American Education*. New York: Dell Publishing, 1974, pp. 293-316.

Hartman, M. and Banner, L.W. (eds.). *Clio's Consciousness Raised: New Perspectives on the History of Women*. New York: Harper and Row, 1974.

Hartmann, Heidi. "The Family as the Locus of Gender, Class and Political Struggle: The Example of Housework." *Signs*, 6, 3 (1981), 366-394.

Hartmann, Heidi. "The Unhappy Marriage of Marxism and Feminism: Towards a More Progressive Union." In L. Sargent (ed.), *Women and Revolution*. Boston: South End Press, 1981, pp. 1-44.

Hartsock, Nancy. "The Feminist Standpoint: Developing the Ground for a Specifically Feminist Historical Materialism." In S. Harding and M. Hintikka (eds.), *Discovering Reality*. Boston: D. Reidel Publishing, 1983, pp. 283-310.

Hartsock, Nancy. "Fundamental Feminism: Process and Perspective." *Quest*, 2, 2 (1979), 46-63.

Hartsock, Nancy. "Feminist Theory and the Development of Revolutionary Strategy." In Z. Eisenstein (ed.), *Capitalist Patriarchy and the Case for Socialist Feminism*. New York: Monthly Review Press, 1978, pp. 56-77.

Haskell, Thomas. *The Emergence of Professional Social Science: The American Social Science Association and the Nineteenth-Century Crisis of Authority*. Urbana: University of Illinois Press, 1977.

Hawkins, Ruth. "The Odds Against Women." Editors of *Change* Magazine *Women on Campus*. New York: Change Magazine, 1975, pp. 28-34.

Hein, H. "Women and Science: Fitting Men to Think About Nature." *International Journal of Women's Studies*, 4, (1981), 369-377.

Held, Virginia. "Marx, Sex, and the Transformation of Society." In S. Bishop and M. Weinzweig (eds.), *Philosophy and Women*. California: Wadsworth Publishing, 1979, pp. 159-163.

Helson, Ravenna. "The Changing Image of the Career Woman." *Journal of Social Issues*, 28, (1972), 33-46.

Henley, Nancy. "Power, Sex and Non-Verbal Communication." In B. Throne and N. Henley (eds.), *Language and Sex: Difference and Dominance*. Rowley, Mass.: Newbury House, 1975, pp. 184-202.

Henley, Nancy. *Body Politics*. New Jersey: Prentice Hall, 1977.

Henley, Nancy. "Assertiveness Training: Making the Political Personal." Paper written for the annual meetings of the Society for the Study of Social Problems, Boston, Harvard University, May 1979.

Herndon, James. *How to Survive in Your Native Land*. New York: Simon and Schuster, 1971.

Hickerson, Nathaniel. *Education For Alienation*. New York: W. W. Norton, 1966.

Hintikka, M.B. and Hintikka, J. "How Can Language Be Sexist?" In S. Harding and M. Hintikka (eds.), *Discovering Reality*. Boston: D. Reidel Publishing, 1983, pp. 139-148.

Hochschild, Arlie Russell. "A Review of Sex Role Research." In J. Huber (ed.), *Changing Women in a Changing Society*. Chicago: University of Chicago Press, 1973, pp. 249-267.

Hochschild, Arlie Russell. "Inside the Clockwork of Male Careers." F. Howe (ed.), *Women and the Power to Change*. New York: McGraw-Hill, 1975, pp. 47-80.

Hole, J. and Levine, E. *The Rebirth of Feminism*. New York: Quadrangle Books, 1971.

Hole, J. and Levine, E. "The First Feminists." In J. Freeman (ed.), *Women: A Feminist Perspective*. Palo Alto, California: Mayfield Publishing, 1979, pp. 436-447.

Holt, John. *How Children Fail*. New York: Delta, 1967.

Holt, John. *How Children Learn*. New York: Delta, 1968.

Hopkins, Elaine. "Unemployed! An Academic Woman's Saga." Editors of *Change* Magazine, *Women on Campus*. New York: Change Magazine, 1975, pp. 140-151.

Hopkins, Nancy. "The High Price of Success in Science." *Radcliffe Quarterly*, 62, (1976), 16-18.

Horner, Matina. "Femininity and Successful Achievement: A Basic

Inconsistency." In M.H. Garskof (ed.), *Roles Women Play: Readings Towards Women's Liberation.* Belmont, Cal.: Brooks/Cole, 1971, pp. 97-122.

Horner, Matina. "Toward an Understanding of Achievement-Related Conflicts in Women." *Journal of Social Issues,* 28, 2 (1972), 157-175.

Horning, Lilli S. "Issues of Educational Equity in the 1980's: Multiple Perspectives." In P.J. Perun (ed.), *the Undergraduate Woman: Issues in Education Equity.* Mass.: Lexington Books, 1982, pp. 399-419.

Howe, Florence (ed.). *Women and the Power to Change.* New York: McGraw-Hill, 1975.

Howe, Florence. "Women and the Power to Change." In F. Howe (ed.), *Women and the Power to Change.* New York: McGraw Hill, 1975, pp. 127-171.

Howe, Florence. *Female Studies II.* Pittsburgh: KNOW, Inc., 1970.

Howe, Florence. "Report on the First Women's Studies Evaluation Conference." *women's Studies Newsletter,* 3, (1974), 4.

Howe, Florence. "Toward Women's Studies in the Eightees" *Woman's Studies Newsletter,* 8, 1 (1980), 2.

Howe, Florence. "Seven Years Later: Women's Studies Programs in 1976." Washington: National Advisory Council on Women's Education Program, 1977.

Howe, F. and Attlum, C. "Women's Studies and Social Change." In A. Rossi and A. Calderwood (eds.), *Academic Women on the Move.* New York: Russell Sage, 1973, pp. 393-423.

Howe, F. and Lauter, P. "The Impact of Women's Studies on the Campus and the Disciplines." *Women's Studies Monograph Series.* (Washington, D.C.:), U.S. Department of Health Education and Welfare, N.I.E.T., 1980, p. 4.

Howell, Mary. "Can We Be Feminists and Professionals?" *Women's Studies International Quarterly,* 2, 1 (1979), 1-8.

Hubbard, Ruth, et al. (eds.). *Women Look At Biology Looking at Women.* Cambridge, Mass.: Schenkman Publishing, 1979.

Hubbard, Ruth. "Have Only Men Evolved?" In S. Harding and M. Hintikka (eds.), *Discovering Reality.* Boston: D. Reidel Publishing, 1983, pp. 45-69.

Huber, Joan (ed.). *Women in a Changing Society.* Chicago: University of Chicago Press, 1973.

Huber, Joan. "Sociology." *Signs,* 1, (1976), 685-697.

Hughes, H. *Consciousness and Society: The Re-orientation of European Social Thought.* New York: Vintage Books, 1977.

Hughes, Patricia. "Fighting the Good Fight: Separation or Integration?" In A. Miles and G. Finn (eds.), *Feminism in Canada: From Pressure to Politics.* Montreal: Black Rose Books, 1982, pp. 283-297.

Hughes, Patricia. "Towards the Development of Feminist Theory." *Atlantis*, 16, (1979), 16-28.

Hunter, Virginia. "Women and the Class Question." *Canadian Forum*, (1974), 39-40.

Hurn, J. Christopher. *The Limits and Possibilities of Schooling: An Introduction to the Sociology of Education.* Boston: Allyn and Bacon, 1978.

Hymes, Dell H. *Pidginization and Creolization of Languages.* Cambridge, Mass.: Cambridge University Press, 1972.

Illich, Ivan. *Deschooling Society.* Boston: Beacon, 1970.

Jacobi Putnam, Mary. *The Question of Rest for Women during Menstruation.* New York, 1877.

James, Selma. *Women, the Unions and Work.* Bristol: Falling Wall Press, 1972.

Janeway, Elizabeth. *Man's World: Women's Place: A Study in Social Mythology.* New York: Delta, 1971.

Janeway, Elizabeth. "Women on Campus: The Unfinished Liberation." Editors of *Change* Magazine *Women on Campus.* New York: Change Magazine, 1975, pp. 10-27.

Janeway, Elizabeth. "Man's World, Women's Place." In S. Ruth and S. Tobias (eds.), *Issues in Feminism: A First Course in Women's Studies.* Boston: Houghton Mifflin, 1980, pp. 236-246.

Kahn, Diana Grossman. "Interdisciplinary Studies and Women's Studies: Questioning Answers and Creating Questions", In B. Reed (ed.), *The Structure of Knowledge: A Feminist Perspective: Proceedings of the Fourth Annual Great Lakes Colleges Association Women's Studies Conference.* Ann Arbor, Mich.: Great Lakes Colleges Association Women's Studies Program, 1979, pp. 20-24.

Kahn, A. and Jean, P. "Integration and Elimination or Separation and Redefinition: The Future of the Psychology of Women." *Signs*, 8, 4 (1983), 659-671.

Kanter, R.M. "Women and the Structure of Organizations: Explorations in Theory and Behaviour." In M. Millman and R.M.

Kanter (eds.), *Another Voice*. New York: Anchor Press/Doubleday, 1975, pp. 34-74.

Karabel, J. and Halsey, A. (eds.). *Power and Ideology in Education*. New York: Oxford University Press, 1977.

Kealey, Linda. "Introduction." In J. Acton et. al. (eds.), *Women at Work, Ontario, 1850-1930*. Toronto: Canadian Women's Educational Press, 1974, pp. 1-11.

Keller, Evelyn Fox. "The Cognitive Repression in Contemporary Physics." *American Journal of Physics*, 47, (1979), 718-721.

Keller, Evelyn Fox. "Feminism and Science." In E. Abel and E.K. Abel (eds.), *The Signs Reader: Women, Gender and Scholarship*. Chicago: University of Chicago Press, 1983, pp. 109-122.

Keller, Evelyn Fox. "Gender and Science." In S. Harding and M. Hintikka (eds.), *Discovering Reality*. Boston: D. Reidel Publishing, 1983, pp. 187-205.

Kelly-Gadol, Joan. "The Social Relation of the Sexes: methodological Implications of Women's History." *Signs*, 1, 4, (1976), 809-824.

Kelly-Gadol, Joan. "Did Women Have a Renaissance?" In R. Bridenthatl and C. Koonz (eds.), *Becoming Visible: Women in European History*. Boston: Houghton Mifflin, 1977.

Kelly-Gadol, Joan. "The Social Relation of the Sexes: Methodological Implications of Women's History." In E. Abel and E. Abel (eds.), *The Signs Reader*. Chicago: University of Chicago Press, 1983, pp. 11-25.

Keohane, N., Rosaldo, Z.M. and Gelpi, C.B. (eds.). *Feminist Theory: A Critique of Ideology*. Chicago: University of Chicago Press, 1982.

Kersey, Shirley Nelson. *Classics in the Education of Girls and Women*. Methuchen, N.J.: Scarecrow Press, 1981.

Kessler-Harris, Alice. *Out to Work: A History of Wage-Earning Women in the United States*. New York: Oxford University Press, 1982.

King, J. and Scott, M. (eds.). *Images of Women in the Media*. London: Virago Press, 1977.

Klein, Viola. *The Feminine Character*. Urbana: University of Illinois Press, 1971.

Klein, Viola. "Feminism: The Historical Background." In J. Freeman (ed.), *Women: A Feminist Perspective*. Palo Alto., Cal.:

Mayfield Publishing, 1979, pp. 419-435.

Knudsin, R.B. (ed.). *Women and Success: The Anatomy of Achievement.* New York: William Morrow, 1974.

Kohlstedt, Sally Gregory. "In From the Periphery: American Women in Science, 1830-1880." *Signs,* 4, 1 (1978), 81-96.

Komisar, Lucy. *The New Feminism.* New York: Warner Publishing, 1971.

Kramarae, Chris and Thorne, Barrie and Henley, Nancy. (eds.). *Language, Gender and Society.* Rowley, Mass.: Newbury House, 1983.

Kramer, C. "Women's Speech: Separate But Unequal?" In B. Thorne and N. Henley (eds.), *Language and Sex: Difference and Dominance.* Rowley, Mass.: Newbury House, 1975, 43-56.

Kuhn, A. and Wolpe, A.M. (eds.). *Feminism and Materialism.* London: Routledge and Kegan Paul, 1978.

Ladd, F.C. "Issues of Education Equity in the 1980's: Multiple Perspective." In P.J. Perun (ed.), *The Undergraduate Woman: Issues in Educational Equity.* Mass.: Lexington Books, 1982, pp. 399-419.

Lahey, Kathleen. "Book Review: Feminist Theorists: Three Centuries of Women's Intellectual Tradition." *Resources for Feminist Research,* 13,2 (1984).

Laidlaw, Toni. "Concepts of Femininity, 1880-1930: Reflections of Cultural Attitudes in Psychological Theories." Unpublished doctoral dissertation, University of Alberta, Edmonton, 1978.

Lakoff, R. "Language and Woman's Place." *Language in Society,* 2, (1973), 45-80.

Lakoff, R. *Language and Woman's Place.* New York: Harper and Row, 1975.

Lange, Lynda. "Reproduction in Democratic Theory." In W. Shea and J. King-Farlow (eds.), *Contemporary Issues in Political Philosophy.* New York: Science History Publications, 1976, pp. 131-146.

Lange, Lynda. "Rousseau: Women and the General Will." In L. Clark and L. Lange (eds.), *The Sexism of Social and Political Theory.* Toronto: University of Toronto Press, 1979, pp. 41-52.

Lange, Lynda. "Woman is Not a Rational Animal: On Aristotle's Biology of Reproduction". In S. Harding and M. Hintikka (eds.), *Discovering Reality.* Boston: D. Reidel Publishing, 1983, pp. 1-15.

Langland, E. and Gove, W. *A Feminist Perspective in the Academy: The Difference It Makes.* Chicago: University of Chicago Press, 1981.

Leach, William. *True Love and Perfect Union: Feminist Reform of Sex and Society.* New York: Harper, 1980.

Leiter, K. *A Primer of Ethnomethodology.* New York: Oxford University Press, 1980.

Lerner, Gerda. "Placing Women in History: Definitions and Challenges." *Feminist Studies*, 3, 1-2, (1975), 5-15.

Lerner, Gerda. "New Approaches to the Study of Women in American History." In B.A. Carroll (ed.), *Liberating Women History: Theoretical and Critical Essays.* Urbana, Illinois: University of Illinois Press, 1976, pp. 349-356.

Lerner, Gerda. *The Female Experience: An American Documentary.* Indianapolis: Bob-Merrill, 1977.

Levine, Helen. "The Personal is Political: Feminism and the Helping Professions." A. Miles and G. Finn (eds.), *Feminism in Canada: From Pressure to Politics.* Montreal: Black Rose Books, 1982, pp. 175-209.

Light, Beth and Prentice, Alison. (eds.). *Pioneer and Gentle Women of British North America.* Toronto: New Hogtown Press, 1980.

Lips, Hilary. "Women and Power: Psychology's Search for New Directions." *Atlantis*, 5, 1 (1979), 1-13.

Lips, Hilary. *Women, Men and the Psychology of Power.* New Jersey: Prentice-Hall, 1981.

Lips, H. and Colwill, N.L. (eds.). *The Psychology of Sex Differences.* New Jersey: Prentice-Hall, 1978.

Lips, J. and Colwill, N.L. "The Paradox of Power." In H. Lips and N.L. Colwill (eds.), *The Psychology of Sex Differences.* New Jersey: Prentice-Hall, 1978.

Lofland, L.H. "The 'Thereness' of Women: A Selective Review of Urban Sociology." In M. Millman and R.M. Kanter (eds.), *Another Voice.* New York: Anchor Press/Doubleday, 1975, pp. 144-170.

Lopata, Helen Z. *Occupation Housewife.* New York: Oxford University Press, 1971.

Lopata, Helene A. "Review Essay: Sociology." *Signs*, 2, 1 (1976), 165-176.

Lowe, M. and Hubbard, R. (eds.). *Woman's Nature: Rationalizations of Inequality.* New York: Pergamon Press, 1983.

Lown, Judy. "Not So Much a Factory, More a Form of Patriarchy Gender and Class During Industrialization." In E. Gamarnikow et al. (eds.), *Gender Class and Work*. London: Heinemann, 1983, pp. 28-45.

Lundberg, Norma. "How Can We Dismantle the Master's House?" *Resources for Feminist Research*, 13, 3 (1984).

Maccoby, E. *The Development of Sex Differences*. Stanford: Stanford University Press, 1966.

Maccoby, E. and Jacklin, N.C. *The Psychology of Sex Differences*. Stanford: Stanford University Press, 1974.

MacDonald, Madeleine. "Curriculum and Cultural Reproduction", *E202*. Milton Keynes: Open University Press, 1977.

MacDonald, Madeleine. "Socio-Cultural Reproduction and Women's Education." In R. Deem (ed.), *Schooling for Women's Work*. London: Routledge and Kegan Paul, 1980, pp. 13-26.

MacDonald, Madeleine. "Schooling and the Reproduction of Class and Gender Relations." L. Barton et al. (eds.), *Schooling, Ideology and the Curriculum*. Barcombe: Falmer Press, 1981, pp. 29-49.

Mackie, Marlene. *Exploring Gender Relations: A Canadian Perspective*. Toronto: Butterworth, 1983.

MacKinnon, Catherine. "Feminism, Marxism, Method, and the State: An Agenda for Theory." *Signs*, 7, 1 (1982), 515-544.

MacKinnon, Catherine. "Feminism, Marxism, Method, and State: Toward Feminist Jurisprudence." *Signs*, 8, 4 (1983), 635-658.

Malmo, Cheryl. "Beyond the Other: Identifying Problems in Feminist Research." Unpublished paper, 1978.

Malmo, Cheryl. "Women's Experience as Women: Meaning and Context, Volume 1." Unpublished Ph.D. dissertation, University of Alberta, 1983.

Marcil-Lacoste, Louise. "The Trivialization of the Notion of Equality." In S. Harding and M. Hintikka (eds.), *Discovering Reality*. Boston: D. Reidel Publishing, 1983, pp. 121-137.

Marcuse, Herbert. *An essay on Liberation*. Boston: Beacon Press, 1969.

Marcuse, Herbert. *Counterrevolution and Revolt*. Boston: Beacon Press, 1972.

Martin, D. "Battered Women: Society's Problem." In J.R. Chapman and M. Gates (eds.), *The Victimization of Women*. Beverley Hills: Sage Publications, 1978, pp. 111-141.

Martyna, Wendy. "Beyond the He/Man Approach: The Case for Nonsexist Language." *Signs*, 5, 3 (1980), 482-493.

McRobbie, Angela. "Working Class Girls and the Culture of Femininity." *Women's Students Groups*. Birmingham: CCCS, 1978.

Mead, Margaret. *Blackberry Winter*. New York: Pocket Books, 1972.

Mednick, M., Tangri, S.S. and Hoffman, L. (eds.). *Women and Achievement: Social and Motivational Analyses*. Washington, D.C.: Hemisphere Press, 1975.

Mednick, S. and Tangri, S. "The New Social Psychological Perspectives on Women." *Journal of Social Issues*, 28, 2 (1972), 1-16.

Mednick, S. and Weissman, H. "The Psychology of Women: Selected Topics." *Annual Review of Psychology*, 12, (1975), 1-18.

Miles, Angela. "Ideological Hegemony in Political Discourse: Women's Specificity and Equality." A. Miles and G. Finn (eds.), *Feminism in Canada*. Montreal: Black Rose Books, 1982, pp. 213-227.

Miles, Angela. "Dissolving the Hyphen: From Socialist Feminism to Feminist Feminism." *Atlantis*, 9, 2 (1984), 77-94.

Miles, A. and Finn, G. (eds.). *Feminism in Canada: From Pressure to Politics*. Montreal: Black Rose Books, 1982.

Miles, A. and O'Brien, M. "Editorial" *Resources for Feminist Research*, 8, 1 (1979).

Miller, J.B. *Psychoanalysis and Women*. Harmondsworth: Penguin Books, 1974.

Miller, J.B. *Toward a New Psychology of Women*. Boston: Beacon Press, 1976.

Miller, J.L. "Women: The Evolving Consciousness". *Journal of Curriculum Theorizing*, 2, 1 (1980), 28-46.

Miller, C. and Swift, K. *Words and Women: New Language in New Times*. New York: Anchor Press Doubleday, 1977.

Miller, C. and Swift, K. *The Handbook of Nonsexist Writing: For Writers, Editors and Speakers*. New York: Barnes and Noble Books, 1980.

Millett, Kate. *Sexual Politics*. New York: Equinox Books/ Avon, 1970.

Millman, Marcia. "She Did It All For Love: A Feminist View of the Sociology of Deviance." In M. Millman and R.M. Kanter (eds.), *Another Voice*. New York: Anchor Press/Doubleday, 1975, pp. 251-279.

Millman, M. and Kanter, R.M. (eds.). *Another Voice: Feminist Per-*

spective on Social Life and Social Science. New York: Anchor Press/Doubleday, 1975.

Ministry of Colleges and Universities. *A Report on the Status of Women in Ontario Universities.* Toronto, 1982.

Mitchell, Juliet. *Women's Estate.* New York: Pantheon Books, 1971.

Mitchell, Juliet. *Psychoanalysis and Feminism.* New York: Vintage Books, 1975.

Mitchell, Juliet. "Women: The Longest Revolution." In N. Glazer and H.Y. Waehrer (eds.), *Woman in a Man-Made World.* Chicago: Rand McNally, 1977, pp. 169-179.

Moulton, Janice. "A Paradigm of Philosophy: The Adversary Method." S. In Harding and M. Hintikka (eds.), *Discovering Reality.* D. Reidel Publishing, 1983, pp. 149-163.

Moulton, Janice. "The Myth of the Neutral 'Man'." In M. Vetterling Braggin et al. (eds.), *Feminism and Philosophy.* Totowa, N.J.: Littlefield, Adams & Co., 1977, pp. 124-137.

Nash, J. and Safa, H. (eds.). *Sex and Class in Latin America.* New York: Praeger Press, 1976.

Nisbet, R. and Bottomore, T. (eds.). *A History of Sociological Analysis.* New York: Basic Books, 1978.

Norris, Joan. "Book Review: Women, Men and the Psychology of Power." *Atlantis,* 7, 2 (1982), 154-159.

Norris, F. (ed.). *Women's Health Needs Project.* Prepared for Women's Heal;th Action Network and Alberta Social Services and Community Health Lifestyles Program. Edmonton, Alberta, April 1980.

Oakley, Ann. *Sex, Gender and Society.* London: Maurice Temple Smith, 1972.

Oakley, Ann. *The Sociology of Housework.* London: Martin Robinson, 1974.

Oakley, Ann. *Housewife.* London: Penguin Books, 1977.

Oakley, Ann. *Subject Women.* Oxford: Martin Robertson, 1981.

Oakley, Ann. *Taking It Like a Woman.* London: Jonathan Cape, 1984.

O'Brien, Mary. "The Politics of Impotence." In W. Shea and J. King-Farlow (eds.), *Contemporary Issues in Political Philosophy.* New York: Science History Publications, 1976, pp. 147-162.

O'Brien, Mary. "Education: A Review." In *Resources for Feminist Research,* 12, 1 (1984), 3-17.

O'Brien, Mary. *The Politics of Reproduction.* Boston: Routledge and

Kegan Paul, 1981.

O'Brien, Mary. "Feminist Praxis: Feminism and Revolution, Feminist Theory and Feminist Practice." In A. Miles and G. Finn (eds.), *Feminism in Canada*. Montreal: Black Rose Books, 1982, pp. 251-268.

O'Brien, Mary. "Feminist Theory and Dialectical Logic." In N. Keohane, et al. (eds.), *Feminist Theory: A Critique of Ideology*. Chicago: University of Chicago Press, 1982, pp. 99-112.

O'Brien, Mary. "Review Article: Feminism and Education: A Critical Review Essay." *Resources for Feminist Research*, 12, 3, (1983), 3-16.

Odum, Eugene. *Fundamentals of Ecology*. New York: Saunders, 1971.

Okin, Susan Moller. *Women in Western Political Thought*. Princeton, N.J.: University Press, 1979.

O'Leary, V. and Hammack, B. "Sex-Role Orientation and Achievement Context as Determinants of the Motive to Avoid Success." *Sex Roles*, 1, (1975), 225-234.

Oleson, A. and Voss, J. (eds.). *The Organization of Knowledge in Modern America, 1860-1920*. Baltimore: John Hopkins University Press, 1979.

O'Neil, Onora. "How Do We Know When Opportunities Are Equal?" In M. Vetterling-Braggin et al. (eds.), *Feminism and Philosophy*. Totowa, N.J.: Littlefield, Adams & Co., 1977, pp. 177-189.

Oppenheimer, K. "Demographic Influence on Female Employment and the Status of Women." *American Journal of Sociology*, 78, (1973), 946-961.

Oppenheimer, K. "The Life-Cycle Squeeze: The Interaction of Men's Occupational and Family Life Cycles." *Demography*, (1974), 227-246.

Oppenheimer, K. "The Sociology of Women's Economic Role in the Family." *American Sociological Review*, 42, (1977), 387-405.

Ortner, S.B. "Is Female to Male as Nature is to Culture?" In M. Rosaldo and L. Lamphere (eds.), *Woman, Culture and Society*. Stanford: Stanford University Press, 1974, pp.

Ortner, S.B. and Whitehead, H. (eds.). *Sexual Meanings: The Cultural Construction of Gender and Sexuality*. Cambridge: Cambridge University Press, 1981.

Palmeri, Ann. "Charlotte Perkins Gilman: Forerunner of a Feminist Social Science." In S. Harding and M.B. Hintikka (eds.), *Discov-*

ering Reality. Boston: D. Reidel Publishing, 1983, pp. 97-119.

Parlee, M.B. "Review Essay: Psychology." *Signs,* 1, 1 (1975), 119-138.

Parlee, M.B. "Introduction." *The Scholar and the Feminist IV: Connecting Theory, Practice and Values,* 104, (1976).

Parlee, M.B. "Introduction." *The Scholar and the Feminist IV: Connecting Theory, Practice and Values, 106, (1977).*

Perrucci, C.C. "The Female Engineer and Scientist: Factors Associated With the Pursuit of a Professional Career." Unpublished report, Washington, D.C., 1968.

Perun, P.J. (ed.). *The Undergraduate Woman: Issues in Educational Equity.* Mass.: Lexington Books, 1982.

Philipsen, G. "Speaking 'Like a Man' in Teamsterville: Cultural Patterning of Role Enactment in an Urban Neighborhood." *Quarterly Journal of Speech,* 61, (1975), 13-22.

Piercy, Marge. *Going Down Fast.* New York: Ballantine Books, 1969.

Piercy, Marge. *Small Changes.* New York: Fawcett Crest, 1972.

Piercy, Marge. *Vida.* New York: Fawcett Crest, 1979.

Piercy, Marge. *Braided Lives.* New York: Fawcett Crest, 1982.

Pierson, Ruth and Prentice, Alison. "Feminism and the Writing and Teaching of History." A. Miles and G. Finn (eds.), *Feminism in Canada.* Montreal: Black Rose Books, 1982, pp. 103-118.

Pollert, Anna. "Women Gender Relations and Wage Labour." In E. Gamarnikow et al. (eds.), *Gender Class and Work.* London: Heinemann, 1983, pp. 96-114.

Prentice, Alison. "The Feminization of Teaching in British North America and Canada, 1845-1975." *Social History,* 8, 15 (1975), 5-20.

Prentice, Alison. "Education and the Metaphor of the Family: An Upper Canadian Example." *History of Education Quarterly,* 12, (1972), 281-303.

Prentice, Alison. *The School Promoters.* Toronto: McClelland and Stewart, 1977.

Prentice, Alison. "Women and Men at the Provincial Normal School of Ontario, 1847-1876: A Preliminary Social Portrait." Paper presented to the joint meeting of the Canadian Education Society, Vancouver, B.C., October 1983.

Prentice, Alison and Houston, Susan (eds.). *Family, School and Society in Nineteenth-Century Canada.* Toronto: Oxford University Press, 1975.

Queens, Gazette. *The Status of Women at Queen's.* Kingston, Ontario, 1979.

Quijano, G. "Dealing With Discrimination Based on Sex and/or Marital Status in the University." University of British Columbia, position paper prepared for the Learned Societies Meeting, Montreal, Quebec, May 28 - June 1, 1972.

Reed, B. (ed.). *The Structure of Knowledge: A Feminist Perspective: Proceedings of the Fourth Annual Great Lakes Colleges Association Women's Studies Conference.* Ann Arbor, Michigan: Great Lakes College Association Women's Studies Program, 1979.

Rendel, M. "How Many Women Academics?, 1912-1276." In R. Deem (ed.), *Schooling for Women's Work.* London: Routledge and Kegan Paul, 1980, pp. 142-162.

Report of Royal Commission on Status of Women. Canada: Ottawa, 1971.

Rich, Adrienne. "Toward a Woman-Centered University." In F. Howe (ed.), *Women and the Power to Change.* New York: McGraw-Hill, 1975, pp. 15-46.

Rich, Adrienne. *Of Woman Born: Motherhood as Experience and Institution.* New York: W.W. Norton, 1976.

Rich, Adrienne. *On Lies, Secrets and Silence: Selected Prose.* New York: W.W. Norton, 1979.

Rich, J.M. *Innovations in Education: Reformers and Their Critics.* Boston: Allyn and Bacon, 1975.

Richards, A. *Sigmund Freud: 4, The Interpretation of Dreams.* London: Penguin Books, 1976.

Riesman, David. "Introduction." In E. Friedenberg, *The Vanishing Adolescent.* New York: Dell, 2nd Edition 1970.

Rist, Ray. "Social Class and Teacher Expectations: The Self-Fulfilling Prophecy in Ghetto Education." *Harvard Education Review,* 40, (1970), 411-451.

Roberts, Joan. (ed.). *Beyond Intellectual Sexism: A New Woman, A New Reality.* New York: David MacKay, 1976.

Roberts, Joan. "Beyond Intellectual Sexism." In S. Ruth (ed.), *Issues in Feminism: A First Course in Women's Studies.* Boston: Houghton Mifflin, 1980, pp. 21-26.

Roberts, Helen. "Some of the Boys Won't Play Anymore: The Impact of Feminism on Sociology." D. Spender (ed.), *Men's Studies Modified.* England: Pergamon Press, 1981a, pp. 73-81.

Roberts, Helen. *Doing Feminist Research*. Boston: Routledge and Kegan Paul, 1981b.

Roby, Pamela. "Structural and Internalized Barriers to Women in Higher Education." C. Safilios-Rothschild (ed.), *Toward a Sociology of Women*. Lexington, Mass.: Xerox College Publishing, 1972, pp. 121-140.

Roby, Pamela. "Institutional Barriers to Women Students in Higher Education." A. Rossi and A. Calderwood (eds.), *Academic Women on the Move*. New York: Russell Sage Foundation, 1973, pp. 37-56.

Roe, A. "Women in Science." *Personnel and Guidance Journal*, 44, (1966), 784-787.

Rooney, Frances. "Mother Tongue." *Resources for Feminist Research*, 13, 3 (1984), 1.

Rosaldo, Z.M. "Woman, Culture and Society: A Theoretical Overview." In Z.M. Rosaldo and L. Lamphere (eds.), *Woman, Culture, and Society*. Stanford: Stanford University Press, 1974, pp. 1-28.

Rosaldo, Z.M. "The Use and Abuse of Anthropology: Reflections on Feminism and Cross-Cultural Understanding." *Signs*, 5, 3 (1980), 389-417.

Rosaldo, Z.M. and Collier, J.F. "Politics and Gender in Simple Societies." In S.N. Ortner and H. Whitehead (eds.), *Sexual Meanings: The Cultural Construction of Gender and Sexuality*. Cambridge: Cambridge University Press, 1981.

Rosaldo, Z.M. and Lamphere, L. (eds.). *Women, Culture, and Society*. Stanford, California: Stanford University Press, 1974.

Rosenberg, Rosalind. "In Search of Woman's Nature, 1850-1920." *Feminist Studies*, 3, 1-2 (1975), 141-154.

Rosenberg, Rosalind. "The Academic Prism: The New View of American Women." In C. Berkin and M.B. Norton (eds.), *A History of Women in America*. Boston: Houghton Mifflin, 1979, pp. 318-341.

Rosenberg, Rosalind. *Beyond Separate Spheres: The Intellectual Roots of Modern Feminism*. New Haven: Yale University Press, 1982.

Rosenfelt, S.D. (ed.). *Female Studies VII: Going Strong - New Courses, New Programs*. OID Westbury, New York: Feminist Press, 1973.

Ross, Dorothy. "The Development of the Social Sciences." In A. Oleson and J. Voss (eds.), *The Organization of Knowledge in Modern America, 1860-1920*. Baltimore: John Hopkins University Press, 1979, pp. 61-99.

Ross, Heather. *Time of Transition*. Washington, D.C.: Urban Institute, 1975.

Rossi, Alice. "The Roots of Ambivalence in American Women." J.M. Bardwick (ed.), *REadings on the Psychology of Women*. New York: Harper and Row, 1972, pp. 114-133.

Rossi, Alice. "Women in Science: Why So Few?" In C. Safilios-Rothschild (ed.), *Toward Sociology of Women*. Lexington, Mass.: Xerox College Publishing, 1972, pp. 141-153.

Rossi, Alice. "Sex Equality: The Beginnings of Ideology." In C. Safilios-Rothschild (ed.), *Toward a Sociology of Women*. Lexington, Mass.: Xerox College Publishing, 1972, pp. 344-353.

Rossi, Alice (ed.). *Essays on Sex Equality*. Chicago: University of Chicago Press, 1970.

Rossi, A.S. and Calderwood, A. (eds.). *Academic Women on the Move*. New York: Russell Sage Foundation, 1973.

Rossiter, Margaret. "Women Scientists in America before 1920." *American Scientist*. 62, 3(1974), 312-323.

Roszak, Theodore (ed.). *The Dissenting Academy*. New York: Pantheon Books, 1967.

Rowbotham, Sheila. *Women's Consciousness, Man's World*. London: Pelican Books, 1973.

Rowbotham, Sheila. *Woman, Resistance, and Revolution*. Harmondsworth, Middlesex, England: Penguin Books, 1974.

Rowbotham, Sheila and Wainwright, Hilary. *Beyond the Fragments: Feminism and the Making of Socialism*. London: Merline Press, 1979.

Rudolph, Frederic. *The American College and University: A History*. New York: Harper and Row, 1962.

Ruth, S. (ed.). *Issues in Feminism: A First Course in Women's Studies*. Boston: Houghton Mifflin, 1980.

Safilios-Rothschild, C. (ed.). *Toward a Sociology of Women*. Lexington, Mass.: Xerox College Publishing, 1972.

Sanguiliano, I. *In Her Time*. New York: Morrow Quill, 1980.

Sarup, Madan. *Marxism and Education*. London: Routledge and Kegan Paul, 1978.

Sargent, Lydia (ed.). *Women and Revolution: A Discussion of the Unhappy Marriage of Marxism and Feminism*. Boston: South

End Press, 1981.

Schapiro, Judith. "Sexual Hierarchy Among the Yanomama." In J. Nash and J. Safa (eds.). *Sex and Class in Latin America*. New York: Praeger Press, 1976, pp. 86-101.

Schapiro, N. "The Schapiro Report: An Analysis of Salaries of Men and Women Faculty at Ohio State University." Columbus, Ohio: Ohio State University, 1976.

Scheman, Naomi. "Individualism and the Objects of Psychology." S. Harding and M. Hintikka (eds.), *Discovering Reality*. Boston: D. Reidel Publishing, 1983, pp. 225-244.

Schepner-Hughes, Nancy. "Introduction: The Problem of Bias in Androcentric and Feminist Anthropology." *Women's Studies"*, 10, 2 (1983), 109-117.

Schwartz, P. and Lever, J. *Women at Yale: Liberating a College Campus*. London: Allen Lane, 1971.

Seccombe, W. "The Housewife and Her Labour Under Capitalism." *New Left Review*, 83, (1974), 3-24.

Senate Task Force on the Status of Women. *Report on Academic Women*. University of Alberta, Edmonton, 1980.

Shea, W. and King-Farlow, J. (eds.). *Contemporary Issues in Political Philosophy*. New York: Science History Publications, 1976.

Sheinin, Rose. "Women in Science: Issues and Actions." *Canadian Women's Studies*, 5, 4 (1984), 70-77.

Sherman, Julia. *On the Psychology of Women: A Survey of Empirical Studies*. Springfield, Ill.: Charles C. Thomas, 1971.

Sherman, J. and Beck, E. Torton (eds.). *The Prism of Sex: Essays in the Sociology of Knowledge*. Madison: University of Wisconsin Press, 1977.

Sherman, Susan. "Women's Studies as a Scholarly Discipline: Some Questions for Discussion." In R.L. Siporin (ed.), *Female Studies V*. Pittsburgh: KNOW Inc., 1972, pp. 114-116.

Sherwin, Susan. "From Feminism to a New Conception of Ethics." Paper presented at the Canadian Research Institute for the Advancement of Women Annual Conference, Vancouver, November 11, 1983.

Shils, L. "On Learning and Research." In A. Oleson and J. Voss (eds.), *The Organization of Knowledge in Modern America, 1860-1920*. Baltimore: John Hopkins University Press, 1979, pp.

Silberman, Charles. *Crisis in the Classroom*. New York: Random

House, 1970.

Simon, J. Rita and Clark, M.S. and Galway, K. "The Woman Ph.D.: A Recent Profile." In J. Bardwick (ed.), *Readings on the Psychology of Women.* New York: Harper and Row, 1972, pp.

Siporin, R.L. (ed.). *Female Studies V.* Pittsburgh: KNOW Inc., 1972.

Smith, D.E. "Women Perspective as a Radical Critique of Sociology." *Sociological Inquiry,* 44, 1 (1974a), 7-13.

Smith, D.E. "The Ideological Practice of Sociology", *Catalyst,* 8, (1974b),

Smith, D.E. "An Analysis of Ideological Structures and How Women Are Excluded: Considerations for Academic Women." *The Canadian Review of Sociology and Anthropology,* 12, (1975), 353-369.

Smith, D.E. *Feminism and Marxism.* Vancouver: New Star Books, 1977a.

Smith, D.E. "Some Implications of a Sociology for Women." In N. Glazer and H.Y. Waehrer (eds.), *Women in a Man-Made World.* Chicago: Rand McNally, 1977b, pp. 15-29.

Smith, D.E. "A Sociology for Women." In J. Sherman and E. Beck (eds.), *The Prism of Sex.* Madison: University of Wisconsin Press, 1977c, pp. 135-187.

Smith, D.E. "A Peculiar Eclipsing: Women's Exclusion From Man's Culture." *Women's Studies International Quarterly,* 1, 4 (1978), 281-196.

Smith, D.E. "Using the Oppressor's Language." *Resources for Feminist Research.* Special Publications: In Search of the Feminist Perspective: The Changing Potency of Women, 1, 2 (1979).

Smith-Rosenberg, C. "The New Woman and the New History." *Feminist Studies,* 3, 1-2 (1975), 185-198.

Snyder, E.C. (ed.). *The Study of Women: Enlarging Perspectives of Social Reality.* New York: Harper and Row, 1979.

Speizer, J.J. et al. "Issues of Educational Equity in the 1980's: Multiple Perspectives." In P.J. Perun (ed.), *The Undergraduate Woman.* Mass.: Lexington Books, 1982, pp. 399-419.

Spender, Dale. "Man-Made Knowledge: Problems of Research in Feminism." *Women's Studies International Quarterly,* 1, 1 (1977), 107-130.

Spender, Dale. "Education or Indoctrination?" In D. Spender and E. Sarah (eds.), *Learning to Lose.* London: Women's Press, 1980a, pp. 22-31.

Spender, Dale. *Man Made Language*. London: Routledge and Kegan Paul, 1980b.

Spender, Dale (ed.). *Men's Studies Modified: The Impact of Feminism on Academic Disciplines*. London: Pergamon Press, 1981.

Spender, Dale. "Education: The Patriarchal Paradigm and the Response to Feminism." In D. Spender (ed.), *Men's Studies Modified*. England: Pergamon Press, 1981a, pp. 155-173.

Spender, Dale. "The Gatekeepers: A Feminist Critique of Academic Publishing." In H. Roberts (ed.), *Doing Feminist Research*. Boston: Routledge and Kegan Paul, 1981b, pp.

Spender, Dale. *Invisible Women: The Schooling Scandal*. London: Writers and Readers Publishing, 1982.

Spender, Dale. *Women of Ideas*. London: Ark Paperbacks, 1983.

Spender, D. and Sarah, E. (eds.). *Learning to Lose*. Women's Press, 1980a.

Stacey, J., Bereaud, S. and Daniels, J. (eds.). *And Jill Came Tumbling After: Sexism in American Education*. New York: Dell Publishing, 1974.

Stanley, L. and Wise, S. *Breaking Out: Feminist Consciousness and Feminist Research*. London: Routledge and Kegan Paul, 1983.

Stanley, Liz. "Who the social science research process discriminates against Women." In S. Acker and D. Warren Piper (eds.), *Is Higher Education Fair to Women?* Great Britain: SRHE and NFER - Nelson, 1984, pp. 289-210.

Stanley, L. and Wise, S. *Breaking Out: Feminist Consciousness and Feminist Research*. London: Routledge and Kegan Paul, 1983.

Statistics Canada. *Teachers in Universities*. Ottawa, Canada, 1983.

Stein, A.H. and Bailey, M.M. "The Socialization of Achievement Orientation in Females." *Psychological Bullentin*, 80, (1973), 345-366.

Stiehm Hicks, Judith. "The Unit of Political Analysis: Our Aristotelian Hangover." In S. Harding and M. Hintikka (eds.), *Discovering Reality*. Boston: D. Reidel Publishing, 1983, pp. 31-43.

Stimpson, Catherine. "The New Feminism and Women's Studies." In (Editors of *Change* Magazine), *Women on Campus*. New York: Change Magazine, 1975, pp. 69-84.

Stimpson, Catherine. "The Power to Name: Some Reflections on the Avant-Garde." In J. Sherman and E. Torton Beck (eds.), *The Prism of Sex*. Madison: University of Wisconsin Press, 1977, pp. 55-77.

Stimpson, Catherine. "Women's Studies: An Overview." *University of Michigan Papers in Women's Studies*. May, 1978.

Strainchamps, Ethel. "Our Sexist Language." In V. Gornick and B. Moran (eds.), *Women in Sexist Society*. New York: New American Library, 1971, pp. 240-250.

Strong-Boag, Veronica. *Woman of Purpose: The Diaries of Elizabeth Smith*. Toronto: McClelland and Steward, 1980.

Sugnet, Charles. "The Uncertain Progress of Affirmative Action." in (Editors of *Change* Magazine), *Women on Campus*. New York: Change Magazine, 1975, 53-68.

Symons, T.H.B. and Page, J.E. "The Status of Women in Canadian Academic Life." In *Some Questions of Balance: Human Resources Higher Education and Canadian Studies*. AUCC, Ottawa, 1984.

Tangri, S.S. "Determinants of Occupational Role Innovation Among College Women." *Journal of Social Issues*, 28, 2 (1972), 177-199.

Teitelbaum, M. (ed.). *Sex Differences: Social and Biological Perspectives*. New York: Anchor Press, 1976.

Thibault, Gisele. "Women and Education: On Being Female in Male Places." In W. Tomm (ed.), *Sexism in Research*. Sir Wilfred Laurier Press, (in press).

Thomas, Claire. "Girls and Counter School Culture." Unpublished manuscript, Australia: McQuarrie University, 1978.

Thorne, b. and Henley, N. (eds.). *Language and Sex: Difference and Dominance*. Rowley Mass.: Newbury House, 1975.

Thompson, (Woolley) Helen. *Psychological Norms in Men and Women*. Chicago: University of Chicago Press, 1903.

Timascheff, N. *Sociological Theory: Its Nature and Growth*. New York: Random House, 1967.

Tobias, Sheila (ed.). *Female Studies I*. Pittsburgh: KNOW Inc., 1970.

Tobias, Sheila. "Women's Studies: Its Origins, Organization, and Prospects." *Women's Studies International Quarterly*, 1, 1 (1978), 85-97.

Touraine, Alain. *The Academic System in American Society*. New York: McGraw Hill, 1974.

Trebilcot, Joyce (ed.). *Mothering: Essays in Feminist Theory*. Totowa, N.J.: Rowman and Allanheld, 1984.

Trofimenkoff, M.S. and Prentice, A. (eds.). *The Neglected Majority: Essays in Canadian Women's History*. Toronto: McClelland and

Steward, 1977.

University of Waterloo Information Service. *Women and Engineering*, 30, October 1974.

Vaughter, Ressa. "Review Essay: Psychology." *Signs*, 2, 1 (1976), 120-146.

Valian, Virginia. "Linguistics and Feminism." In M. Vetterling-Braggin et al. (eds.), *Feminism and Philosophy*. Totowa, New Jersey: Littlefield, Adams & Co., 1977, pp. 154-170.

Veroff, Joseph. "Process Versus Impact in Men's and Women's Achievement Motivation." *Psychology of Women Quarterly*, 1 (1976), 283-293.

Vetterling-Braggin, M. Elliston, F. and English, J. (eds.). *Feminism and Philosophy*. Totowa, New Jersey: Littlefield, Adams & Co., 1977.

Veysey, Laurence. *The Emergence of the American University*. Chicago: University of Chicago Press, 1965.

Vickers, Jill McCalla. "Memoirs of an Ontological Exile: The Methodological Rebellions of Feminist Research." In A. Miles and G. Finn (eds.), *Feminism in Canada: From Pressure to Politics*. Montreal: Black Rose Books, 1982, pp. 27-46.

Vickers, J. McCalla and Adam, June. *But Can You Type?, Canadian Universities and the Status of Women*. Ontario: Clark, Irwin, 1977.

Villeneuve, Raymond. *The State of Women's Studies of Quebec Universities*. Secretary of State, Quebec Women's Program, Montreal: 1982.

Walker, Beverly. "Psychology and Feminism — If You Can't Beat Them, Join Them." In D. Spender (ed.), *Men's Studies Modified*. England: Pergamon Press, 1981, pp. 111-124.

Walker, S. and Barton, L. (eds.). *Gender, Class and Education*. New York: Falmer Press, 1983.

Warren, M.A. "Secondary Sexism and Quota Hiring." In S. Bishop & M. Weinzweig (eds.), *Philosophy and Women*. California: Wadsworth Publishing, 1979, pp. 237-247.

Watkins, Bari. "Women and History." In Editors of *Change* Magazine, *Women on Campus*. New York: Change magazine, 1975, pp. 95-101.

Watkins, Bari. "Feminism: A Last Chance for the Humanities." In G. Bowles and R. Duelli-Klein (eds.), *Theories of Women's Studies*. Berkeley: Women's Studies, University of California, Berkeley,

1980, pp. 79-87.

Webb, Marilyn. "Feminist Studies: Frill or Necessity?" In J. Stacey et al. (eds.), *And Jill Came Tumbling After*. New York: Dell Publishing, 1974, pp. 410-422.

Weinbaun, Batya. *The Curious Courtship of Women's Liberation and Socialism*. Boston: South End Press, 1978.

Weisstein, Naomi. "Psychology Constructs the Female" or the "Fantasy life of the Male Psychologist." In M. Garskof (ed.), *Roles Women Play: Readings Toward Women's Liberation*. California: Wadsworth Publishing, 1971, pp. 68-83.

Weitz, S. *Sex Roles: Biological, Psychological and Social Foundations*. New York: Oxford University Press, 1977.

Weitzman, L.J. *Sex Role Socialization: A Focus on Women*. Palo Alto, Cal.: Mayfield Publishing, 1979.

White, Martha A. "Psychological and Social Barriers to Women in Science." In C. Safilios-Rothschild (ed.), *Toward a Sociology of Women*. Lexington, Mass.: Xerox College Publishing, 1972, pp. 300-308.

Willinsky, John. *The Well-Tempered Tongue: The Politics of Standard English in the High School*. New York: Peter Lang, 1984.

Wilson, Edward O. *Sociobiology: The New Synthesis*. Cambridge, Mass.: Harvard university Press, 1975.

Wilson, J.D. (ed.). *Canadian Education in the 1980's*. Calgary: Detselig Enterprises, 1981.

Wilson, J.J. *Women, the Family, and the Economy*. Toronto: Mc-Graw-Hill Ryerson, 1982.

Wine, Jerri. "Gynocentric Values and Feminist Psychology." In A. Miles and G. Finn (eds.), *Feminism in Canada*. Montreal: Black Rose books, 1982, pp. 67-88.

Wirth, L. "The Social Sciences." In M. Curti (ed.), *American Scholarship in the Twentieth Century*. New York: Russell and Russell, 1967, pp. 69-119.

Wolpe, Ann Marie. "Education and the Sexual Division of Labour." In A. Kuhn and A.M. Wolpe, (eds.), *Feminism and Materialism*. London: Routledge and Kegan Paul, 1978, pp. 290-328.

Women's Studies: A Resource Guide for Teachers, Vancouver: Department of Education, B.C., n.d.

Wood, Caroline Sherif. "Bias in Psychology." In J. Sherman and E. Beck (eds.), *the Prism of Sex*. Madison: University of Wisconsin Press, 1977, pp. 93-134.

Woolf, Virginia. *Three Guineas.* London: Hogarth Press, 1938.

Woolf, Virginia. *A Room of One's Own.* London: Hogarth Press, 1928.

Worsley, A. *Introducing Sociology.* New York: Penguin Books, 1970.

Young, Michael D. (ed.). *Knowledge and Control: New Directions for the Sociology of Education.* London: Collier-MacMillan, 1971.

Zangrando, S. Joanna. "Women Studies in the U.S.: Approaching Reality." *American Studies International,* 14, 1 (1975), 15-36.

Zaretsky, Eli. "Capitalism, the Family and Personal Life." *Socialist Review,* 13 and 14, (1973).

Zimmerman, D. and West, C. "Sex Roles, Interruptions and Silences in Conversation." In B. Thorne and N. Henley (eds.), *Language and Sex: Difference and Dominance.* Mass.: Newbury House, 1975, pp. 105-129.

Frances E. Mascia-Lees

TOWARD A MODEL OF WOMEN'S STATUS

American University Studies: Series XI, (Anthropology/Sociology), Vol. 1
ISBN 0-8204-0054-8   146 pages   paperback US $ 14.60*

*Recommended price - alterations reserved

Many difficulties have been encountered by researchers attempting to assess women's status in contemporary societies. One major obstacle has to do with the problems encountered in developing indices of status that can be used as objective measures of women's position. Due to such obstacles, many, if not most, studies of women's status have concentrated on qualitative analyses of single cultures or culture areas, making comparisons across societies unsystematic and, therefore, of limited applicability. Yet it is just such systematic studies that are required if the conditions perpetuating women's status around the world are to be identified and changed. This work presents a first attempt to develop measures of women's status, using existing statistics, that are applicable across nations and make possible comparisons in time and space. This volume reviews the literature on the determinants of women's status in contemporary societies, analyzes the range of variation in women's position in the public sector, provides quantitative measures of women's status in the political, economic, educational, and family spheres, and identifies factors important in explaining and predicting women's position on a world-wide scale.

PETER LANG PUBLISHING, INC.
62 West 45th Street
USA - New York, NY 10036